Essential Test Tips Video from Trivium Test Prep

Dear Customer,

Thank you for purchasing from Trivium Test Prep! Whether you're looking to join the military, get into college, or advance your career, we're honored to be a part of your journey.

To show our appreciation (and to help you relieve a little of that test-prep stress), we're offering a **FREE *PECT Essential Test Tips* Video** by Trivium Test Prep. Our video includes 35 test preparation strategies that will help keep you calm and collected before and during your big exam. All we ask is that you email us your feedback and describe your experience with our product. Amazing, awful, or just so-so: we want to hear what you have to say!

To receive your **FREE *PECT Essential Test Tips* Video**, please email us at 5star@ triviumtestprep.com. Include "Free 5 Star" in the subject line and the following information in your email:

1. The title of the product you purchased.
2. Your rating from 1 – 5 (with 5 being the best).
3. Your feedback about the product, including how our materials helped you meet your goals and ways in which we can improve our products.
4. Your full name and shipping address so we can send your **FREE *PECT Essential Test Tips* Video**.

If you have any questions or concerns please feel free to contact us directly at 5star@triviumtestprep.com.

Thank you, and good luck with your studies!

PECT PreK-4 Exam Study Guide

2 Practice Tests and PECT Prep Book for the Pennsylvania Educator Certification

Eric Canizales

ISBN-13: 9781637983614

Table of Contents

Cirrus
The Authority in Teacher Certification

Online Resources

Trivium includes online resources with the purchase of this study guide to help you fully prepare for the exam.

Practice Test

The second practice test can be taken in the book or online for an interactive experience. Since many exams today are computer based, practicing your test-taking skills on the computer is a great way to prepare.

Flash Cards

Trivium's flash cards allow you to review important terms easily on your computer or smartphone.

From Stress to Success

Watch "From Stress to Success," a brief but insightful YouTube video that offers the tips, tricks, and secrets experts use to score higher on the exam.

Reviews

Leave a review, send us helpful feedback, or sign up for Cirrus promotions—including free books!

Access these materials at: www.cirrustestprep.com/pect-prek4-online-resources

Introduction

Congratulations on choosing to take the PECT PreK – 4 exam! By purchasing this book, you've taken the first step toward becoming a teacher in Pennsylvania.

This guide will provide you with a detailed overview of the PECT PreK – 4 exam, so you will know exactly what to expect on test day. We'll take you through all of the concepts covered on the exam and give you the opportunity to test your knowledge with practice questions. Even if it's been a while since you last took a major test, don't worry; we'll make sure you're more than ready!

What is the PECT?

The Pennsylvania Educator Certification Test: PreK – 4 exam is a criterion-referenced test used to assess the expertise of prospective PreK – 4 teachers.

What's on the PECT PreK – 4 exam?

The exam contains solely selected response questions. Each item has four answer choices and one correct answer. The exam is broken into three modules.

PECT PreK – 4 Test Content		
Module	**Number of Questions**	**Time**
Module I ▪ Child Development, Learning, and Assessment ▪ Collaboration and Professionalism	36	45 minutes
Module II ▪ Language and Literacy Development ▪ Social Studies, Arts, and Humanities	45	75 minutes
Module III ▪ Mathematics, Science, and Health	45	90 minutes
Total	**126 questions**	**3 hours and 30 minutes**

How is the PECT PreK – 4 exam scored?

Each module is computer-scored.

Raw scores are first calculated, and then scores are transformed to scaled scores from 100 – 300 for each module. An overall score of 197 is the passing score for Module 1. An overall score of 193 is the passing score for both Modules 2 and 3.

Once an examinee passes each module, that particular module does not need to be taken again in the event that the exam must be retaken because all parts were not passed; however, examinees must wait thirty days to retest. Scores are reported within ten days of testing and are available from your online account for two years after the score report date. After two years, you can request a copy using the reprint request form.

Did You Know?

The "founding father" of behaviorism, psychologist B.F. Skinner, was also a pioneer in educational technology. In 1954, he invented a prototype for what he called the "teaching machine." The machine used a system of hole punches and tapes to give students immediate feedback after answering a question, much like today's educational technology platforms.

How is the PECT PreK – 4 exam administered?

The PECT PreK – 4 exam is computer-based and available at testing centers in Pennsylvania and throughout the United States. Online proctoring is also available. A total of 45 minutes is permitted to complete Module 1; 75 minutes are allowed to complete Module 2; and 90 minutes are given to complete Module 3. Examinees taking all three modules at once will also receive a 15-minute break between modules. An on-screen calculator is available for use during Module 3.

About Cirrus Test Prep

Cirrus Test Prep study guides are designed by current and former educators and are tailored to meet your needs as an incoming educator. Our guides offer all of the resources necessary to help you pass teacher certification tests across the nation.

Cirrus clouds are graceful, wispy clouds characterized by their high altitude. Just like cirrus clouds, Cirrus Test Prep's goal is to help educators "aim high" when it comes to obtaining their teacher certifications and entering the classroom. We're pleased you've chosen Cirrus to be a part of your professional journey!

1. Child Development

Theories of Learning and Development

Many theories on cognitive and social development drive instructional practices. Furthermore, many theorists have contributed to current practices and their impact on student learning. **Cognitive development** refers to the way in which people think and develop an understanding of the world around them through genetics and other learned influences. The areas of cognitive development include information processing, reasoning, language development, intelligence, and memory.

Social development refers to learning values, knowledge, and skills that allow children to relate to others appropriately and effectively and contribute to family, the community, and school in positive ways. Social development is directly influenced by those who care for and teach the child; it is indirectly influenced through friendships, relationships with other family members, and the culture that surrounds them. As children's social development progresses, they begin to respond to influences around them and start building relationships with others.

Many theories about child cognitive and social development fall into one of two broad categories: behaviorism and constructivism. **Behaviorism** concerns observable stimulus-response behaviors and suggests that all behaviors are learned through interactions with the environment through classical or operant conditioning. Therefore, our mind is a *tabula rasa*, or blank slate, at birth. In contrast, **constructivism** presents the idea that learning is an active process and knowledge is constructed based on personal experiences. The learner is not a "blank slate" as suggested by behaviorism; instead, the learner uses past experiences and cultural factors to gain knowledge in new situations.

Practice Question

1) Which of the following describes a behaviorist approach to classroom management?
   - A. Students work together to create classroom rules.
   - B. Students are asked to reflect on their behavior at the end of the school day.
   - C. The teacher uses rewards (e.g.,) stickers and consequences (e.g., time-outs).
   - D. The teacher models appropriate behavior for students in an ongoing capacity.

Piaget and Cognitive Constructivism

Cognitive development in children has been studied in many ways throughout the years. In 1936, the prominent theorist **Jean Piaget** proposed his **theory of cognitive development**. Piaget's theory came from several decades of observing children in their natural environments. He posited that a child's knowledge develops from schemas, or units of knowledge that use past experiences to understand new experiences.

According to Piaget, schemas constantly change due to two complimentary processes: assimilation and accommodation. **Assimilation** is taking in new information and relating it to an existing schema, or what the child already knows. **Accommodation** occurs when schema changes to accommodate new knowledge. Piaget states that there is an ongoing attempt to balance accommodation and assimilation to gain equilibration.

The core of Piaget's theory is the idea that cognitive development happens in four stages of increasing sophistication and abstract levels of thought. The stages always happen in the same order and build upon learning that occurred in the previous stage.

The first stage is the **sensorimotor stage**, which takes place in infancy. During this stage, infants demonstrate intelligence through motor activities and without using symbols. They have limited knowledge of the world around them; however, their world knowledge is developing through physical interactions and experiences. At around seven months of age, children understand **object permanence** (that an object still exists even when it cannot be seen). The increase in physical development, or mobility, in this stage allows for the progression of new intellectual abilities. Symbolic language abilities begin to develop at the end of this stage

The second stage, the **pre-operational stage**, takes place from toddlerhood to early childhood. This stage is characterized by the demonstration of intelligence through symbols. Furthermore, language abilities mature at this stage, and memory and imagination are developing rapidly. Thinking, however, is nonlogical, nonreversible, and egocentric.

The **concrete operational stage** is the third stage and takes place from the elementary years to early adolescence. In this stage, children begin to use actions that are logical and rational when thinking and solving problems. They start to understand **conservation**, or the concept that weight, volume, and numbers may remain the same even though appearance may change. In this stage, operational, or reversible thinking, develops and egocentric thinking is reduced.

The final stage is the **formal operational stage** that occurs from adolescence through adulthood. During this stage, children become able to independently navigate through problems and situations. They should be able to adapt to different situations by applying learned knowledge. A major cognitive transition occurs in this stage in that adolescents are better able to think in more advanced, efficient, and complex ways.

Practice Question

2) A kindergarten teacher wants to assess whether or not students understand conservation. Which activity is most appropriate?

A. pouring the same amount of water into cups of different sizes and asking the child which cup has more
B. weighing a heavy object and a lighter object and asking students which object has greater mass
C. hiding a toy behind a blanket and asking the child if the ball is still there
D. moving a stack of books from a table onto the floor and asking the child if the books still weigh the same amount

Vygotsky and Social Learning

The theorist **Lev Vygotsky** introduced the **social development theory** and the zone of proximal development. This theory is characterized by the idea that social development plays a critical role in cognitive development. Vygotsky believed that learning cannot be extricated from its socio-cultural context. Adults teach children language, signs, and symbols as tools to be used in learning that children then **internalize**. Children then form their own "tool kit" of sorts that aids them in continued development as they interact with the culture in which they live.

Vygotsky also theorized that there is a zone of proximal development which cognitive development depends upon. The ZPD is achieved when children are engaged in social behavior with adults or peers. According to Vygotsky, cognitive development is better achieved through interactions or help from peers or an adult than what can be accomplished alone.

The **zone of proximal development (ZPD)** is the distance between a child's actual developmental level, as demonstrated by independent problem-solving, and the potential developmental level as demonstrated under adult or peer guidance. Children will typically follow an adult's or a more capable peer's example and eventually be able to complete certain tasks alone.

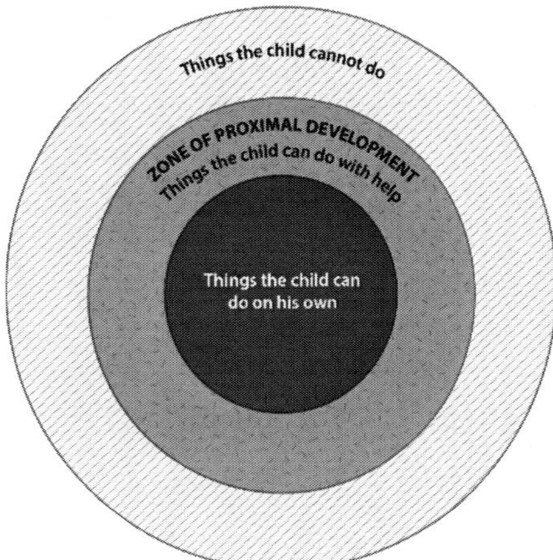

Figure 1.1. The Zone of Proximal Development

Vygotsky's ZPD has been modified and changed over the years and forms the foundation for the concept of scaffolding. **Scaffolding** is when a teacher or more capable peer provides guidance and support to the child in his ZPD, as appropriate, and gradually scales back the support when it is no longer necessary.

Practice Question

3) Per Vygotsky, how does a child internalize new knowledge?

A. through repeated visual exposure
B. through interactions with adults
C. through neural pathway development
D. through physical rewards

Gardner and Multiple Intelligences

A third theorist contributing to the field of child development is **Howard Gardner**. Dr. Gardner is a professor of education at Harvard University whose **theory of multiple intelligences** was published in 1983. This theory suggests that the traditional method of testing intelligence, IQ testing, is limited and that there are eight different types of intelligence to characterize the ways in which children and adults develop skills and solve problems. One's potential is correlated to her learning preferences. Dr. Gardner's suggested intelligences are as follows:

- verbal-linguistic intelligence
- logical-mathematical intelligence

- spatial-visual intelligence
- bodily-kinesthetic intelligence
- musical intelligence
- interpersonal intelligence
- intrapersonal intelligence
- naturalist intelligence
- existential intelligence

Check Your Understanding

Which developmental domains would be addressed within each of Gardner's multiple intelligences?

Dr. Gardner states that, although today's schools and culture focus heavily on linguistic and logical-mathematical intelligence, we should equally focus on other intelligences. The theory of multiple intelligences encourages educators to reflect on how schools operate and implement changes to ensure teachers are trained to deliver instruction in a variety of ways to meet the intelligence needs of all children. Implementing this theory can develop children's strengths and build confidence as well as provide teachers with a set of teaching and learning tools that reach beyond the typical lecture, textbook, and worksheet methods.

Practice Question

4) Which statement BEST demonstrates a commitment to meeting the needs of students with multiple intelligences?

A. A teacher follows direct instruction with guided and independent practice.
B. A teacher uses heterogenous grouping to encourage students to help each other.
C. A teacher provides students with a digital version of the textbook.
D. A teacher allows students to choose a paper, diorama, or group skit for a project.

Bruner and Learning Modes

Jerome Bruner is yet another significant theorist. According to Bruner, there are **three modes of representation** in which learners interpret the world: enactive, iconic, and symbolic. He explains that these modes are followed in sequence; however, in contrast to other theorists, they are not age-dependent. The modes of representation are dependent upon how familiar the learner is with the subject matter. Thus, Brunner presents the idea that what is being taught must be appropriate and ready for the learner instead of the learner being ready for the subject matter. In other words, any subject can be taught to any individual at any age, but the material must be modified to the appropriate form and stage for the learner.

Bruner's enactive stage is characterized by the idea that knowledge is stored through motor responses. This stage not only applies to children but adults as well. Some tasks completed as adults would be difficult to describe in the iconic (picture) mode or the symbolic (word) form. Next, the iconic stage is characterized by the idea that knowledge is stored through visual images. Finally, in the symbolic stage, knowledge is stored through words, mathematical symbols, or other symbol systems.

Practice Question

5) A first-grade teacher wants to introduce subtraction via Bruner's three modes of representation. Which process reflects each mode?

A. taking away one block, striking out one picture of a block, writing $2 - 1 = 1$.
B. adding one block, taking one block away, writing $1 + 1 = 2$ and $2 - 1 = 1$.
C. learning the word *subtraction*, writing $2 - 1 = 1$, saying "two minus one equals one"
D. writing $2 - 1 = 1$, drawing two objects, covering up one object

Bandura and Social Learning Theory

Another important theorist is **Albert Bandura** and his **social learning theory**, which presents the idea that people learn best by observing, imitating, and modeling behaviors, attitudes, and emotional reactions. In contrast to some theorists, Bandura's social learning theory includes a social element—the idea that people can learn new information and behaviors simply by observing other people.

Three core concepts encompass this theory. The first is that people can learn by observation through three basic models: a live model, a verbal instructional model, and a symbolic model. A live model is an individual demonstrating or acting out a behavior. The verbal instructional model provides descriptions and explanations of a behavior. The symbolic model is when real or fictional characters portray behaviors in books, movies, television, or online media.

The second core concept is the idea that a person's mental state and motivation can determine whether a behavior is learned or not. Bandura presents the idea that external environmental reinforcement contributes to learning along with intrinsic reinforcement, or internal reward.

The final concept of Bandura's theory is the idea that even though a behavior is learned, there may not be a change in behavior. In contrast to behaviorist learning, which states that there is a behavioral change once something new is learned, observational learning states that new information can be learned without behavioral changes.

Bandura's theory is said to combine the cognitive and behavioral learning theories with four requirements for learning: attention, retention, reproduction, and motivation. The first requirement is attention. To learn new information, one must be paying attention—any distractors will negatively affect observational learning. The next is retention, or the ability to store and retrieve information at a later time. The third requirement is reproduction, which is performing the observed and learned behavior. The last requirement is motivation. One must be motivated to reproduce the observed behavior, either by external or intrinsic motivators.

Practice Question

6) A fourth-grade teacher wants to help students prepare for measuring liquids in graduated cylinders. Which activity would involve the use of Bandura's symbolic model?

A. teacher demonstration
B. lecture
C. video
D. written directions

Erikson and Psychosocial Development

Erik Erikson is another theorist who contributed to the field of child development with his **theory of psychosocial development,** which outlines eight stages from infancy through adulthood. Each stage is characterized by a psychosocial crisis that will have a positive or negative effect on personality development. This theory suggests that a healthy personality is developed by the successful completion of each stage; an inability to successfully complete a stage may lead to the inability to complete upcoming stages. This may result in an unhealthy personality and sense of self; however, this can be successfully resolved in the future.

Erikson's first stage, **trust versus mistrust**, takes place during a child's first eighteen months of life. This stage is characterized by an infant's uncertainty about the world around her. These uncertain feelings can be resolved by a primary caregiver who provides stability and consistent, predictable, and reliable care that will help develop a sense of trust and secure feelings in the infant, even when threatened. However, if an infant has received care that is inconsistent, unpredictable, or unreliable, she can develop a sense of mistrust and carry the feeling into other relationships, which may lead to anxiety and insecurities.

Erikson's second stage is **autonomy versus shame and doubt**. This stage is characterized by a child's physical development and occurs between the ages of eighteen months and three years. During this stage, children begin to assert their independence and autonomy and discover their many skills and abilities. Erikson believes that parents and caregivers should exhibit patience and allow children to explore their independence by providing support and encouragement. If children are supported and encouraged, they will become confident and secure with their abilities; however, if they are criticized, controlled, or not allowed to exhibit independence, they may have feelings of inadequacy, shame, and doubt, and become dependent upon others.

The third stage is **initiative versus guilt**, which occurs between the ages of three and five and is characterized by children continuing to assert their independence more frequently while interacting with other children. During this stage, children develop interpersonal skills through play by planning and initiating activities or making up games with other children. If these skills are encouraged, a child will feel secure in taking initiative; however, if a child is not allowed to develop these skills, he can develop a sense of guilt (e.g., feeling like a nuisance) and lack self-initiative.

Industry versus inferiority is the fourth stage of the psychosocial development theory. During this stage—between the ages of five and twelve—teachers play an important role since children are now in school. Additionally, friends begin to play a significant role in a child's self-esteem during this time as children begin to seek the approval of their peers. If children are encouraged by parents, teachers, and peers, they begin to develop a strong sense of confidence. In contrast, if children are not encouraged, they can begin to feel inferior and doubt their abilities.

> **Check Your Understanding**
>
> How do free-choice learning and play centers align with students in the initiative versus guilt stage?

Four final stages characterize psychosocial development during the transitions from childhood to adolescence and adulthood through the older adult years.

Table 1.1. Erik Erikson's Psychosocial Development Theory

Age	Birth – Age 2	Ages 2 – 3	Ages 3 – 6	Ages 6 – 11
Stage	**trust v. mistrust**	**autonomy v. shame and doubt**	**initiative v. guilt**	**industry v. inferiority**
Virtue	trust	will	purpose	competence
Children learn...	Can people be trusted?	Am I allowed to be myself?	Am I allowed to do the things I want to do?	Can I be successful?

Practice Question

7) What happens in each of Erickson's stages of development?

A. rebellion against authority
B. parental encouragement
C. physical changes
D. psychosocial crisis

Maslow's Hierarchy of Needs

Abraham Maslow is another theorist with significant contributions to the field of early childhood development. Maslow is best known for the **hierarchy of needs,** a motivational theory that consists of five needs: physiological, safety, love, esteem, and self-actualization. He presented the idea that basic human needs are arranged hierarchically. In order for one to be able to attain the highest level—self-actualization—one must reasonably meet the growth needs in each stage.

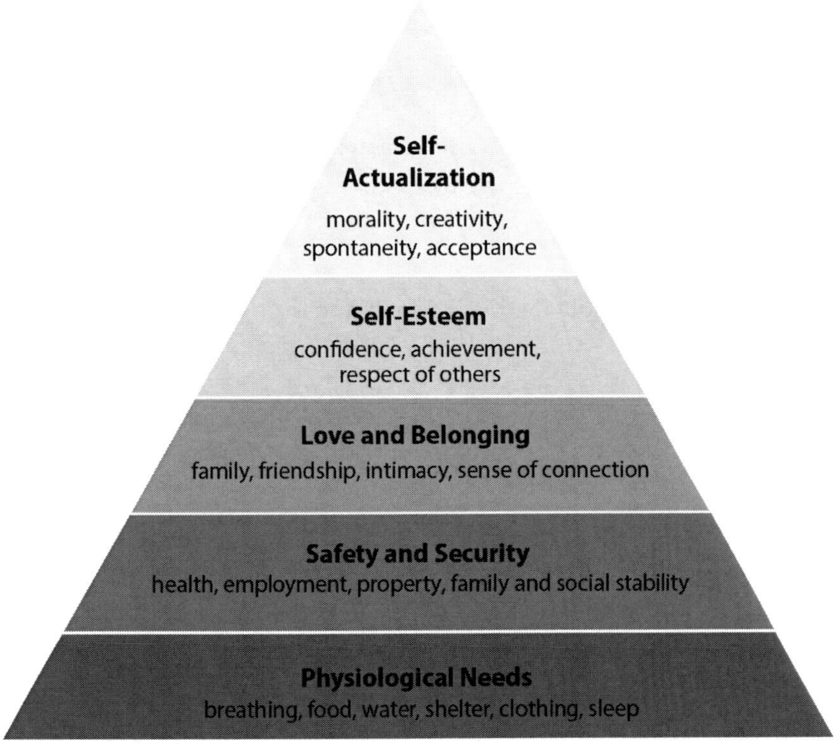

Self-Actualization
morality, creativity, spontaneity, acceptance

Self-Esteem
confidence, achievement, respect of others

Love and Belonging
family, friendship, intimacy, sense of connection

Safety and Security
health, employment, property, family and social stability

Physiological Needs
breathing, food, water, shelter, clothing, sleep

Figure 1.2. Maslow's Hierarchy of Needs

These needs are presented in a hierarchical order and shown in a pyramid, with physiological needs at the bottom of the pyramid and self-actualization at the top. Physiological needs, placed at the bottom of the pyramid, include basic needs such as air, food, drink, shelter, warmth, and sleep. Following physiological needs are safety needs, which include order, law, stability, protection from elements, security, and freedom from fear. Next is love and a feeling of belonging, or friendships, intimacy, trust, receiving and giving affection, and feelings of acceptance or feeling like a part of a group. Maslow divided esteem needs—which appear after love—into two categories: esteem for oneself and the need for respect from others. Children and adolescents have a greater need for respect and reputation as these arrive before real self-esteem, or dignity, can develop. The final level is self-actualization, or a feeling of personal growth, self-fulfillment, or reaching maximum personal potential.

Maslow describes that everyone has the capability and desire to move up the hierarchy; however, sometimes progress can be disrupted by the inability to meet lower-level needs. One's life experiences can influence progression up the hierarchy and some may even move back and forth between levels, which means everyone will progress in different ways.

Practice Question

8) How could a teacher help meet students' needs in alignment with the base of Maslow's hierarchy?

A. recognizing differences between individualist and collectivist cultures
B. organizing school fundraisers for improved facilities
C. planning professional development centered on language learning
D. giving information about the free lunch program to parents

Bloom's Taxonomy and Mastery Learning

Finally, **Benjamin Bloom** made major contributions to classifying educational objectives and the theory of **mastery learning**. In mastery learning, students work on material until they master it, regardless of the pace at which peers are working. Material that is not mastered is practiced further; only when material is mastered do students move on to new material.

Bloom is also known for developing **Bloom's taxonomy,** which is a hierarchy of skills that build upon each other from simple to complex and concrete to abstract. Bloom created the original taxonomy in 1956. It was revised in 2001 to include more action words to describe the cognitive processes through which learners work through knowledge.

The original taxonomy categories included knowledge, or the simple recall of information; comprehension, or the ability to understand and use information; application, or being able to use abstract thinking in concrete situations; analysis, or the ability to break down an idea or concept into parts and recognize the relationships between ideas or concepts; synthesis, or putting together elements or parts to make a whole; and evaluation, or the ability to judge material and the method of its purpose.

In 2001, a group of professionals across the fields of education and psychology revised Bloom's original taxonomy to include action words to label the categories and subcategories and describe the process in which learners work through knowledge. The first category is remembering, or the ability to recognize and recall. Next is understanding—interpreting, exemplifying, classifying, summarizing, inferring, comparing, and explaining. The third category is applying, or being able to execute or implement. The fourth is the ability to analyze or differentiate, organize, or attribute. The fifth category is evaluating, or checking or critiquing. The final category is creating—generating, planning, and producing.

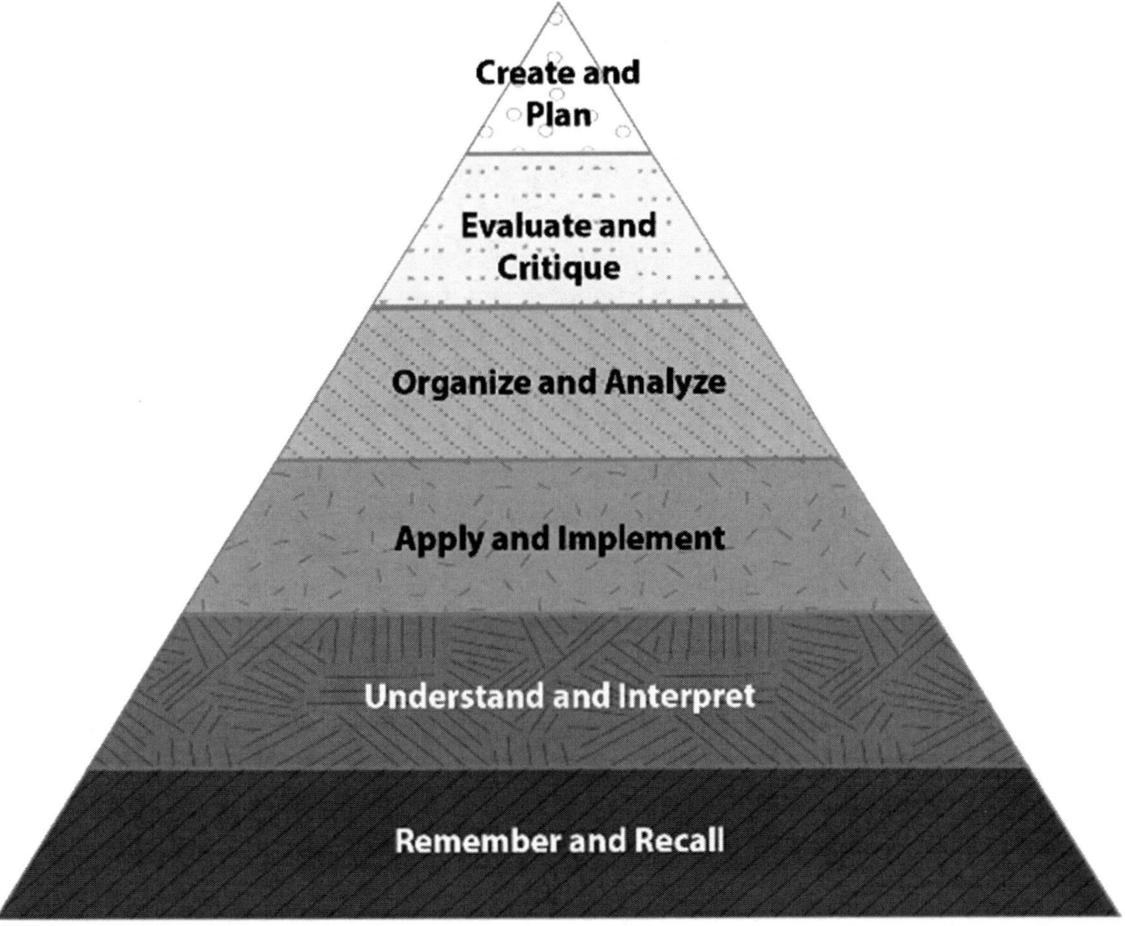

Figure 1.3. Bloom's Taxonomy

Incorporating Bloom's taxonomy into current practices includes many benefits. One of these is establishing objectives or learning goals so that teachers and students understand the purpose of instruction. A second benefit is that Bloom's taxonomy provides teachers with a framework with which to organize objectives. From these objectives teachers can plan and implement appropriate instruction, design and implement purposeful and valid assessments, and ensure that instruction and assessments are objective-driven.

Practice Question

9) Which question is the MOST cognitively rigorous per Bloom's taxonomy?

A. What does "opportunity cost" mean?
B. How many sides does a triangle have?
C. How many syllables are in the word *treehouse*?
D. What is the difference between morphemes and syllables?

Bronfenbrenner and Ecological Systems Theory

Another development theorist in the field of early childhood is Urie Bronfenbrenner. He developed what came to be known as the **ecological systems theory**. This theory provides an excellent lens through which to view the multiple social systems and interactions that impact a child. The theory defines five systems at work in the lives of children:

- The **microsystem** is that which is closest to the child, such as the family, school, temple, mosque, church, synagogue, and any other institutions in the community with which the child is in direct contact.
- The **mesosystem** is the network of relationships among different microsystems that also affect the child. The relationships between parents and teachers and the school and families are crucial mesosystem relationships that will either aid or detract from the development of the child.
- **Exosystems** are relationships between a child and others in her social orbit that do not involve the child directly. For example, a parent who has an unpleasant relationship with her boss might impact the child by bringing the stress from this relationship into the household.
- **Macrosystems**, which can be broadly defined as the overall cultural constructs in which a child lives, may include race and ethnicity, socioeconomic status, political systems, and the general larger environment in which the child lives.
- **Chronosystems** represent environmental changes and transitions that happen over the course of a child's life. These might impact microsystems, such as when parents divorce, or macrosystems, such as when a family moves to a foreign country.

Check Your Understanding

Draw your own concentric circles based on Bronfenbrenner's theory and label the most important parts of your own microsystem, mesosystem, exosystem, macrosystem, and chronosystem.

The ecological systems theory, sometimes called the **bioecological model**, is very important for teachers to consider both when teaching socio-emotional development and when teaching broader social studies concepts. Teachers should consider that multiple systems outside of the classroom are affecting children and can have a significant impact on each child's social and emotional identity.

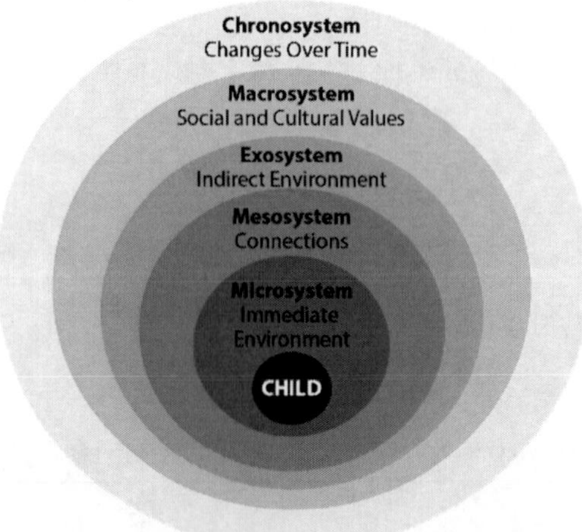

Figure 1.4. Urie Bronfenbrenner's Ecological Systems Theory

Practice Question

10) Which of the following is an example of a macrosystem that might impact a child?

A. family
B. school
C. ethnicity
D. church

Bowen and Family Systems Theory

Most children grow up in some kind of family unit, and psychiatrist Murray Bowen sought to describe this family unit in eight concepts to describe the way in which families operate:

1. **Triangles:** Triangles in families are relationships among three people. Bowen believes three-way relationships are inherently more stable because they can tolerate tension, which can be more evenly spread among three people than two people. As tension develops, triangles may change in order to absorb that tension.

2. **Differentiation of self:** Differentiation of self refers to an individual's ability to resist groupthink and define oneself outside of his approval, acceptance, or domination over others.

3. **Nuclear family emotional process:** This describes four basic relationship patterns:

- Marital conflict: Spouses react to family tension by focusing on what is wrong with the spouse and trying to control the spouse.
- Dysfunction in a spouse: One spouse concedes to pressure to change; if tension increases, the subordinate spouse can have continued anxiety.
- Impairment of one or more children: Anxieties are focused on a child or children, who may internalize this anxiety.
- Emotional distance: People distance themselves from each other.

4. **Family projection process:** This is when a parent's emotional problems become those of the child. It usually follows three steps:

- The parent believes something is wrong with the child and therefore focuses on the child.
- The parent believes the child's actions confirm a problem.
- The parent then starts to treat the child as though there is an actual problem.

At this point, the child then begins to actually exhibit the problem.

5. **Multigenerational transmission process:** This describes the way children in families develop a self-identity that is similar to or different from that of their parents or other family members.

6. **Emotional cutoff:** This describes people cutting off emotional contact with family members when there are unresolved emotional issues. This may be by reducing or eliminating physical contact or by simply avoiding the discussion of any "hot button" issues with family members.

Check Your Understanding

While many early childhood programs screen children for atypical development, some students may not have participated in such programs. Prekindergarten and kindergarten teachers must therefore be aware of typical developmental trajectories.

7. **Sibling position:** The sibling position (oldest, middle, youngest) can impact how an individual functions.

8. **Societal Emotional Process:** Behavior is governed by emotional systems within a society. Families often respond to broader societal factors as part of child-rearing.

Practice Question

11) Which example illustrates part of the family projection process?
   A. A parent believes one child may have an emotional disturbance, so the parent watches the child closely.
   B. A child sees her father working on a computer, so the child pretends to work on a computer.
   C. A child keeps her distance from her mother because her mother does not accept her career choice.
   D. A parent believes the problem in the family is her spouse.

Child Development

Overview of Developmental Domains

Another area of child growth and development in which early educators must be knowledgeable is **developmental domains**. The early childhood years are marked by rapid growth and development with five main areas that develop concurrently:

- social-emotional
- cognitive
- language
- physical
- moral

Within each domain are typical stages and milestones that children should reach within a certain time frame; however, each child develops at her own pace, and some children may meet the stages and milestones earlier while some will meet them later. Conversely, early educators must also be aware of **atypical development**, or when behaviors fall outside of the expected range of development.

Educators should use these five developmental domains, the milestones and stages within them, and information on typical and atypical development when considering each child's overall development. Additionally, when planning lessons and activities, each developmental domain (described in Table 1.2.) should be addressed.

Table 1.2. Summary of Developmental Milestones

Developmental Milestone	Definition	Typical Development	Atypical Development
Social-emotional	feelings, emotions, self-concept, self-esteem, autonomy, relationship-building skills	ability to manage feelings, understand the feelings of others, and engage in positive interactions	difficult to comfort when upset; inability to self-soothe; difficulty self-regulating; difficulty adapting to new situations; acting withdrawn; avoids eye contact

Table 1.2. Summary of Developmental Milestones

Developmental Milestone	Definition	Typical Development	Atypical Development
Cognitive	how children process thoughts; maintain attention; remember, understand, plan, predict, regulate, and evaluate tasks and situations	shows progress in observation and interactions with world around them; engages in goal-directed behavior; displays progress in how to store, process, and use information; increased imaginative play	difficulty solving problems; difficulty acquiring new or basic information; difficulty learning advanced concepts; difficulty generalizing information
Language	how children understand, process, and produce language	increasing vocabulary, answers questions about a story, communicates easily, follows multi-step directions, has developing phonological skills, understands rhyming, has an increased ability to read sight words, puts sounds together to read words	difficulty developing speech-sound system; difficulty understanding or producing new language; limited vocabulary; limited working memory; difficulty with comprehension; struggles to remember sight words; uses short, simple sentences; limited social-play skills
Physical	development of fine motor (small muscles) and gross motor (large muscles) skills; includes development of the five senses	balanced muscle tone; ability to sit, stand, run, jump, skip, and throw; ability to grasp and pick up object; holds a pencil or crayon; turns off a light; plays with toys	difficulty running, jumping, throwing, or catching; difficulty with muscle tone (too high or too low); difficulty with motor coordination; delays in vestibular and proprioceptive systems; difficulty grasping objects; inability to eat with utensils; difficulty dressing or undressing; difficulty cutting, writing, or drawing
Moral	sense of right versus wrong and understanding how to make the right choices	understands difference between right and wrong; understands importance of family values; understands others' viewpoints; is considerate; shows empathy; understands rules and consequences	inability to show empathy; disregards rules and consequences; inability to understand other's viewpoints; inappropriately expresses and manages emotions; difficulty forming relationships; difficulty controlling inhibitions

Practice Question

12) A kindergarten teacher notes that a student is unable to turn the light switch in the classroom bathroom on and off and struggles to hold a crayon. Which of the following should the teacher conclude?

A. The student has atypical development in the social-emotional domain.
B. The student has atypical development in the physical domain.
C. The student has typical development for his age and grade level.
D. The student has typical physical development but atypical social-emotional development.

Social-Emotional Domain

The **social-emotional** domain is described as feelings and emotions, self-concept, self-esteem, autonomy, and behaviors and skills used to build and maintain positive relationships. Typical social-emotional development is the ability to manage one's own feelings, understand the feelings and needs of others, and positively interact with others. The milestones associated with social-emotional development are described in Table 1.3.

Table 1.3. Milestones in Socio-Emotional Development

Age/Grade	Milestones
Three years old	able to separate from parents in familiar situations able to take turns shows affection able to dress, undress, and feed self increasing independence—may refuse help
Four years old	prefers play with peers to playing alone will enjoy make-believe able to recognize unsafe behaviors
Kindergarten	knows the difference between real and make-believe (most of the time) initiates play and conversation wants to visit a friend's house can understand classroom rules
First grade	changing circle of friends ability to recognize feelings in others can solve some conflicts with peers without adult help understands the rules and norms of most situations
Second and third grades	development of empathy seeks out social interaction

Table 1.3. Milestones in Socio-Emotional Development	
Age/Grade	**Milestones**
	spends the bulk of social time with peers may feel insecure at times and need reassurance
Fourth and fifth grades	may develop a first crush (or pretend to have one) may have very strong friendships, such as a "best friend" has most social skills needed to be successful in the classroom

Atypical social-emotional development may emerge in many different ways. Some indicators of atypical social-emotional development include the following:

- difficulty to comfort or calm when upset
- an inability to calm oneself down
- the inability to self-soothe
- little or no self-regulation
- difficulty adapting to changing situations
- avoiding eye contact with others
- showing a similar level of affection to caregivers and strangers
- hurting oneself or others
- acting withdrawn

Social-emotional development that is misaligned with developmental milestones can be an indication of serious developmental difficulties and should be addressed immediately.

Practice Question

13) A prekindergarten teacher has a classroom of four-year-old students. Which behavior should the teacher expect students to have mastered?

A. an understanding of all classroom rules
B. an ability to resolve conflicts with peers without adult intervention
C. an ability to take turns with peers while playing with a toy
D. an understanding of the feelings of peers

Cognitive Development

Cognitive development is described as the way in which children process thoughts, maintain attention, remember, understand, and plan, predict, regulate, and evaluate tasks and situations. Typical cognitive development shows the progression of children in observing and interacting with the world around them. It includes engagement in goal-directed, intentional behaviors; progression in how children process, store, and use information; and an increase in imaginative play. Milestones in cognitive development are described in Table 1.4.

Table 1.4. Milestones in Cognitive Development

Age/Grade	Milestones
Three years old	plays with toys with moving parts (buttons, levers, puzzles) understands two is more than one can turn pages of a book can copy simple shapes on paper with crayon or large pencil can remove jar lids and open doors
Four years old	can identify some colors, shapes, and numbers can sort items that are the same and those that are different understands concepts of *before* and *after* can use scissors can copy letters of first name is developing concepts of print understands basic story events
Kindergarten	can count to twenty and identify most shapes and colors can write numbers to twenty can categorize shapes understands the concepts of largest and smallest can print name can focus on a single activity for around fifteen minutes is in the beginning stages of literacy
First grade	can begin decoding and sight word recognition is able to write many words and basic sentences understands the passing of time (days, weeks, months) can use logical reasoning can add and subtract basic numbers
Second and third grades	asks many in-depth questions often develops collections can plan ahead and make predictions understands cause and effect makes the transition from learning to read to reading to learn

Table 1.4. Milestones in Cognitive Development	
Age/Grade	**Milestones**
Fourth and fifth grades	makes in-depth connections understands broad or complicated cause/effect relationships seeks out new information from many sources

Atypical development may take the following forms:

- difficulty with problem-solving skills
- deficits in acquiring new or basic information (e.g., colors and shapes)
- difficulty in learning advanced concepts (e.g., counting, reading, and writing)
- difficulty generalizing information from one situation to the next
- difficulty adapting to new situations
- delays in early concepts (e.g., object permanence or recognizing the function of objects)

Practice Question

14) A first-grade teacher is asked to observe a student closely and record any behaviors that may indicate the need for further evaluation for possible atypical cognitive development. Which behavior should the teacher make note of?

A. The student struggles to understand complex cause and effect relationships.
B. The student is still in the process of learning to read.
C. The student struggles to plan ahead.
D. The student is still in the process of learning to count to five.

Language Development

Language development describes the way in which children understand, process, and produce language. This involves communication behaviors, such as listening and talking; literacy skills, such as reading, writing, comprehension, and expression; and nonverbal communication skills.

Although children develop language and speech at varying rates, typical development follows a predictable progression. Children are said to have typical language development when they have an increasing vocabulary; are able to answer questions about a story read independently or aloud; can easily communicate with adults and peers; can follow multiple-step directions; have developing phonological skills, such as knowledge of letters and sounds, can understand rhyming, or putting sounds together to form words; and have an increasing ability to remember and read sight words. Milestones in language development are described in Table 1.5.

Table 1.5. Milestones in Language Development

Age/Grade	Milestones
Three years old	follows 2 – 3-step instructions can say the name of most everyday objects can say own name can speak 2 – 3 sentences can hold a simple conversation
Four years old	can use most pronouns and many verbs and nouns correctly (in speech) can recite a familiar song or rhyme can say first and last name can answer *who*, *what*, *when*, *where* questions
Kindergarten	can form future and past tenses (in speech) can tell a story using several sentences can say name, address, and phone number can use language purposefully
First grade	can clearly communicate past and present events (in speech) can express themselves orally and in writing understands connection between written and spoken language
Second and third grades	can understand language use that it not literal can communicate purposefully in writing tries out many new words
Fourth and fifth grades	proficient oral language skills more advanced skills with written language

Check Your Understanding

What are some particular language development issues that early childhood educators will need to keep in mind when working with English language learners?

Children displaying atypical language development may have difficulty with different aspects of language in varying situations and during numerous stages of language development. Some children may have a challenging time with phonological development, or the speech-sound system; trouble understanding and producing language; a limited working memory; a hard time remembering sight words; experience frustration trying to comprehend a story while reading or while being read to; difficulty understanding questions; limited vocabulary; only use short, simple sentences; make frequent grammatical errors; have limited social play skills; and have a tough time carrying on conversations or choose to avoid them altogether.

Practice Question

15) Which of the following describes typical language development for a first grader?
   A. begins to name most familiar objects
   B. begins to focus on one activity for 5 – 10 minutes
   C. understands and follows multi-step directions
   D. has an interest in writing poetry

Physical Development

Physical development includes fine motor skills (the use of small muscles) and gross motor skills (the use of large muscles) as well as the development of the five senses: hearing, seeing, touching, tasting, and smelling. Typical motor development follows a predictable sequence that starts from the inner body, develops to the outer body, and moves from top to bottom. For example, children will gain control of their arms before their fingers and control their head first before their legs and arms. Children with typical gross motor development have balanced muscle tone and are able to sit, stand, walk, run, jump, skip, and throw an object along with performing other activities within certain timeframes. Children with typical fine motor development are able to grasp and pick up objects, hold a pencil or crayon, turn off a light, or play with toys. Milestones in physical development are described in Table 1.6.

Table 1.6. Milestones in Physical Development

Age/Grade	Milestones
Three years old	takes appropriately sized bites of food can run fairly easily can walk up stairs, climb, and pedal can build a tower of six blocks can draw and scribble begins potty training
Four years old	can use spoon and fork can pour liquids can drink from a cup and straw can catch a ball bounced at them has completed potty training
Kindergarten	can tiptoe, walk on a balance beam, jump rope can catch a ball can use the bathroom and wash hands independently shows hand dominance can use all eating utensils
First grade	can kick and catch easily

Table 1.6. Milestones in Physical Development

Age/Grade	Milestones
	can tie shoelaces handwriting becomes more readable has more stamina when writing
Second and third grades	can fasten buttons, zippers, and snaps can run and play longer without resting can ride a bike begins to lose baby teeth
Fourth and fifth grades	growth spurt hand dominance is fully formed may begin to enter puberty

Children with atypical gross motor development may have difficulty with the following:

- walking, running, jumping, or hopping
- throwing, rolling, or catching a ball
- irregular muscle tone (either low or high muscle tone)
- challenges with motor coordination
- delays in the vestibular system, which provides one's sense of balance
- delays in the proprioceptive system, which is the awareness of where one's body is in space

Atypical fine motor development may involve difficulty grasping objects; an inability to eat with utensils; difficulty dressing or undressing oneself; or challenges cutting with scissors, drawing, or writing.

Practice Question

16) A preschool teacher notices that some students alternate between writing or coloring with their right and left hands. How should the teacher proceed?

A. Do nothing since hand dominance typically does not emerge until kindergarten.
B. Do nothing since these students most likely have the ability to write with both hands.
C. Monitor for atypical physical development since hand dominance begins at around age two.
D. Monitor for atypical physical development since hand dominance should be set by age three.

Moral Development

Moral development is described as the sense of right versus wrong and the understanding of how to make the right choices. Moral development is influenced by experiences at home and within the daily environment, as well as the development of physical, cognitive, emotional, and social skills. Early social and emotional experiences and interactions with primary caregivers, as well as other children and adults, are indicators of moral development.

Typical moral development is when children understand the difference between right and wrong and behave accordingly; understand the importance of family values; understand that others have viewpoints; learn how to be considerate; show empathy; and understand the necessity of rules and the consequences for breaking them.

Atypical moral development may take the form of an inability to show empathy; disregarding rules and consequences; an inability to understand and accept the viewpoints of others; difficulty forming relationships; inappropriately expressing and managing emotions; and difficulty controlling inhibitions.

Practice Question

17) A first-grade teacher observes students at lunchtime and recess during the first week of school. Which situation most strongly suggests a student may have atypical moral development?

A. A student cries after falling down on the cement.
B. A student takes and eats a peer's pudding cup.
C. A student wants to borrow a peer's sweater.
D. A student appears to have already made a best friend.

Factors Affecting Child Development

As a young child grows, many factors can positively or negatively influence her progression in all developmental domains. An early childhood educator must be informed of the factors that may affect the children in their classroom and how they are developing.

One important factor that may affect young children's development is **genetics**, or inherited characteristics. Heredity plays a key role in growth and development. Children typically inherit at least some of their parents' characteristics of temperament; cognitive functions, such as intelligence, aptitudes, mental disorders or ailments; and physical abilities, such as height, weight, hair and eye color, and body structure.

> **Did You Know?**
>
> Many developed nations like France, Norway, and Sweden offer free or highly subsidized federally funded early childhood education programs for all children.

Brain development can also impact a child's development. Ninety percent of a child's brain develops within the first five years of life. At birth, an infant already has all the neurons, or brain cells, he will ever have; however, brain cells alone are not enough. Children need connection, or **synapses**, between brain cells. Synapses are made in droves during the early childhood years *if* children are given sufficient care and stimulation in the early years of life. Children who are neglected and/or experience few positive early learning experiences may lag behind in brain development.

Nutrition also plays a critical role in growth and development as growth is directly impacted by nutrition. A child's nutritional health has been linked to their parents' income and education and can have lifelong lasting effects. Children who are malnourished tend to be underweight, shorter than average, and slower to grow. Additionally, inadequate nutrition can impair cognitive and motor development. Furthermore, if children come to school lacking proper nutrition, they struggle to focus and complete activities as they are preoccupied with feeling hungry. Nutritional deficits are often irreversible.

Another important component of child development is a child's overall **health**. Overall health includes physical health, mental health, and social-emotional health. Social and economic factors, such as family income, education, nutrition, quality of housing, household and community safety, and access to resources can dramatically affect a child's overall health. Healthy child development contributes to school readiness and appropriate coping and social skills, which ultimately reduce academic, social, and behavioral difficulties.

Conversely, inadequate health experiences can lead to poor health outcomes throughout life, which may include cognitive limitations, behavioral problems, poor physical and mental health, cardiovascular disease and stroke, hypertension, diabetes, obesity, and mental health disorders. Intervening early by providing resources and education to families can interrupt an unhealthy life cycle and lead to improved child health and development that spans a lifetime.

Another important factor affecting child development is **public policy**. Under President Barack Obama, the Preschool for All bill was passed. The legislation establishes partnerships between federal and state governments to improve funding to provide high-quality preschool for four-year-olds from low- and moderate-income households.

However, national policies and practices still fall behind the incredible body of research and science regarding the benefits of access to high-quality early childhood education. Critical steps must be taken to ensure all families have access to this high-quality care. The first is providing appropriate funding in any state or setting. The second step is ensuring that all families can choose and afford high-quality, early childhood programs that are most appropriate for them. Finally, national policies must ensure that all early childhood professionals are diverse and effective leaders who are adequately compensated.

The **environment** in which children are raised also plays a key role in their development and shapes behavior, thinking, relationships with others, growth, and how emotions are processed. Environmental influences include social, cultural, and economic factors, characteristics of the family and household, urbanization, nutrition, pollutants, and the physical environment, such as climate, altitude, and temperature. A nurturing environment promotes positive development with fewer developmental obstacles. Children learn to appropriately process, regulate, and verbalize their emotions; cope with stress; and build and maintain relationships with adults and peers.

Consequently, several environmental factors can adversely affect a child's growth and development. An impoverished environment can lead to stunted growth and inadequate weight gain, poor academic performance, difficulty focusing and controlling impulses, physical health problems, and mental health disorders. Impoverished environments are also associated with child abuse and an increased incidence in physical injuries. Within a challenging home environment where children are exposed to parental stress, inappropriate discipline methods, discord, and parental mental health issues, children can have difficulty processing emotions and controlling their own behaviors.

Part of a child's environment is the **culture** in which the child is raised and the values of that culture. For example, some researchers believe that there are collectivist cultures, common in much of Asia, Central and South America, and Africa. **Collectivist** cultures value community needs over the needs of individuals. **Individualist** cultures on the other hand, which are common in Western Europe and North America, value independence and individual action. Whether a child is raised in a collectivist or individualist culture can shape the child's beliefs. For example, children raised in individualist cultures may feel very strongly that they are unique and distinct from all others. Children raised in a collectivist culture may dislike competitive games.

Another critical factor that may affect child development is **substance abuse**. Unfortunately, too many children are exposed to family members or caregivers who abuse alcohol or misuse legal drugs, or who use, manufacture, or distribute illegal drugs. Children exposed to substance abuse have a higher risk of behavior and medical problems, experience developmental and educational delays or mental health disorders, and may eventually abuse drugs or alcohol themselves. Additionally, parents who abuse drugs and alcohol often struggle to provide a safe and nurturing environment and prioritize their children's basic physical, physiological, and emotional needs.

Physical abuse is yet another factor that can affect children's overall development and, unless properly addressed, can last a lifetime. The primary effects begin during or immediately after physical abuse has taken place with pain, medical issues, and sometimes even death. The lasting effects of physical abuse may include brain damage leading to cognitive delays, vision loss, hearing loss, and the development of severe emotional, behavioral, or learning problems. Furthermore, the effects of physical abuse can manifest into high-risk, unhealthy, and dangerous behaviors. Individuals may engage in excessive promiscuity, smoking, and alcohol and drug abuse to cope with the physical and emotional pain.

The emotional effects can manifest into numerous psychological problems. Children who have been abused struggle significantly with their home lives, at school, and when developing relationships with peers. They are more likely to suffer from low self-esteem, fear, anxiety, and act aggressively toward peers, and other family members, especially siblings.

Physical abuse can also have damaging effects on children's social development. These children may struggle with trusting others, building and maintaining relationships, communicating appropriately, and might turn to aggression to solve problems. If not resolved, these issues can negatively influence their adult lives as well. Thus, it is critical for early childhood professionals to recognize the signs and symptoms of abuse and report any suspected abuse immediately.

Emotional distress is another facet of a child's life that can affect growth and development. Several factors can cause emotional distress: poverty, repeated abuse, loss of a loved one, parental substance abuse or mental illness, exposure to violence, a natural disaster, a serious injury, or a frightening experience like a car accident or getting robbed. If a child has experienced one of these situations but is protected by supportive adult relationships, their stress levels can return to normal.

However, if a child experiences prolonged exposure to stressful situations without supporting and caring adults, stress can become toxic and disrupt normal brain development. And, the more adverse the situation, the greater the likelihood is that a child will experience developmental delays and other issues. Providing children with stable, caring, and responsive relationships as early as possible is key in preventing or reversing the damage caused by toxic stress.

Finally, **economic factors** can affect children's development across all domains. The term *socioeconomic status* (SES) includes a person or family's income, educational achievement, occupational achievement, and social class and status. SES is proven to be a reliable indicator of outcomes throughout a person's life. SES impacts where a child lives, quality and quantity of food, and learning experiences the child has inside and outside of the home. Children who come from families with low-to-moderate SES typically have fewer opportunities and privileges than do their higher SES counterparts, which can lead to difficulties in psychological and physical health, education, and family well-being. However, there are many programs, including charter schools and after-school programs, that seek to change these trends through education and intervention.

Practice Question

18) Which of the following is a genetic condition that impacts a child's cognitive development?

A. Down syndrome
B. cystic fibrosis
C. poverty
D. low birth weight

Answer Key

1) C: Behaviorism is rooted in stimulus-response behaviors, so rewards would reinforce good behavior and consequences would lead to the extinction of poor behavior.

2) A: Pouring the same amount of water into cups of different sizes and asking the child which cup has more would assess whether the child understands that volume is the same even if it changes form or appearance.

3) B: By observing and interacting with adults, young children internalize the "tools" of learning (e.g., language and symbols).

4) D: This option shows that the teacher is providing opportunities for students to leverage multiple intelligences (e.g., verbal-linguistic, spatial-visual, and interpersonal).

5) A: The student uses a motor response by taking away one block, uses pictures to subtract one block, and then uses a standard math symbolic algorithm to subtract one from two.

6) C: Students can learn how to use graduated cylinders by watching people use these devices in a video, which is a symbolic model of the desired behavior.

7) D: Whether or not the psychosocial crisis is resolved satisfactorily determines the child's development per Erickson.

8) D: The base of Maslow's hierarchy is physiological needs (e.g., food), so giving information about the free lunch program to parents would be the best activity to help meet students' needs in alignment with the base of Maslow's hierarchy.

9) D: Knowing the difference between morphemes and syllables describes understanding and comparing, which are more cognitively rigorous than the other options, which describe simple recall.

10) C: Macrosystems are broad cultural constructs that may impact a child.

11) A: The family projection process begins with a parent believing there is a problem with a child even when there is not. The parent then observes the child, believes the problem has been confirmed, and treats the child as though there is a problem—even when there may not be one.

12) B: An inability to turn on and off a light or hold a crayon describes atypical physical development for a kindergarten student.

13) C: The ability to take turns is typically mastered at age three, so a four-year-old prekindergarten student should have mastered this if development is typical.

14) D: By kindergarten, most students with typical cognitive development will have learned to count to twenty; if a first-grade student is still learning to count to five, it could signal possible atypical cognitive development.

15) C: A first grader who understands and follows multi-step directions is displaying typical development in receptive language.

16) A: Preschool students are still developing fine motor skills and may not show preference for one hand over the other until kindergarten.

17) B: Taking and eating a peer's pudding cup shows an inability to control inhibitions and a disregard for appropriate social interactions.

18) A: Down syndrome is a genetic condition that impacts cognitive development.

2. Collaboration & Professionalism

Collaboration

Family Partnerships

Because of the multiple family systems that may exist within an early childhood classroom or program, it is critical to implement a variety of strategies to involve families in their child's development and learning. Developing strong relationships with families is a key component of developmentally appropriate practice and leads to improved social, behavioral, and academic outcomes for children. Furthermore, families who communicate regularly and in a variety of ways with their child's program feel more involved and knowledgeable about their child's education. And, teachers who establish partnerships with families feel more satisfied in their roles. Developing family partnerships can greatly improve program quality.

Several strategies are available to ensure that all families are involved in classroom activities and their child's overall program. When implementing family activities, it is important to consider each family's time constraints, access to technology, home language, and communication preferences. Within the early childhood program, one way to involve families is with a family center, or a dedicated place where families can gather, talk informally with their child's teacher, and have access to a computer and the internet. This space can also be used to conduct family-teacher conferences.

Another strategy is a monthly or weekly newsletter. The newsletter should be available in multiple languages as appropriate and in multiple formats, such as electronic and paper copies. Program events, curriculum information, community resources, and researched information on child development are some examples of content that may be included in such a newsletter.

Incorporating program events is another way to involve families. Program events offer activities in which all family members can attend and participate. Additionally, the program can encourage families to become involved in planning such events. Some events may include an open house to showcase the program, classrooms, and children's work; a family movie night; a family science night where families can come and participate in different simple science activities together; fall fun night with fall-themed activities for families to work on together; family fitness night, where health and nutrition information are presented and fitness activities are available; and family field trips.

A program may also develop a website to communicate information about classroom activities, share photos of children, and provide daily information as well as links to additional community resources and events. An individual classroom can incorporate family involvement strategies on such a site as well. Other family involvement ideas include the following:

- inviting families for breakfast, lunch, or snack
- a parent questionnaire for families to complete when beginning a program

- a limited-access class website
- text message reminders
- daily notes home
- frequent phone calls
- conversations at drop-off and pickup
- group email
- classroom newsletter provided in multiple languages and formats
- family-teacher conferences to discuss child progress and information sharing
- take-home activity kits that children and families complete together at home
- home visits
- inviting family input in program planning as appropriate (e.g. best days/times for events or extracurriculars, types of homework support desired)

Regardless of the activity, regular and direct communication will ensure that families receive information that is relevant, accurate, and timely.

> **Helpful Hint**
>
> At the beginning of the school year, it is a good idea to ask families how they prefer communications (e.g., phone, text, e-mail).

Families will be culturally diverse, and teachers must be able to interact with families from various backgrounds. The ability to communicate with and understand people from a culture different from one's own is called **cross-cultural competence**. Developing cross-cultural competence is important so that teachers do not presume that the values, beliefs, and practices of students' families are identical to their own. Some strategies for cross-cultural competence include the following:

- Learn about families: What are their goals for their child? What do they teach and learn at home?
- Adapt service delivery when necessary: Can materials be translated into other languages? Can communication styles be adapted to cultural norms?
- Value diversity: How can students and families share parts of their culture?
- Be open and seek to understand: Do I have all the information? Have I spoken directly with the parent or family member?
- Be honest and humble: Do I admit when I lack knowledge of those who are different? Do I seek out this knowledge?

Striving to form genuinely trusting relationships with families from different cultures exemplifies for students' **global awareness,** or the capacity to competently navigate the cross-cultural world in which we live.

Because family systems are so diverse, it is also important for programs and teachers to encourage and provide information on community involvement and resources. A characteristic of a high-quality program is linking families to resources within the community that can extend learning beyond the classroom. This information should be provided in multiple formats to ensure all families have access.

Community activities may include health, nutrition, and fitness resources; educational resources, fairs, and activities; community events; public library information and activities; cultural events like plays, concerts, or museum events; sporting events; and organizations and resources within the community that support children and families. A great indicator of a high-quality educational program is the way in which it develops relationships, involves families, and links families to community resources. How families perceive the school environment and staff determines their level of involvement in their child's school experiences. Creating an environment of trust, respect, open communication, and one where families feel welcome is critical to successful family involvement.

Did You Know?

Students whose parents are involved in their education adapt well to school; have better social skills; and have higher grades, scores, and attendance rates—regardless of income or background.

Practice Question

1) A fourth-grade teacher is planning a parent education night to talk about "strategies to nourish a love of reading." Which option would help the teacher show cultural competence during this event?

A. recognizing that interest in reading is limited to individualist cultures
B. providing handouts translated into other languages
C. encouraging students to attend with their parents
D. holding the event at a venue off school grounds

Other Partnerships

PK – 4 teachers do not work in a vacuum. Rather, they are part of a group of many stakeholders invested in positive outcomes for students. Teachers will find themselves partnering with other teachers, school administrators and counselors, and special education personnel.

One way in which teachers must partner with colleagues is as part of an **individualized education plan (IEP) team**. The general education teacher is part of this team and must

- know the IEP;
- understand the expectations to implement it;
- know who is available to help;
- identify accommodations that could be used in the general education classroom;
- implement the IEP;
- communicate with parents, other teachers, and professionals; and
- monitor student progress.

In some general education classrooms, **paraprofessionals** may be assigned. These individuals may be offering instructional, language, or behavioral supports to individuals or small groups of students. They may also assist students who need physical or medical support in the classroom. One role of the general education teacher is to guide paraprofessionals as necessary to ensure all students' needs are met. Paraprofessionals are best able to support students when they receive clear information on the core curriculum as well as the resources available to help students succeed.

School counselors are other professionals with whom general education teachers may collaborate. Counselors participate in IEP programs, help in the placement of students moving on to the next level of education, and help guide the social-emotional development of students. Counselors can be a great resource to partner with general education teachers in the case of a dispute among students that requires an outside mediator or a bullying situation that the general education teacher has struggled to resolve.

General education teachers will also partner with **community members** in a variety of ways. Sometimes the needs of students and families cannot be met in the school alone. Individuals like social workers, health care workers, and nonprofit associates can be important resources for students and families.

As part of partnering with students and families, another role of an education professional is advocating for children, families, and early childhood education programs. **Advocacy** is not just a political tool; it involves supporting, raising awareness, defending, or speaking out in the best interests of an individual or group. Early educators are responsible for advocating on a daily basis because they are aware of the needs of children, families, and programs. They are also familiar with trends and changes in the profession and how these changes affect the profession.

As advocates for children and families, educators should build a team of people who know what is in the best interest of the child and family; know the family's goals for the child; and understand the family's strengths, needs, and available resources to formulate a plan for the child. In addition, they should utilize multiple resources and services to provide support and information to families and collaborate with families on strategies that can be used at home to strengthen the child's skills.

Practice Question

2) A first-grade teacher suspects that one of her students may be homeless based on conversations with the child and his father. In order to provide support and advocate for her student, the teacher should do which of the following?

A. ask the student if he is homeless during a private conference
B. speak to an administrator and the school counselor about acquiring resources for the family
C. ignore her concerns; this is a private matter and none of her business
D. invite the child and his father to stay with her until they can find a place to stay

Professional Guidelines

Laws Affecting K – 4 Teachers

One law all educators must abide by is the Family Educational Rights and Privacy Act (FERPA). **FERPA** has the following provisions:

- Parents or students aged eighteen or older (or those attending school beyond high school) may inspect and review educational records.
- Parents or students aged eighteen or older (or those attending school beyond high school) may request amendments to inaccurate or misleading records. If no amendment is made, a statement of disagreement may be placed in the record by the parent or student.

- Written permission from parents or students aged 18 or older (or those attending school beyond high school) must be obtained before any information from an education record may be released UNLESS
    - it is released to a school to which the student is transferring;
    - it is used for audit or evaluation purposes;
    - it is released to a school official with a "legitimate educational interest";
    - it is released to parties providing financial aid to the student;
    - it is given to organizations involved in certain school research;
    - it is given to accrediting organizations;
    - it is released per court order or subpoena;
    - it is given to officials for a health or safety emergency;
    - it is lawfully given to state or local authorities in the juvenile justice system; and
    - it is "directory" information (student name, address, phone number, date and place of birth, honors and awards, dates of attendance), in which case parents and students must be informed of this ahead of time and given enough time to request that information not be included.

Another responsibility of educators is to identify and analyze the impact of federal and state laws on education in the classroom. Several laws have significantly impacted PK – 4education. The most recent law to impact the profession is the **Every Student Succeeds Act (ESSA),** which replaced the No Child Left Behind Act in 2015. This law's commitment to equal opportunity for all students has made significant progress in recent years due to the efforts of educators, parents, students, and the community.

ESSA focuses on equality for all students by protecting disadvantaged and high-needs students; requires high academic standards be taught to all students in order to prepare them for college and career readiness; ensures that educators, students, families, and communities have the critical information needed by administering statewide assessments that measure performance on academic standards; maintains and builds upon the Obama administration's investment in improving access to high-quality preschool; expects accountability and action in low-performing schools to have positive effects on graduation rates and students who are not progressing; and works to support and expand local innovations that include evidence-based and place-based interventions created by local leaders and educators.

Another important law educators must understand is the **Individuals with Disabilities Act (IDEA)**. This law makes certain that children with disabilities in the United States receive free and appropriate services in the **least restrictive environment,** which means that to the maximum extent appropriate, children with disabilities should be educated with peers who are not disabled. Children who receive special education services should not be removed from the general education classroom unless education in the general education classroom cannot be achieved. IDEA oversees state and public agencies and how early intervention, special education, and related services are provided to eligible infants, toddlers, children, and youth with special needs. IDEA is divided into two parts: Part B and Part C:

- Part B provides special education services to children and youth ages three to twenty-one.
- Part C provides early intervention services to infants and toddlers with disabilities from birth through two years and their families.

Making referrals and implementing interventions is a major responsibility of educators and is required by law. If a child has a possible disability, a parent or public agency, such as a teacher or other caregiver, can request an **initial evaluation**. After the initial request, the evaluation must be completed within sixty days and must follow procedures to

- determine if the child does have a disability under IDEA,
- determine the needs of the child, and
- develop an IEP for children under Part B and an individualized family service plan (IFSP) for children under Part C.

Study Tip

To remember the ages of children served in Part B and Part C of IDEA, think of Part B as **b**ig kids, or those aged three to twenty-one, and Part C as **c**hildren who are small—birth to age two.

After the initial referral and evaluation, an IEP or an IFSP is developed in collaboration with team and family members who understand the best interests of the child. Teachers must know the intricacies of each child's IEP or IFSP. The IEP includes the child's present level of academic and functional performance (PLAAFP); measurable academic and functional goals; how and when progress toward goals will be measured; the special education services, aids, and other related services provided to the child; and the necessary accommodations required to measure academic achievement and functional performance.

The IFSP includes present levels of the child's physical, cognitive, communicative, social/emotional, and adaptive development; information on the family's resources, priorities, and concerns; results or outcomes that are measurable and expected for the child and family to achieve, how progress will be determined, and what modifications need to be made, if any. Finally, it includes a statement of specific services the child and family will receive.

An additional law affecting teachers requires that suspected abuse or neglect be reported. Teachers by law are mandated reporters, and if abuse or neglect is suspected, a report must be filed to the **Pennsylvania ChildLine**. Reports can be made by phone or online; however, mandated reporters making an oral report must also make a written report within forty-eight hours and may use the form provided on the Pennsylvania Department of Human Services website.

Did You Know?

An IEP is implemented in the educational setting and is focused on the child only. The IFSP can be implemented in any appropriate setting, and services include the child's family as well.

Financial penalties may occur for failing to report. When reporting, educators should provide as much information and facts as possible.

Practice Question

3) A kindergarten student comes to school with dark bruises on the back of his neck and has suddenly become withdrawn and quiet. When asked by his teacher, the student responds that he "was bad" and "got punished" by his dad. What should the teacher do?

A. assume the bruises are from something else
B. talk to the students' parents about the issue
C. tell a colleague and have her report the bruises and behavior
D. report the abuse online and provide as much information as possible

Standards for K – 4 Teachers

In addition to roles and responsibilities and laws affecting K – 4 teachers, regulations for program licensing, ethical guidelines, and state and professional standards are also in place.

Some early childhood programs that are not part of public schools are under federal regulation by the **Office of Head Start (OHS)**. These programs must follow the Head Start Program Performance Standards. Other centers are regulated by the **Pennsylvania Department of Health and Human Services**. Elementary schools are typically overseen by the Pennsylvania Department of Education (PDE).

Ethical guidelines provide specifics on how educators are expected to act and what they should and should not do. The Pennsylvania Professional Standards and Practices Commission (PSPC) and the National Association for the Education of Young Children (NAEYC) have specific guidelines for ethical and professional responsibilities.

The **Code of Professional Practice and Conduct for Educators**, established by the commonwealth of Pennsylvania, contains three major sections:

- Commitment to Students (thirteen guidelines)
- Commitment to Colleagues (eight guidelines)
- Commitment to the Profession (eleven guidelines)

These guidelines must be followed; violations of any guideline will be used as supporting evidence for disciplinary action.

The NAEYC Code of Ethical Conduct contains ideals and principles related to ethical responsibilities to children, ethical responsibilities to families, ethical responsibilities to colleagues, and ethical responsibilities to community and society.

Teachers must also teach the **Pennsylvania Core Standards** for all subjects for students in grades PK – 4. These standards are intentionally designed to build on each other each subsequent year. Teachers must also familiarize themselves with the **assessment anchors**, anchor descriptors, and eligible content aligned to the Pennsylvania Core Standards. This will ensure that students receive instruction and classroom assessments aligned with state standards.

Individual schools or districts will also have a **technology or IT policy** that teachers must abide by. This may include provisions for keeping student data secure, using school devices only for school-related purposes, and policies on the use of school or class websites.

Practice Question

4) Which of the following is a guideline in the Code of Professional Practice and Conduct for Educators?

A. shall not be on school premises or at a school-related activity involving students, while under the influence of, possessing, or consuming alcoholic beverages or illegal or unauthorized drugs
B. shall not provide students guidance or advice on preparation for college or the college testing and admissions process but will leave this work to designated officials
C. shall not acknowledge a student or his family if the student appears in a public space at which the teacher is also present
D. shall not require students to purchase any materials, such as notebooks, paper, or pencils for use in the classroom

Instruction

The concept of developmentally appropriate practice drives everyday instruction, classroom management, and child guidance in the classroom. **Developmentally appropriate practice (DAP)** is based on current research about how children learn and develop as well as effective practices in early education. In DAP, teachers meet children at their current developmental level both individually and as a group, guiding each child toward challenging yet attainable learning goals. There are three core considerations of DAP:

- knowledge about child development and learning
- knowledge of what is individually appropriate
- knowledge of cultural importance

When implementing DAP, an educator should incorporate a **universal design for learning (UDL)**. A UDL provides all children with the opportunity to access, participate, and make progress in the general curriculum by modifying how information is presented, selecting available materials and activities, and choosing how they demonstrate and engage in learning. In a UDL, the traditional curriculum should provide multiple, varied, and flexible options to accommodate the needs of all children. In return, children become experts who are in control of their own learning. They can assess their own learning needs, monitor progress, and regulate and maintain their own interest, effort, and persistence.

Table 2.1. Universal Design for Learning Guidelines

Multiple Means of Engagement	Multiple Means of Representation	Multiple Means of Action and Expression
allow choices to meet multiple interests and encourage authentic learning	provide alternatives for visual and auditory information and multiple ways of presenting information	vary response interactions and provide access to tools and assistive technology
allow choices to drive effort and persistence via collaboration, community, and feedback	clarify and illustrate language and symbols for all learners	use multimedia tools for expression, communication, and composition

Table 2.1. Universal Design for Learning Guidelines

Multiple Means of Engagement	Multiple Means of Representation	Multiple Means of Action and Expression
allow choices for self-regulation, self-assessment, and reflection	drive comprehension via provision of background knowledge, main ideas, visualization, and generalization	support executive functioning through planning, goal setting, strategy use, and progress monitoring

As part of DAP and UDL, PK – 4teachers will have to select and adapt existing instructional materials and activities as well as design their own. This process will vary based on the content area, the student population, and the needs of individual students. Quality instructional materials

- are accurate,
- align to standards,
- are easy to use,
- are easy to modify,
- provide learning opportunities at different cognitive levels,
- include assessment components,
- are differentiated for different skill levels and language abilities,
- are culturally relevant and provide all needed background information,
- include diverse activities, and
- are engaging to students.

Did You Know?

Many educational publishers use teacher reviewers to help ensure their products meet the needs of educators before they release and sell these materials.

The goal of UDL is to develop learners who are purposeful and motivated, resourceful and knowledgeable, and strategic and goal-directed. This is part of providing a **positive social context** for learning. When there is a positive social context, students have strong relationships with teachers and each other. Best practices for creating a positive social context for learning include

- exhibiting patience with students,
- showing respect to students,
- listening to students,
- getting to know students,
- driving student interest in the subject matter,
- teaching with demonstrations,
- having a good sense of humor, and
- making modifications to help all students.

More specific strategies include the following:

- Show welcoming and inclusion by
  - knowing all students' names and pronouncing them correctly,
  - avoiding any stereotypes or generalizations about any student group,
  - learning about each student's cultural background, and
  - learning a few key phrases in the native language of ELL students.
- Show sensitivity by
  - recognizing students' anxiety with challenging material,
  - recognizing mood shifts, and
  - giving consequences without singling anyone out in front of the class.
- Show openness by
  - giving students choices,
  - encouraging student self-reflection,
  - allowing students to provide input,
  - holding class meetings, and
  - embracing new technology.
- Show fairness by
  - avoiding favorites,
  - acknowledging individuality,
  - modeling tolerance, and
  - setting clear grading guidelines.

Practice Question

5) A third-grade teacher wants to ensure that all students in the class will be successful in reading a literary passage about baseball. Which strategy could BEST ensure students are successful?

A. dividing the text into chunks and assigning student groups a small chunk of the passage
B. having students use reader's theatre to read the passage aloud
C. introducing background knowledge (e.g., key vocabulary) needed to understand the passage
D. asking students to write a summary of the passage after they have completed silent reading

Assessment

Formal Assessments

Some assessments that are used for educational purposes are considered formal and some are informal. **Formal assessments** measure student progress using standardized measures. Both achievement and aptitude tests are examples of formal assessments. Formal assessments may be oral, written, or computer-based. For example, annual state tests and Wechsler Scales are commonly used formal assessments. Generally, formal assessments are purchased from a publisher who has specified both administration and scoring procedures. An advantage to using a formal test is that a great deal of effort has gone into making sure that it accurately measures what it claims to measure; however, formal assessments are expensive and time-consuming, and are therefore not practical for daily application.

Formal assessments are frequently used to make educational placement decisions and measure the effectiveness of educational programs, while informal tests are used to help districts, schools, and teachers make informed classroom decisions.

Depending on the goal of the assessment instrument, teachers may use formative, summative, or diagnostic assessments. **Diagnostic assessments** are formal or informal assessments given before a learning experience that provide teachers with a baseline of student's skills. Formal diagnostic assessments include Developmental Reading Assessments (DRAs); Dynamic Indicators of Basic Early Learning Skills (DIBELS); and Comprehension, Attitude, Strategies, Interests (CASI). Each of these formal diagnostic assessments provides teachers with information about student reading levels; however diagnostic assessments may also be used in other content areas.

Screening assessments are a type of diagnostic assessment given to all students to identify the need for interventions. Screening assessments must be accurate and sensitive enough to identify students who may be at risk for difficulties. Screening assessments are often part of a response to intervention (RtI) framework.

Standardized assessments are formal assessments that fall into two categories: norm-referenced and criterion-referenced. Norm-referenced assessments measure an individual student against a group of other test takers, typically those of the same age or grade level. Results are reported in a percentile ranking.

Norm-referenced tests are most often used to measure achievement, intelligence, aptitude, and personality. Achievement tests are a type of norm-referenced test that measure which skills a student has mastered. These often fall under categories like reading and mathematics. Popular achievement tests include

- the Iowa Test of Basic Skills (ITBS),
- the Peabody Individual Achievement Test,
- the Wechsler Individual Achievement Test (WIAT-III), and
- the Stanford Achievement Test.

Criterion-referenced tests measure an individual's performance as it relates to criteria or a predetermined benchmark. These tests are generally used to measure a student's progress toward meeting certain objectives. They do not compare test takers to one another but rather compare student knowledge against the set criteria. Criterion-referenced tests include everything from annual state tests to those created by teachers or educational publishers to assess mastery of learning objectives.

> **Study Tips**
>
> Formative assessments are used while students are *forming* their knowledge; summative assessments are used to add up all of student learning into one lump *sum*.

One new incarnation of the criterion-referenced test used to meet federal mandates is **standards-referenced testing** or **standards-based assessment**. These tests measure a student's performance against certain content standards as defined by each grade level and subject. They are typically scored in categories such as basic, proficient, and advanced; or unsatisfactory, satisfactory, and advanced. Most annual state accountability tests such as PSSA are standards-based, criterion-referenced tests.

Practice Question

6) A third-grade student took the Stanford Achievement Test, and a score report was sent home. The student's parents ask the teacher for help understanding what the 65th percentile means. How should the teacher explain this?

A. The student answered 65 percent of the questions correctly.
B. The student outperformed 35 percent of other students.
C. The student outperformed 65 percent of other students.
D. The student answered 35 percent of the questions correctly.

Informal Assessments

Informal assessments are regularly used to evaluate classroom performance and drive instruction. Typically, informal assessments are created by teachers or committees of teachers but have not gone through the rigorous validation processes of formal assessments. Most districts use informal benchmark tests but provide some degree of standardization in the administration and scoring of the test.

Formative assessments are used throughout the learning experience to help teachers make instructional decisions and to provide feedback to students. Examples of formative assessments include anecdotal records, questioning techniques, and pop quizzes. Generally, formative assessments do not provide quantifiable data, but they are valuable for providing teachers with information in order to tailor instruction to specific student needs.

Table 2.2. Examples of Formative Assessments	
anecdotal records	notes that teachers keep that indicate student performance according to learning or behavior goals
observation	watching students perform a learning activity to determine strengths and weaknesses so that students may receive targeted remediation
pop quiz	a short, unexpected assessment used to indicate student strengths and weaknesses regarding newly learned material; is more useful for giving the teacher and student feedback than it is for grading
ticket out the door (exit ticket)	open-ended questions that students must answer when ending a lesson; provides insight about student strengths and challenges in relation to new learning
think/pair/share	involves all students thinking about a question related to content and then articulating their answers to a partner, allowing them to practice active listening and learn from one another; serves as a formative assessment when teachers observe discussions and ask partner groups to share their answers

Table 2.2. Examples of Formative Assessments	
journals/learning logs	kept by students throughout a learning experience to journal their thoughts and questions; used by teachers to assess student understanding
discussion	informs the teacher about students' general understanding of learning topics; must be facilitated in a way that prevents some students from dominating the conversation while others avoid participation
questioning	helps teachers gain insight into student understanding; requires maintaining student engagement by calling on students at random and giving ample think time to the class
signaled response/choral response	signaled response: when a student performs a gesture to answer a question; could include giving a thumbs up or thumbs down, standing up or sitting down, or walking to a certain corner of the classroom; requires everyone to engage on a physical level, though some students may copy one another rather than think independently choral response: when everyone in the class gives the answer at the same time; can improve student engagement for short answer questions; involves explicitly telling students prior to each learning experience whether the expectation is to raise their hand or call out answers

Summative assessments may be formal or informal and evaluate student achievement after learning takes place. Standardized state tests are an example of a formal summative assessment. End-of-unit tests and benchmark tests are examples of informal summative assessments. Summative assessments may be used for accountability and grades as they are a measure of student performance in relation to the objectives.

One of the most common types of classroom assessments is a **curriculum-based assessment (CBA)**. This is an assessment of student progress through the curriculum. In other words, it is an assessment of the curriculum that has been taught in the classroom. CBA may be formative or summative. Formative CBA is essential for **progress monitoring**, or the ongoing assessment of student progress toward learning goals.

A middle ground between a formative assessment and a summative assessment is the **benchmark assessment**. This type of assessment is more formal than a formative assessment but is not a high-stakes standardized summative assessment. Benchmark assessments are sometimes called interim assessments or predictive assessments. They track student progress and determine the degree to which students are on track to perform well on future summative assessments. Benchmark assessments may be formal (created and field-tested by an educational publisher) or informal (created by individual teachers).

> **Check Your Understanding**
>
> Why would a teacher use a diagnostic assessment?

Regardless of the type, an assessment will only be accurate if it is aligned with the instructional objectives and learning activities; therefore, how the teacher will use formative and summative assessments is a crucial part of the planning process that should not be overlooked.

Practice Question

7) A second-grade teacher gives a weekly spelling test. The teacher reads the word out loud, and students write it down on a sheet of paper. What is this an example of?

A. an informal curriculum-based assessment
B. a formal summative assessment
C. an informal diagnostic assessment
D. a formal screening assessment

Creating Assessments

For each type of assessment, there are a variety of formats that may be used to evaluate student learning.

Convergent questions may be used as summative tests. These are questions that have clear, correct answers. **Selected response**, or multiple-choice questions, are the most common example of convergent questions. They can be used in any subject to provide information about student content knowledge; however, they have limitations.

Convergent questions are beneficial in assessing a student's literal and interpretive comprehension. They are also versatile and easy to grade, making them a popular choice among educators. For example, in reading, a teacher might give a test with convergent questions to assess a student's understanding of the plot of a book or of lower-order, concrete skills like spelling or grammar; in math, a teacher may present a series of math problems.

The majority of district- and state-administered assessments primarily use convergent questions; however, convergent questions can be difficult to write. Furthermore, they do not allow for creativity and have limited analytical possibilities, as it is also difficult to determine the reason for student error, making remediation a challenge. These assessment types are not well suited to all subjects and are most appropriate where there is only one right answer (e.g., in math, science, grammar, vocabulary, and certain instances in social studies).

In reading and writing assessments, **cloze questions** are often used in addition to multiple-choice questions. Also called "fill-in-the-blanks," these are questions in which certain words or phrases are left out of a text. Students must then fill in the appropriate word or phrase. Cloze tests are primarily used to assess students' vocabulary and their ability to use context for comprehension. Depending on the goals of the assessment, cloze tests can be objective—meaning they have one specific correct answer—or subjective—meaning there are multiple ways to correctly complete the text.

> **Helpful Hint**
>
> Quality assessments also contain various levels of cognitive rigor. A common framework is Depths of Knowledge (DOK). DOK 1 = recall; DOK 2 = skills/concepts; DOK 3 = strategic thinking; and DOK 4 = extended thinking.

To assess a student's critical or creative comprehension and writing skills, teachers should use **divergent questions**. Divergent questions are open-ended and designed to assess a student's ability to analyze, evaluate, and create. These typically come in the form of **constructed responses** in which the teacher gives the students a prompt to which the students respond. Essay tests are easy to write, but time-consuming and subjective to grade and are therefore more practical to use either as a summative assessment or in conjunction with other types of questions. They may also be used as formative assessments that can be quickly reviewed. Such divergent questions are best suited to English/language arts and social studies.

When discussing a prompt, it is important that the teacher considers the objectives to assess. Test instructions should clearly focus students on those objectives. For example, when completing a unit on descriptive language, the teacher may give the students the prompt, "Write a paragraph about the first day of school." The teacher should also include a statement like, "Include at least three examples of descriptive language" or, more effectively, the teacher should provide a rubric that describes the criteria of assessment in detail (see below for more information on rubrics). Otherwise, students might focus more on factual accuracy, plot development, or grammar than on developing effective descriptive language.

One important trend in student assessment is authentic assessment. **Authentic assessment** measures the student's ability to use knowledge in a direct, relevant, often real-world way.

In an authentic literacy assessment, students apply reading and writing skills in a pragmatic or practical way. For example, high school students might work on writing a resume or a profile on a professional networking platform. These are both examples of an authentic assessment of skills in writing for a formal audience. Or, a fifth-grade teacher might give students brochures for places to explore on a field trip and ask them to read and summarize the high points of each brochure. These are authentic literacy assessments since they measure literacy skills in a pragmatic context.

Authentic assessments offer opportunities to go much deeper than traditional written tests. There are numerous examples—many of them cross-curricular—that can be used to assess reading and writing skills in an authentic context. Teachers across multiple disciplines can collaborate to design projects that assess multiple skills. For example, a science teacher and an English teacher might work together to have students research and summarize a scientific article to earn a grade for English and then design an experiment based on the article for a grade in science.

Practice Question

8) A third-grade teacher wants to prepare students for the format of the PSSA. Which type of assessment should the teacher give?

A. authentic assessment
B. selected-response
C. cloze
D. exit ticket

Other Assessment Types

Not all assessment methods are written tests. **Rubrics** are fixed scales that measure performance, offering detailed descriptions of criteria that define each level of performance. Rubrics set the expectations of an assignment, thereby clarifying the standards of quality work and improving consistency and reliability in evaluations. Rubrics work best with writing, projects, and performance-based learning activities.

Analytical checklists outline student performance criteria; as students show mastery of each required skill in standards-based

> **Helpful Hint**
>
> Rubrics may be holistic or analytic. Holistic rubrics assess the totality of the work as a whole while analytic rubrics break the work into categories that each receive a rating that is then totaled for the overall score.

education, teachers can mark off that skill. Checklists should be written in language easily understood by students and their parents but should be based on state standards. Analytical checklists only note if a student has mastered a skill; they do not provide information regarding the degree to which the student has met proficiency. Typically, the teacher would date the checklist so that progression can be seen over time. Checklists work best in activities that require the incremental mastery of skills, such as athletics, instrumental music, languages, math fluency, and pre-reading skills.

Table 2.3. Sample Analytical Checklist: Pre-K

Objective	Date of Mastery
rides a tricycle	
matches objects by shape	
matches objects by color	

Anecdotal notes will frequently accompany checklists. **Anecdotal notes** are written records of the teacher's observations of a student. Records should be specific, objective, and focused on outlined criteria. Anecdotal notes provide cumulative information about how each individual performs and may include information about learning and/or behavior. Anecdotal notes are particularly useful for targeting remediation; however it can be overwhelming for a teacher to attempt to observe every action of every student in this way.

Scoring guides are similar to rubrics because they outline criteria for quality work and define levels of proficiency; however, they differ from rubrics in that each criterion is weighted with a multiplier. For example, a rubric may measure writing scores based on mechanics, word choice, and organization. On the other hand, a scoring guide may indicate that word choice is more important than mechanics, so the score on the word choice portion of the rubric will be multiplied by two.

Rating scales are used to rate attitudes and opinions on a continuum. Typically, a **rating scale** will ask participants to rate an idea or an experience on a number scale or a category, such as "strongly agree," "agree," "neutral," "disagree," and "strongly disagree." The most commonly used rating scale is the Likert Scale. The advantage of using rating scales is that students are required to rate the degree to which they feel a certain way; however, students are not always honest. Rating scales can be used for self-assessment, peer assessment, or to gain student input to evaluate learning activities and overall understanding of concepts. For example, the teacher may ask students to rate the participation of their peers during a cooperative learning activity.

Portfolio assessments are especially effective in art, although they may also be used in language arts and potentially other subjects. Students collect a variety of artifacts as evidence of learning to be evaluated when using **portfolio** assessments. Written work, photographs of projects, and video evidence may all be used as artifacts in a portfolio. Portfolios have the advantage of providing a holistic view of student learning but are time-consuming and difficult to grade. An example of a portfolio assessment might be used in a technology class where students are asked to submit their best work from each of the applications used.

Observation is when a teacher watches a student engaged in a learning activity to find evidence of learning. Like conferences, observation does not leave a paper trail and is difficult to grade, but can provide information to make instructional decisions. Anecdotal records, checklists, or rubrics should be used when employing this method of assessment. Observation is effective in all subjects.

To gather information about challenging behaviors, a teacher can develop a **behavior scale**. To create a behavior scale, the teacher should clearly identify the behavior to be observed. Typically, a teacher targets between one and three behaviors. Next, a method for measuring the behavior must be developed. Is information about frequency, duration, and/or intensity going to be part of the data collected? From there, a baseline is established by measuring the behavior before any interventions begin, and then goals are set. For example, if a student typically has three temper tantrums every hour, the first goal might be to reduce the number of temper tantrums to one per hour.

The teacher is the primary evaluator, but there are times when training students to be evaluators will improve outcomes. When students evaluate their own work and the work of their peers, they are using metacognitive skills that help them to internalize the distinguishing characteristics of a quality work product from one of lesser quality. Students become active participants in the evaluation process and develop into autonomous learners.

Self-assessment describes methods by which students monitor their own progress towards learning goals. Students must have a clear understanding of their learning goals to be able to determine if they are making adequate progress. Goals should follow the SMART goal format. In other words, they should be specific, measurable, attainable, relevant, and time-bound. With the use of learning contracts, students and teachers work together to determine how students will monitor their own progress. Students may use checklists or rubrics as they develop a portfolio to document their growth.

Many of the same benefits of self-assessment occur with peer assessment. **Peer assessment** is when students evaluate one another and offer feedback. Students need a great deal of training to properly use peer assessment as they are unable to help one another if they do not have a clear understanding of what constitutes quality performance. It is recommended that students participate in guided practice by using a sample of writing provided by the teacher prior to their first independent peer assessment. Rubrics, checklists, and rating scales may be used as guides to help students evaluate one another. Peer assessment requires a safe learning atmosphere in which students trust one another and feel comfortable providing and receiving critical feedback. Frequently, peer assessment is used as part of group work and may improve the participation of all group members. Peer assessment improves critical thinking skills since students must not only be able to evaluate one another's work but also articulate and defend the reasons behind the scores they assign.

Practice Question

9) A second-grade teacher wants to identify how well students work as a group to complete a science activity. Which assessment tool is MOST appropriate?

A. self-assessment
B. portfolio
C. scoring guide
D. observation

Responsible Use of Assessments

No assessment is perfect; each has a distinct limitation in that it only captures learning as a snapshot in time. Learning, by its very nature, is ever-changing. Further, some students are savvy test-takers who may have learning needs not uncovered by a certain assessment tool; others may know more than their test scores suggest. These limitations mean that teachers must use assessment tools both practically and responsibly.

> **Check Your Understanding**
>
> In what cases could student assessment results be released per FERPA guidelines?

First and foremost, assessments must always be used in an ethical manner. This means that assessments should only be used for their intended purpose and only by those authorized to administer them. The results of assessments should also be kept confidential per FERPA policies. Although it is impossible to avoid all bias in assessments as they are products of the culture in which they have been created, every effort should be made to avoid bias when administering or creating assessments. This includes but is not limited to

- avoiding any gender, racial, or ethnic stereotypes;
- limiting background knowledge demands;
- field testing or pilot testing assessment tools for reliability and validity; and
- using multiple methods of assessment to meet the needs of all learners.

In using multiple methods of assessment, teachers should consider the learning preferences of all students. Teachers may even use or create learning preference assessments for this purpose to help students identify the ways through which they prefer to receive information. Consideration should also be made for individual student needs with a realization that assessment methods may have to be modified. For example, if an oral presentation is planned as a summative assessment at the end of a social studies unit, a student who is afraid of speaking in front of the class may be permitted to submit an essay or poster instead.

Students with IEPs, 504 plans, and ESL plans may qualify for special **accommodations** on the PSSA or Keystone exams. These accommodations may include

- presentation accommodations (e.g., braille or auditory tests);
- response accommodations (e.g., scribes or audio-recorded responses);
- setting accommodations; and/or timing or scheduling accommodations.

Accommodation decisions are made by the IEP team, which includes the student, parents, special education teacher, LEA representative, and others who are aware of the student's learning needs. No accommodation decisions may be made outside of the team. These individuals will consider the student's characteristics, the tasks expected of the student on the assessment, and the alignment to IEP goals.

On state tests, students only receive accommodations, which do not change learning expectations; they do not receive modifications on the PSSA. Further, these accommodations may not be limited to use during assessments and must also be used during instructional periods. A full list of allowable accommodations is available in the PDE *Accommodations Guidelines* booklet.

Assessment results can be used for a variety of purposes. Formative assessment results can and should be used for ongoing progress monitoring and to assess the effectiveness of instruction and need for reteaching. Summative assessment results should also be used for these purposes as well as identifying students' strengths and needs and to plan targeted interventions.

Data from assessments may be collected and interpreted with technology; such tools may help teachers identify trends. For example, if assessment data shows that student scores trend downward each year once subtraction with regrouping is introduced, the teacher could consider how to better prepare students for this topic and/or how to offer more practice and reinforcement.

In keeping and tracking student performance records, multiple types of data should be included. Running records, anecdotal records or notes, and even notes from parent conferences are all useful sources of information to review when planning instruction for a specific student.

When communicating assessment results to families, it is imperative that they understand how to interpret score reports and for what the assessment data will be used. This can mitigate the possibility of panic or concern.

Practice Question

10) Which statement BEST describes how PSSA assessment accommodations should be handled?

A. Accommodations should be modified during the test as needed.
B. Accommodations should be offered only on this assessment.
C. Accommodations should be developed by the IEP team.
D. Accommodations should be kept hidden from the student.

Professional Development

To be effective, PK – 4teachers must stay apprised of current research and trends in education and must therefore commit to lifelong learning.

In the past, teacher **professional development** (PD) was often offered in a "one shot" **workshop** form. Current thinking informed by research suggests that this type of PD is only one of many options. In fact, workshop-style PD may be less effective than other approaches if it is not aligned with teacher needs.

Many districts now offer a variety of opportunities. **Online learning**, both synchronous or asynchronous, can allow teachers to find PD content aligned with their specific goals and needs. **Massive Open Online Courses (MOOCs)** are one option. These are often free, though some of these learning opportunities offer college or university credit for an additional fee. Another trend in educator PD is **micro credentials**, which are self-paced learning opportunities that often culminate in a performance-based task. The National Education Association (NEA) offers many micro-credential opportunities.

Teachers can also **observe** other teachers and/or work with a **mentor** teacher or instructional coach to increase their instructional knowledge and proficiency. As part of this process, teachers often self-reflect on their own teaching through a journal, blog, or some other platform.

Reading research by others, such as educational journals or content on trusted websites, is another means of PD, which allow teachers to look for information on a specific subject they wish to learn more about or a specific instructional strategy they want to try. Teachers can also conduct their own **action research** in the classroom. Action research involves a teacher identifying a classroom problem, collecting and analyzing data, taking action, and then evaluating results. For example, if a teacher notices that first-grade students are struggling with reading words with *r*-controlled vowels, a teacher may give all

Did You Know?

Pennsylvania educators need 180 clock hours of PD every five years for certification renewal.

students an oral assessment on *r*-controlled vowels. After analyzing results, if the teacher realizes that the most challenging words are those with an *-er* pattern, the teacher can then devise instruction accordingly and re-assess students as a way to evaluate the results.

Teachers should also strive to keep up-to-date on policy decisions that impact their students and schools. This will allow teachers to be informed advocates on behalf of their profession and their school communities.

Practice Question

11) A second-grade teacher is struggling with classroom management. What would be the MOST effective PD opportunity for the teacher to seek out?

A. conducting a functional behavioral analysis on a problem student and publishing the results
B. reading an article on the contrast between behaviorist and constructivist theories
C. attending a workshop on atypical development in young children
D. asking a mentor teacher to observe the class and provide feedback

Answer Key

1) B: Providing handouts translated into other languages shows that the teacher is welcoming to parents who may not speak English.

2) B: It is always best practice to speak to an administrator or the school counselor first for tips on how to conference with a family in this situation; these professionals will have a list of trusted resources.

3) D: As a mandated reporter, the teacher is required to report the abuse. Since the teacher has the most information and facts on the child, she should make the report directly—not a colleague.

4) A: Not being under the influence or in possession of alcoholic beverages and/or illegal or unauthorized drugs is a provision in the Code of Professional Practice and Conduct for Educators.

5) C: The teacher cannot assume all students have a background in baseball, so introducing key terms such as *home run* or *bases* will help all students better understand the story.

6) C: The Stanford Achievement Test is a norm-referenced test with a percentile score. The score refers to the percentage of students of the same age and grade whom the student outperformed.

7) A: A weekly spelling test is an informal curriculum-based assessment because it is based on spelling words that are part of the grade-level curriculum; it is not a published instrument.

8) B: The PSSA includes selected-response questions, so this would be the best format to help familiarize students with the exam's format.

9) D: By using direct observation as an assessment, the teacher can more easily evaluate teamwork.

10) C: The IEP team will develop assessment accommodations that the student will use both in the classroom and on the PSSA.

11) D: Asking a mentor teacher to observe the class and provide feedback most targets the issue the teacher is experiencing and would likely yield the most immediate and useful results.

3. Language and Literacy Development

Early Language Development

Language acquisition is the process through which humans develop the ability to understand and create words and sentences to communicate. Many experts believe that children have an innate ability to acquire **oral language** from their environment. Oral language comes in two types: **receptive language** and **expressive language**. Receptive language refers to oral language that is heard and understood; expressive language refers to language that is formed and spoken. Generally receptive language develops before expressive language.

Even before babies can speak, they cry and coo in reaction to environmental stimuli or to communicate their needs. They recognize basic variants in the speech patterns of those around them, such as **articulation**, defined as the distinct sounds of speech; they can also identify contrasts when exposed to new languages. With this awareness, cooing and crying quickly turn into **babbling**, the first stage of language acquisition. This stage generally lasts from six months to around twelve months. In this stage, infants make a variety of sounds but may begin to focus on sounds for which they receive positive reinforcement. For example, babbles such as *baba* and *yaya* tend to garner praise and excitement from parents, so these may be repeated until the coveted *mama* or *dada* is produced.

At around one-year old, but varying from child to child, children start using first words, generally nouns. During this single-word stage, or **holophrastic stage**, these solitary words are generally used to express entire ideas. For example, "Toy!" may mean "Give me the toy." After a few months, this shifts to two-word utterances such as "Mommy go" or "David bad." The **two-word stage** may last through early toddlerhood but generally gives rise to the **telegraphic phase** of oral language development at around age two and a half. In this stage, speech patterns become more advanced, though sometimes prepositions, articles, and other short words are missing. Telegraphic speech includes phrases such as "See plane go!" and "There go teacher." This stage persists until children are mostly fluent in the home language, generally at age three or four.

> **Did You Know?**
>
> Ninety-five percent of all babbling by babies throughout the world is composed of only twelve consonants: *p, b, t, d, k, g, m, n, s, h, w, j*.

What children are able to express also increases as they develop. They are generally able to name familiar objects between the ages of one and one and a half. At around eighteen months old, children will also begin to comprehend sequence or order in spoken language but may not be able to create or form sequences themselves until ages four or five.

A young child's initial expressive language use will be very concrete but advance to the ability to draw conclusions or make inferences by the ages of three to six. During this age range, young children can also comprehend and produce rich oral descriptions.

In early childhood, most typically developing children will develop an increasingly expanding language tool kit, which will include various means of **phonological processing**. Phonological processing includes phonological awareness (the knowledge words are made up of sounds), phonological memory (remembering what these sounds are), and phonological retrieval (being able to retrieve the needed sound).

Practice Question

1) While monitoring recess, a teacher hears a young child utter "go" to ask to go to the playground. The child is likely in which stage of language development?

A. babbling
B. two-word stage
C. telegraphic phase
D. holophrastic stage

Early Literacy Development

Early literacy development begins with print awareness. **Print awareness** involves a basic understanding of the nature of reading: that English is read from left to right and top to bottom, and that words on a page are being read. Very young children without solid print awareness may believe that meaning is gleaned from pictures on a page rather than words. Some younger children may understand that books convey meaning but may not quite know how. Teachers may see these children modeling reading a book upside down.

Key to print awareness are many **concepts of print**. These are the many underlying principles that must be mastered before learning to read. They include things such as knowledge and identification of a word, letter, and sentence; knowledge of the many uses of print; and knowledge of the overarching structure of a book or story (title, beginning, middle, end).

Many students have some print awareness through **environmental print**, or the words printed throughout their everyday environments. Environmental print includes product names, street signs, business names, menus at restaurants, and any other print that students encounter in the normal course of their lives. Teachers can use popular environmental print, such as the names and logos of popular children's products, stores, and restaurants to encourage pre-readers to "read" these names. Teachers should also consider using environmental print in the classroom in each of the home languages of their students. For example, a teacher may label the door in English, Spanish, Thai, and Vietnamese. This builds confidence and familiarity and reinforces the idea that these words in languages other than English also have meaning. This is part of creating a **print-rich environment**, or a classroom environment where students have many opportunities to interact with print in their immediate surroundings.

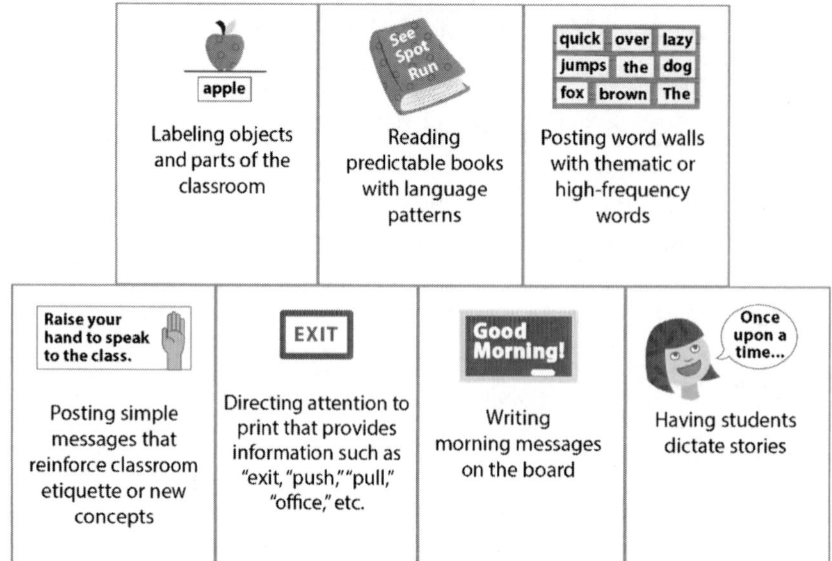

Figure 3.1. Concepts of Print Classroom Strategies

When working with young students, teachers should have students point to words on a page and also point to words (versus pictures) themselves during storybook reading since this will reinforce concepts of print and help students develop print awareness. This will help even very young students begin to understand that, while both the pictures and words on the page contribute to the overall meaning, the part being read is the words, not the pictures.

Early literacy development does not happen by chance; educators must use explicit, research-based instructional strategies. This includes the selection of developmentally appropriate instructional materials, both in print and online. These materials should be interesting and engaging to students and provide multiple opportunities for children to develop an interest in books and reading.

Most prekindergarten and kindergarten classrooms employ some form of **guided or interactive storybook reading,** where the teacher reads a picture book aloud to students in an interactive way. During this exercise, students can be asked to recall or retell story events, identify a sequence of events, make predictions about what will happen next, and connect characters or events in stories to personal experiences. This builds interest in books and stories and drives early literacy development.

Young children can also be encouraged to explore classroom libraries on their own. Even pre-readers can enjoy picture books, which help develop sequencing, comprehension, and inferencing skills. Most importantly, early childhood classrooms should be **communities of readers,** or groups of people who are interested in books and reading.

Students who are not yet fluent readers will need specific assessment techniques to ensure they are mastering foundational skills that form the building blocks of later reading instruction. Since concepts of print are the first stage of reading development, these skills must be mastered thoroughly. Most of the time, these assessments are informal and might include any of the following:

- asking students to point to the parts of a book (e.g., title, front cover, back)
- presenting students with a book and observing as they interact with it

- asking students to point to a word, sentence, or picture

As students progress to developing phonetic awareness or overall phonemic awareness, assessment is also conducted in a highly interactive manner. Students might be asked to clap out sounds or words, think of rhyming words, repeat words or sounds, and so on.

Once students begin to work on letter recognition and sound-symbol knowledge, letter charts or letter-sound charts can be used as assessment tools. Students can cross off each letter or letter sound once it is mastered. The same assessment method with a chart or list can be used for sight words (often with a Dolch word list), consonant blends, digraphs, diphthongs, and other challenging sounds.

There is an important distinction between children's ability to sing the alphabet song or point to and say letters or sounds in order (which many master quite early) and the different (though related) skill of letter and letter-sound recognition in isolation. For this reason, it is a good idea to always assess phonics skills in different contexts. For example, students can be asked to point to certain letters or sounds (*/b/*, */ch/*, */i/*) in a book or story. This type of **embedded phonics** assessment ensures that students can transfer knowledge and apply it in connected texts.

Practice Question

2) A prekindergarten teacher wants to assess students' print awareness at the beginning of the year. Which of the following will help gauge a student's print awareness?

A. asking the student to recount story events
B. asking the student to point to a sentence
C. asking the student to write the letter *P*
D. asking the student what sound the letter *P* makes

Phonemic Awareness

Before instruction in the sounds of language, children must be able to distinguish between environmental sounds, such as the air conditioner or an alarm, and the sounds of human speech. For most children, an awareness of the unique sounds of their native language occurs at around six months of age.

Phonological awareness is the general ability to understand that within the structure of oral language, there are subparts. These parts include individual words; **syllables**, or units (typically containing a single vowel sound) within words; **onsets**, or the beginning consonant sounds of words (*sw*-im); and **rimes**, or the letters which follow (sw-*im*).

> **Helpful Hint**
>
> Remember that onsets are the first part of the word, or the first "button" readers see—the ON button. Rimes are the parts of the word that rhyme such as c-*at*, h-*at*, b-*at*, and so on.

Having phonological awareness is a crucial early stage in learning to read and write, and it can be fostered in the initial levels through singing songs and other oral language activities. Additionally, students can be asked to **segment sentences** or identify the individual words that make up a sentence.

Any activities or speech that seeks to break language into component parts or that help establish an understanding of syllables, onsets, and rimes—"Would *Son*-ya come to circle time?" "Do you want a *c*-at or a *h*-at for your birthday?"—are good choices for helping students begin to recognize the parts within language.

Letter knowledge is another part of early literacy and includes the ability to name and form letters as well as the alphabetic principle and awareness of letter-sound correspondence. The **alphabetic principle** presumes an understanding that words are made up of written letters that represent spoken sounds. In order to proceed with more advanced reading concepts, children must first have a firm grasp of **letter-sound correspondence**, or the knowledge of the sound that each letter makes.

There is no firm rule on the pace at which the letter sounds should be mastered in their entirety, although most experts agree that those with the greatest frequency and those that will allow children to begin sounding out short words quickly should generally be introduced first. It is also sometimes easiest for children to master simple sounds—/t/ and /s/, for example—over more challenging or confusing sounds such as /b/, /d/, and /i/. Regardless of the way in which a curriculum breaks up practice with the alphabetic principle (e.g., a letter of the week or a teaching of the letters and sounds in rapid succession), teachers should recognize that repetition is key and students must be given multiple exposures to each letter and sound. As part of this repeated exposure, students may enjoy hearing books or stories with **alliteration** or several words that have the same beginning sound.

> **Did You Know?**
>
> The alphabet song was copyrighted in 1835 but is actually an adaptation of a Mozart melody.

Phonemes are distinct units of sound and the basic units of language. There are twenty-six letters in the alphabet, and there is some agreement among researchers that there are at least forty-four phonemes in English—some letters represent different phonemes and some phonemes are made up of more than one letter. There are eighteen consonant phonemes, such as /r/ and /t/; fifteen vowel phonemes, such as /Ā/ and /oi/; six *r*-controlled vowels, such as /Ä/; and five digraphs such as /ch/ and /sh/. **Phonemic awareness** refers to the knowledge of and ability to use these phonemes. This awareness generally does not come naturally, and students will need explicit instruction to master these skills. It is often best to differentiate instruction and work with students in smaller groups when working on phonemic awareness because proficiency levels may vary substantially.

Table 3.1. Phoneme Chart

Phoneme	Example	Phoneme	Example	Phoneme	Example
Consonants		***Vowels***		***R-Controlled Vowels***	
/b/	bat	/a/	lap	/ã/	hair
/d/	dog	/ā/	late	/ä/	art
/f/	fish	/e/	bet	/û/	dirt
/g/	goat	/ē/	see	/ô/	draw
/h/	hat	/i/	hit	/ēə/	rear
/j/	jump	/ī/	ride	/üə/	sure
/k/	kick	/o/	hop	***Diagrams/Digraphs***	
/l/	laugh	/ō/	rope	/zh/	measure
/m/	milk	/oo/	look	/ch/	chick
/n/	no	/u/	cut	/sh/	shout
/p/	pot	/ū/	cute	/th/	think
/r/	rat	/y//ü/	you	/ng	bring
/s/	sit	/oi/	oil		
/t/	toss	/ow/	how		

Table 3.1. Phoneme Chart

Phoneme	Example	Phoneme	Example	Phoneme	Example
/v/	vote	/ə/ (schwa)	syringe		
/w/	walk				
/y/	yak				
/z/	zoo				

Various activities can aid students in developing phonemic awareness. Part of phonemic awareness is identifying the **beginning, medial,** and **final sounds** in a word (e.g., /c/ /a/ /t/ or /th/ /i/ /s/. Understanding unique sounds in words beyond onset and rime helps students continue to develop phonemic awareness and lays a strong foundation for later phonics instruction.

Many techniques can help students identify and practice using the sounds of words. **Phoneme blending** involves students putting given sounds together to make words. To work on phoneme blending, teachers can say sounds and ask students what word is made: "I like /ch/ /ee/ /z/. What do I like? That's right, I like cheese." Teachers can also ask students to simply repeat or chorally repeat the sounds in words during circle time or storybook reading: "The car went vvvvv-rrrrr-oooo-m!"

Helpful Hint

Phoneme blending involves students blending sounds together like putting them in a blender to make a word. Phoneme segmentation involves students unblending, or segmenting, each sound like the segments of a worm.

Phoneme segmentation is generally the inverse of phoneme blending and involves students sounding out a word. Phoneme segmentation is important both for reading and spelling a word. More advanced phonemic awareness activities include **phoneme deletion**, in which a phoneme is removed to make a new word (e.g., ramp – /p/ = ram) and **phoneme substitution**, where one phoneme is changed to make a new word (e.g., fla/t/ to fla/p/).

Practice with **rhyming** also helps young children develop phonemic awareness. By age four, many children can identify words that rhyme; by kindergarten, most children can produce their own rhyming words.

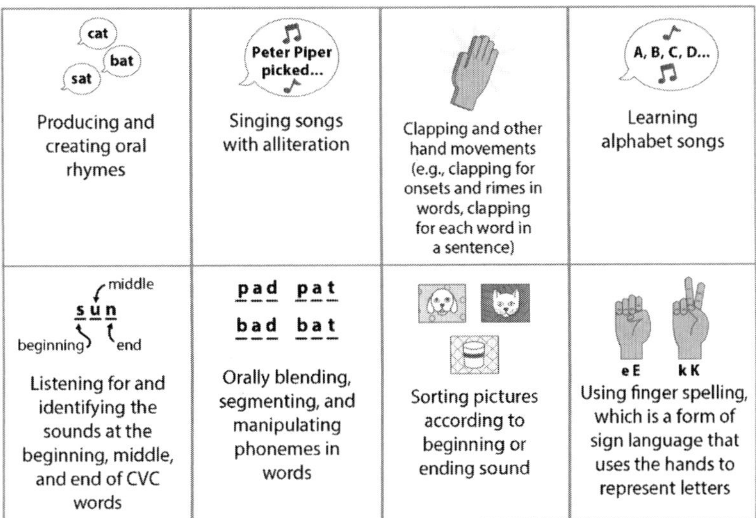

Figure 3.2. Phonological Awareness Classroom Strategies

Early childhood teachers should work on phonemic awareness with students in a variety of contexts. Having students manipulate language orally—"What word could I make if I took away the first letter of *cow?*"—and encouraging students in high-interest literacy activities in centers with alphabet boards, letter cards, alphabet sorters, and other manipulatives will provide multiple opportunities for students. Educators should also remember students will have varying backgrounds, skill levels, English language proficiencies, and possibly speech and language delays and hearing loss. Some students may need modifications for certain activities; this should be considered in the planning of inclusive activities.

Practice Question

3) A kindergarten teacher is lesson planning at the beginning of the year. Which activity would be most appropriate for the teacher to plan to help students practice the alphabetic principle?

A. sorting small animals into tubs based on the initial letter sound of the animal's name
B. asking students to help clap out the syllables in a student's name
C. asking students to point to a sentence on a page
D. having students remove a sound from a word and say the new word

Phonics

Phonics is an age-old strategy for helping students read by connecting written language to spoken language or by correlating certain sounds with certain letters or groups of letters.. Letter-sound correspondence is a foundational skill for effective phonics instruction, as most phonics strategies will require students to draw rapidly on this memory bank of letter sounds. As previously mentioned, most strategies for introducing students to the letter sounds draw on **high-frequency letter-sound correspondence**, where the most frequent and useful letter sounds are taught first. This will allow students to begin reading as soon as possible without having to wait for mastery of each letter sound.

As part of phonics learning, students will learn that the English alphabet contains both **consonants** and **vowels** but that it also contains much more complex structures. It contains consonant blends where two or more consonants make a single sound, such as /bl/ or /tr/.

Students will also require instruction in **graphemes**, or ways of recording a sound. Grapheme units can be a single letter that makes a sound (/i/), or a sequence of letters that makes a sound (/ai/). A single sound can also be represented by multiple graphemes. For example, the long /a/ sound can be made by both the words *r<u>ay</u>* and *w<u>eigh</u>*.

Part of helping students become strong decoders is teaching certain patterns in the English language to help students when they encounter unfamiliar words. One of these patterns involves syllables.

Syllables can be segmented into multisyllabic words.

Table 3.2. Syllable Patterns		
Closed syllables	end in a consonant short vowel sound	hat hip-ster
Open syllables	end with a vowel long vowel sound	go lo-cate
Vowel-consonant-*e* (VC*e*)	end with silent -*e* long vowel sound	take ren-o-vate
Vowel teams	more than one vowel letter makes one sound	sea green-er
R-controlled syllables	vowel + *R*	stir in-jur-ious
Consonant-le (C-le)	consonant + le	ta-ble lit-tle

There are some syllable patterns that do not fall into any of these types such as *-ive*, *-ion*, *-age*, and -*ture*.

Syllable division patterns can also help students decode and spell words:

- VCCV: syllable division is between the two consonants; the accent is on the first or second syllable (in/sect; com/bine; in/sist)
- VCV: syllable division is before the consonant and accent is on the first or second syllable (ro-bin; re/quest; u/nite)

VCCCV: syllable division is after the first consonant and accent is on the first or second syllable (sand/wich; hun/dred; ex/treme)
Students may also benefit from learning about **vowel combinations** (digraphs and trigraphs), as seen in Table 3.3.

Table 3.3. Vowel Combinations (Digraphs and Trigraphs)			
ai	ee	ign	olt
au	ea	ing	oll
ay	eu	oo	ou
aw	ew	oa	ow
augh	ei	oe	ue
all	ey	oi	ui
ald	eigh	oy	oll
alm	le	old	ou
alt	igh	olk	

Students should also learn to analyze the structure of word parts, known as **morphemes**. Morphemes come in various types. **Free morphemes** are words on their own (*help, go, big*), while **bound morphemes** must be added to another morpheme (e.g., *-ly, -ing, un-).* Morphemes can also be derivational or inflectional. **Derivational morphemes** are affixes (prefixes and suffixes) that, when added to another word, create a new word. Derivational morphemes include prefixes like *un-*, *re-*, *pre-* and suffixes like *-able*, *-ive*, and *-ion*. In contrast to derivational morphemes are **inflectional morphemes**. These morphemes simply denote a plural or tense but do not make an entirely new word or change the word to a new part of speech. For example, *-s*, *-ed*, and *-ing* are inflectional morphemes. Knowing the most common inflectional morphemes and their orthography or spelling can help young readers and writers.

Morphemes are distinct from syllables in that syllabication refers to patterns and word divisions related to pronunciation while morphemes refer to patterns based on meaning. Often syllabication is a strategy for sounding out words orally while morphemic analysis is a spelling or vocabulary strategy.

Phonics instruction draws on the strategy of **decoding**, or the ability to pronounce the sounds of written words orally and glean meaning. Because of its focus on the specific sound structures of words, phonics instruction tends to involve more explicit, direct instruction and is not without critics, who believe it overemphasizes the mechanics of reading while sacrificing the enjoyment. However, most classrooms today employ a combination approach that balances inquiry-based student learning, allowing for the open exploration of high-interest literacy games and activities, with more direct phonics instruction. Research has identified explicit, systematic phonics instruction as being highly effective.

> **Helpful Hint**
>
> There are four types of phonics instruction: synthetic phonics instruction (explicit, direct instruction of phonemes and graphemes); analytic phonics instruction (focuses on onset and rime); analogy phonics instruction (focuses on word families); and embedded phonics instruction (teaches phonics via actual books).

Some words are decodable, meaning they follow basic principles of phonics. These words can typically be sounded out effectively if basic structural deviations, like long vowel sounds with a word ending in –*e*, and various digraphs, where two letters make a single sound such as /th/ and /ay/, are mastered.

However, there are some words that deviate from basic sound structures and cannot be sounded out. These words must be presented to students with great frequency so they can simply be memorized. These words must become **sight words,** or words that require no decoding because they are instantly recognized and read automatically.

It is recommended that some high-frequency decodable words, such as *and* and *get*, also be memorized by sight so as to increase reading rate and fluency. There are many lists of such words. The most popular is the Dolch word list, which contains 315 words that are purported to be the most frequently used in English. Early childhood teachers might post some of these high-frequency words around the classroom for maximum exposure or encourage students to play games with sight word flashcards. Repetition will lead to mastery of these words and will help students read more quickly, fluently, and easily.

Helping students practice phonics can involve a variety of strategies and activities, and these should always be developmentally appropriate for the grade level and differentiated to accommodate students with varying needs and skills. A typical phonics progression may look something like this:

1. mastery of high-frequency letter sounds
2. sounding out CVC words

3. mastery of all letter sounds
4. introduction of consonant blends and digraphs
5. long vowel sounds
6. vowel teams
7. *r*-controlled vowels
8. more advanced word parts (e.g., prefixes, suffixes)
9. silent letters

Phonics study is generally undertaken first at the word level. As students move beyond needing to sound out each phoneme or each word, they generally begin reading sentences. Using **connected texts** or groups of related sentences is also part of phonics learning and helps students experience learning to read in more authentic contexts.

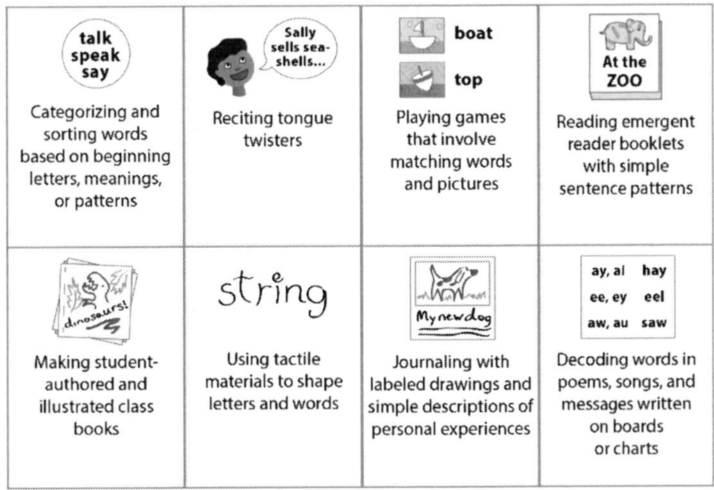

Figure 3.3. Phonics Classroom Strategies

English language learners will need additional practice with phonemes that are unique to English or simply not part of their home language. Students who come from a background with a language that does not use the Latin alphabet may need more background with the alphabetic principle than native speakers. Additionally, strategies (e.g., visual cuing to indicate certain sounds) may be needed to help students who are hard of hearing master phonics.

Teachers may also need to provide extension and application activities for gifted students who may become bored with phonics study if they are already reading at a high level of proficiency. Frequently, these students can be accommodated within an existing lesson framework. For example, a teacher may aim for the bulk of her students to master two sight words per week from the Dolch list, but students who already know the whole list might practice spelling these words instead.

In addition to more structured assessment methods like charts and lists, phonics skills can be assessed through any number of hands-on activities. Students can play with letter/sound cards or magnets and form or dissect words. Students can match up cards with different rimes and onsets or different target consonant or vowel sounds.

In assessing decoding, or the ability to sound out a word and glean meaning, an oral assessment approach continues to be the gold standard. There are many assessment tools designed specifically to aid in assessing such skills, including the popular **Quick Phonics Screener**, which assesses a student's ability to read a variety of sounds and words.

When assessing decoding skills, it is important to note student strengths and weaknesses. But teachers must also develop a general idea of the student's overall approach and "word-attack skills," or methods of decoding unfamiliar words. Attention to how students approach any oral reading task can provide significant information on strategies they are already using, as well as those they do not use but might find beneficial. Though the age of the student certainly comes into play, sometimes older students still mastering decoding might be able to verbalize the way they approach such challenging words. Questions posed to the student about strategy or method can also yield valuable information.

In addition to these methods, there are also several published assessment instruments for pre-readers and emerging readers:

- Letter knowledge and phonemic awareness can be assessed using the **Dynamic Indicators of Basic Early Literacy Skills (DIBELS)** and the **Early Reading Diagnostic Assessment (ERDA)**.
- The **Comprehensive Test of Phonological Processing (CTOPP)** and **Phonological Awareness Test (PAT)** can also be used as instruments to assess phonemic awareness.
- Other instruments that assess early reading skills include the **Texas Primary Reading Inventory (TPRI), Test of Word Reading Efficiency (TOWRE),** and even the kindergarten version of the **Iowa Test of Basic Skills (ITBS)**.

Regardless of the assessment instruments used, assessing emerging readers can be challenging since young children often find assessment scenarios intimidating. Any single assessment is only as useful as the portion of the full picture that it provides. The fullest picture of a student's pre-reading development can best be gleaned through observation and input from both parents and teachers. Portfolios, observational records, checklists, and other informal assessment methods can provide much insight into the development of emergent readers.

Practice Question

4) A kindergarten teacher wants to quickly assess a new student's familiarity with sounding out CVC words. Which word should the teacher ask the student to sound out?

A. gap
B. onto
C. drink
D. and

Fluency

Fluency refers to the rate, accuracy, and expression of a piece when read. Fluency is an important measure of a student's reading development; lack of fluency will hamper overall comprehension as well as the enjoyment of reading. Reading **rate** is a measure of speed and is generally calculated in words per minute. **Accuracy,** or the correct decoding of words, is generally entwined with rate when measuring fluency, as reading quickly but incorrectly is not desirable.

In addition to rate and accuracy, **prosody,** or the overall liveliness and expressiveness of reading, is also a skill to nurture in students. Prosody may involve appropriate pauses and various changes in pitch and intonation based on punctuation and the overall meaning of the piece. Developing prosody in students should involve a combination of modeling by teachers (as they read stories, passages, and even directions aloud) and giving students plenty of opportunities for oral reading practice.

Many situations may threaten students' fluency. Limited phonics knowledge may cause students to struggle with new or challenging words. Other students may have limited sight word knowledge, slowing down their reading rate as they sound out each word. Still others may lack vocabulary knowledge or knowledge of academic language.

The over-arching instructional strategy for helping students develop fluency is practice. This may involve any of the following strategies:

- modeling oral fluency
- using choral reading exercises where a more proficient reader or teacher reads with the student
- teaching finger tracking while reading or using a tracking device
- rereading the same texts multiple times
- increasing sight word recognition
- increasing phonics knowledge

While fluency is not limited to oral reading, it is virtually impossible to assess fluency during silent reading, and most educators rely on frequent oral reading assessments to help determine student progress. While several standard measures exist, one of the most researched is the Hasbrouck-Tindal oral reading fluency chart. This chart is designed to measure progress over the course of the school year and from grade to grade and compares students in percentiles with their peers on a scale of words read correctly per minute. It is important to remember that all students will develop fluency on a different timeline, and assessments of fluency are most accurate when they are developmentally appropriate and when they are not presented as high-stakes testing situations.

Educators may find it challenging to find time for oral reading assessment in the classroom as they balance multiple priorities; however, teachers must make time to regularly listen to all students read aloud, regardless of grade level. While examining written work and performance on independent or group practice activities may give some indication of a student's overall development, to get the fullest picture teachers must gather as much data as possible. Assessing student fluency through oral reading is seminal to an overall understanding of a particular student's learning situation.

Fluency is highly correlated with comprehension because students who struggle to read and decode individual words will have difficulty comprehending entire sentences and paragraphs. Additionally, students who read at a very slow rate may have trouble recalling what they have read. It is well worth the time investment to listen to students read aloud as much as possible.

Helpful Hint

There are various software applications that allow teachers to record and track students' oral reading progress. While this technology cannot replace frequent live listening to students reading, it can augment it and speaks to the importance of oral reading in gauging students' overall literacy development.

Practice Question

5) A second-grade teacher notices that his students often read in monotone during oral reading practice. Which strategy would BEST help his students develop prosody?

A. setting aside timed oral reading each day
B. modeling an appropriate reading rate
C. using ability grouping for silent reading
D. having students act out a play from a script

Vocabulary

Vocabulary knowledge, particularly knowledge of academic language, is essential to both listening comprehension (understanding what is said) and reading comprehension (understanding what is read). Students acquire new vocabulary both through **formal** methods (e.g., classroom instruction) and **informal** methods (e.g., hearing new words spoken or used in context). Vocabulary is also developed via **explicit** instruction (e.g., introducing content-area words to students along with their definitions and examples) and via **implicit** means (e.g., students learning a content area word by independently reading a content area text). Students should be guided to seek out vocabulary knowledge as they read independently. Strategies to promote this include the use of a vocabulary journal or notebook and teaching annotation or note-taking strategies.

Students will be exposed to a wide variety of vocabulary in a literacy-rich classroom, and teachers can further aid vocabulary acquisition through incorporating new words and new meanings into the daily routine. Some vocabulary acquisition will involve learning **content-specific words** that require students to first understand the vocabulary of the subject before applying the knowledge. Consider that even a kindergarten student must master dozens of basic math terms before applying them. For example, the terms *triangle*, *hexagon*, and *rectangle* must all be learned intrinsically before a student can separate or sort items by shape. Additionally, third graders must learn terms like *habitat*, *natural resource*, *metric system,* and *variable* to apply them to science and math assignments.

Student vocabulary must also grow to include the various homonyms, or **multiple-meaning words**, that exist in the English language. The word *interest*, for example, might mean one thing as it applies to a math unit on saving money and another when used in a freewriting assignment on a topic of *interest*.

Students can be taught new vocabulary explicitly via the Frayer model (a specific type of graphic organizer), **semantic maps** (where students connect the word to other ideas in a web), or **word walls** (where students or groups of students look up the word, write a succinct definition, and provide an accompanying image to post in the classroom). Students may also create **analogies** or relationships among words to help them remember and understand new vocabulary.

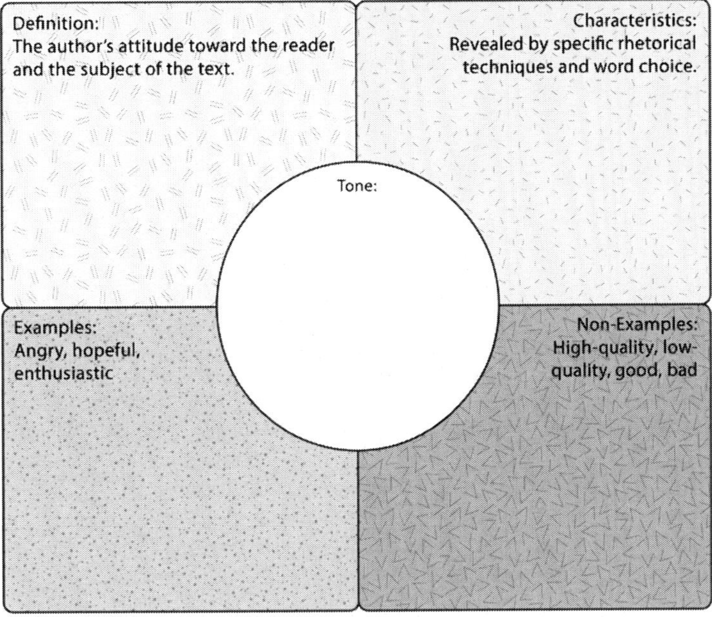

Figure 3.4. Frayer Model

Students should also be trained to learn new words as they encounter them, which may involve the following:

- using context clues such as definition, restatement, **synonym** (another word in the text with a similar meaning), or **antonym** (another word in the text with the opposite meaning)
- looking up the word in a dictionary or glossary
- identifying the category of the word based on its context or structure (e.g., noun, verb, adjective)
- understanding nuances in word meanings such as figurative meanings, multiple meanings, words that are spelled the same but have different meanings (**homographs**), or words that sound the same but have different meanings and spellings (**homophones**)
- using technology, such as built-in dictionary features in digital texts

Using morphology, or word parts, is another way for students to learn new vocabulary. Because they help form new words, derivational morphemes are essential building blocks of the English language. **Derivational morphemes** are added to roots or base words in English. These roots are often derived from Latin or Greek. Related to morphology is **etymology**, or the study of the history or origin of words, which often focuses on tracing the root back to its origin and meaning.

With roots and affixes or derivational morphemes, new words are formed. For example, the word *cent* is a Latin root meaning "one hundred." **Affixes or derivational morphemes** are added to words or roots to change their meanings. For example, the prefix *per-* can be added to *cent* to make the

> **Did You Know?**
>
> Although some English words come from French or German words, those words often originated from Latin words. This means that the great majority of English words have a true Greek or Latin origin.

word *percent*, effectively changing the meaning to "one part in a hundred." Likewise, the suffix *–ury* can be added to *cent* to make the word *century*, effectively changing the meaning to "a period of one hundred years."

Students can be taught to identify roots or base words, common affixes, or derivational morphemes and their etymologies as one strategy to learn new words. For example, if students know that *geo* is Latin for "the earth" or "ground" and that *-logy* means "science," they can conclude that the term *geology* means "the science or study of the ground or earth."

As students read, they should monitor their understanding of vocabulary as part of their overall comprehension. Students learning English as a second language may need additional vocabulary support such as pre-teaching, picture dictionaries, or digital translators.

Practice Question

6) A third-grade student encounters the following sentence in a passage:

I like the paintings for their realism. They look just like photographs.

Which strategy should the teacher recommend to help the student identify the meaning of the underlined word?

A. think about the possibility that the word is being used figuratively
B. find the antonym in the sentence that follows
C. identify the phrase in the next sentence that indicates what the word means
D. consider the category of words that end in *-ism* that this word belongs to

Literacy Learning

Text Types

It is important that students of all ages be exposed to a wide variety of texts. **Informational texts,** or **nonfiction texts,** are texts about the world around us and generally do not use characters to convey information. Science and social studies texts fall into this category. These informational texts are often structured in such a way as to organize information in a format that is accessible and meaningful to students.

> **Think About It**
>
> In selecting books and passages for curricular integration, which genres are most appropriate for social studies, music, or art?

As part of an introduction to different types of texts, a teacher might ask elementary-aged students to analyze elements of their textbooks or workbooks: Do they have bold headings to help the reader understand when new ideas are being introduced? Do they have **sidebars** to give readers additional information alongside the main body of text? Analyzing such elements is one way to build **literacy across the curriculum**.

In contrast, **literary texts**, or **fiction texts**, are usually stories made up by the author. While they may contain true elements or be based on actual events (as in literary nonfiction), they usually include plenty of elements designed to keep and capture the reader's interest. They generally have **characters,** which may be real or imagined people, animals, or creatures, and a **plot**, or sequence of story events. The **setting** of fiction texts may be any time or place past, present, future, real, or imagined. While teachers may put a lot of focus on short stories that are highly accessible for young students, it is also important to expose children to other genres so that students get comprehension practice with texts that are unfamiliar at first.

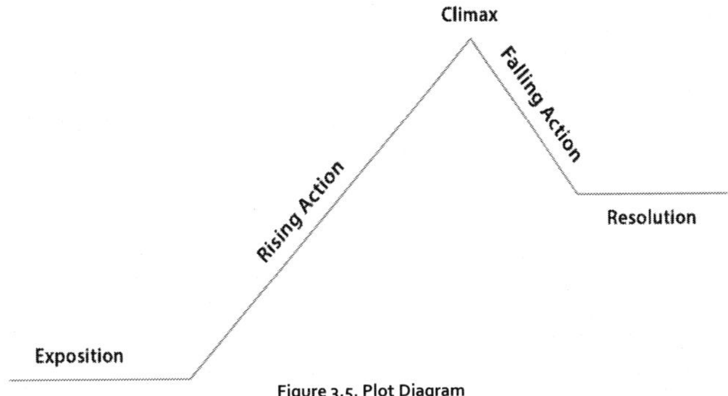

Figure 3.5. Plot Diagram

In **drama**, most of the story is centered around dialogue between characters. They are usually separated into segments (e.g., chapters known as **acts**) and smaller subsegments (generally with a consistent setting) known as **scenes**. Using drama in the classroom is a great way to get students interested in different types of texts. One idea includes setting up a simple **stage** in a kindergarten or elementary classroom as a natural outgrowth of a dramatic play center. When building on students' innate curiosity and imagination, the possibilities are endless. Acting out dramas not only helps students work on expressive reading (prosody), but it also reinforces social and emotional learning as students analyze the emotions and actions of characters.

While poetry may be associated with older children, even young students can appreciate and recognize **rhyme**. Poetry with rhyme can help reinforce phonological awareness and is a natural outgrowth of many young children's love of song. **Meter**—the rhythm, or beat, of the poem—can also be used to engage young students with different texts as a beat can be clapped to, stomped to, or even danced to! Many timeless books for children—such as *One Fish, Two Fish, Red Fish, Blue Fish* and *Each Peach Pear Plum*—have both rhyme and meter and give young children exposure to poetry. Young writers may even begin to write simple poems with one or two **stanzas**, or groups of **lines** similar to paragraphs. Students should be encouraged to recognize and create their own rhyming words as an additional outgrowth of phonological awareness. Asking students to name all the words they can think of that rhyme with *dog*, for example, will allow for continued practice with rhymes.

Children's literature is a genre in its own right. It often includes **myths, legends**, or **folktales** written for a young audience. It tends to have characters who are children; if animals or mythical creatures are the characters, they tend to behave in the way a child would. The genre also tends to focus on characters who learn an important lesson, often one that is applicable to life as a whole. Other characteristics of children's literature include accessible vocabulary and situations or events that children can relate to and find appealing. Many children's books, even those for intermediate readers, often include vivid illustrations to help bring the plot to life.

The structural elements of literature, such as characters, setting, conflict, plot, resolution, point of view, and theme can be introduced alongside other literacy activities, even with students who are pre-readers. Consider bringing these elements into guided storybooks while asking questions the following types of questions:

- "Who are the characters on this page?" (characters)
- "Where does this story happen?" (setting)

- "Why was __________mad/happy/worried, etc?" (conflict/plot)
- "What happened after______?"

"How was (the problem) fixed?" (conflict/plot/resolution)
Although **point of view**, or the perspective from which the story is told (first person, *I*, *we*; third person, *he*, *she*, *it*, or *they*; sometimes second person, *you*), may be harder for very young students to grasp, teachers can begin introducing the basic concept of differing points of view by reading the **narrator's** part in one voice and each different character in a different voice and encouraging students to do the same. For older students, second-person point of view can be practiced by reading and writing letters to other students, the teacher, or administrators, or other school personnel.

Practice Question

7) A third-grade teacher is planning a unit on American Indian myths and legends. Which instructional strategy is MOST important for student success?

A. introducing pertinent background information
B. encouraging students to identify picture cues
C. ensuring students distinguish between fiction and nonfiction
D. requiring oral reading of the setting details

Text Comprehension

Multiple factors will influence students' text comprehension:

- word analysis skills (sometimes called "word attack skills"), which are various strategies for decoding
- prior knowledge, referring to student familiarity with the content and structure of the text
- language background and experience, referring to the level of English language fluency
- previous reading experience, referring to how much exposure to text the student has had
- fluency, the ability to read with appropriate rate, accuracy, and expression
- vocabulary development
- ability to monitor understanding
- text characteristics (such as genre and complexity)

Additionally, any text has multiple levels of meaning at the word, phrase or clause, sentence, and broader discourse levels. Students struggling to read words or sentences will also struggle to comprehend them.

Before students read any text, they should set a **purpose** for reading. This may be to learn about a new person, place, or idea; how to do a task; or to enjoy a fictional story. Also prior to reading, students should engage in other **pre-reading strategies**, such as **previewing** the text; noting the title, headings, graphics, bolded words or other features; **making predictions** about what the text will be about; and **connecting prior knowledge**. For example, if the text is about sailing a boat, students might connect past experience they have had with boats or what they already know about boats. Another consideration is characteristics of certain text types that **identify the genre**. For example, if the text includes a list of steps, students may predict that it will provide some procedural information.

In developing comprehension, a distinction between **literal comprehension**, or that which is stated directly in the text and **inferential comprehension**, or that which must be inferred, should be made. Typically, literal comprehension is easier for young readers than inferential comprehension.

One part of literal comprehension is identifying the **central**, or main, **idea** of a story or article. This is a prerequisite to **summarizing** or condensing the main elements of a story or passage. Literal comprehension also involves recalling key details and identifying basic elements, such as point of view (usually first- or third-person), setting, main characters, and order of story events.

Students can also practice literal comprehension by identifying **facts**, or statements of truth backed by empirical evidence, and **opinions**, or statements of authorial beliefs.

Inferential comprehension involves higher-order thinking skill, such as inferring the **theme** or message of a text, **making predictions** about what will happen next, and **inferring** or concluding something based on text evidence.

Making inferences is an important skill in developing overall comprehension as it allows students to go deeper than the literal meaning and make conclusions based on previously obtained knowledge and experiences. Whenever teachers ask students to make an inference based on a text, they should be sure to ask them to support their inference with evidence. "How do you know this?" "What made you think this?" "Which part of the story/passage made you think this?" are all good follow-up questions for inferring students. As students advance in their comprehension skills, it is also important to ensure that students know that sometimes we all make faulty inferences and that we must constantly evaluate whether we are projecting our own beliefs and experiences onto a text that lacks support for a conclusion we drew.

Beyond literal and inferential comprehension is **evaluative comprehension** wherein students begin to consider their own thoughts and beliefs in relationship to the text as they analyze more deeply. This might involve analysis of a character in a literary text or detecting faulty reasoning in an argumentative text. Evaluative comprehension is often best practiced and assessed through open-ended questions for discussion or an extended constructed response.

It is also highly worthwhile that students comprehend images or graphics embedded in texts. This helps students get the most from informational texts like textbooks and informational websites or educational software. Pointing out and helping students understand how visual elements promote a greater understanding of concepts or ideas that the author is trying to convey will help students be cognizant of these important elements that exist alongside text. Images can also aid struggling readers to decode. While students should not be reliant on pictures, most texts for young readers include ample images to aid in students' overall understanding and enjoyment, and these should be pointed out and discussed when appropriate.

Reading comprehension must be constantly monitored. Students need to be explicitly instructed in **self-monitoring** or **self-evaluation** of their own understanding as they read. These strategies include:

- visualizing
- questioning
- predicting
- drawing conclusions
- making connections to prior knowledge
- summarizing
- annotating
- rereading

> **Think About It**
>
> What strategies could help students develop their ability to visualize as they read?

When students become aware that their comprehension has broken down, they should apply what some call "**fix-up**" strategies. These may include (but are not limited to):

- adjusting the reading rate (slowing down)
- rereading confusing parts
- looking up unknown word,
- reading aloud
- asking for peer or teacher support (typically as a last resort)

To aid students in developing a toolbox for comprehending texts, teachers can implement a variety of techniques. **Think-alouds**, where teachers explain their own self-monitoring as they read, are one strategy. Helping students use maps, webs, or outlines to track key information in a text is another. Other types of graphic organizers, such as **KWL charts**, where students identify what they already know about a topic, what they want to learn, and then what they did learn after reading are also useful and appropriate. Using reading logs or reading journals where students track what they have read and write in response to these texts is another useful instructional tool. Teachers can also put students in small groups, conduct whole-class discussions about texts, or ask students to debate their beliefs about a character or opinion presented in a text.

Sometimes, pre-teaching the important background information needed to fully comprehend a text may be necessary. For example, as students read literature from different cultures, they may first need basic information on that culture, such as where it is located and what life is like there. Texts that include references to languages other than English may also require pre-teaching and/or reference tools, such as a list of commonly used non-English terms in the story and their meanings.

Comprehension while reading silently can be assessed through **cloze exercises**. In these exercises, words are removed from the text and students must fill them in. There are other written exercises aimed at determining level of comprehension. Some students might struggle to answer written questions. Therefore, a full assessment of silent reading comprehension should include an oral component as well.

> **Check Your Understanding**
>
> What are the major phases of oral language development?

As previously mentioned, one of the most common assessments is the informal reading inventory (IRI). There are multiple versions created by various entities. One of the more popular versions is **Pearson's Qualitative Reading Inventory (QRI)**. These assessments include oral reading of word lists that assess accuracy of word identification. The QRI also contains passages and questions that assess both oral and silent reading comprehension. Standardized norm-referenced test batteries such as the Iowa Test of Basic Skills and the Stanford Achievement Test, as well as several criterion-referenced tests such as the PSSA, also test reading comprehension.

Aside from standardized, published instruments, teachers often use curriculum-based assessment (CBA) to evaluate reading comprehension (see Chapter 2). These are generally teacher-created tests.

Comprehension assessment does not require a lengthy formal written test. Simply asking students to recount or retell a story they have read or to recall the most important or interesting parts of a text can provide valuable data. Further, self-assessment should be ongoing and explicitly taught to all readers to monitor comprehension. As students self-assess, they can apply fix-up or fix-it-up strategies as needed when comprehension breaks down.

Practice Question

8) In a lesson with fourth-grade students, the teacher wants to provide a sentence frame to help students identify the theme of a folktale. Which sentence frame would be MOST useful?

A. The message about life in the story is ______________.
B. The parts of nature in the story are ______________.
C. The main character does things like ______________.
D. The setting is a place where people ______________.

Use of Academic Language

Understanding the structure of language is an important part of effective oral and written communication. Language has many functions: emotional expression, play, identity expression, imaginative expression, and communication. Academic language is generally used for communication in a school setting. Depending on a student's background, he may have little past experience with academic language.

Students may not consistently use parts of speech correctly in their writing and speaking until well into their elementary years. Recall that within oral language development are phases in which children leave out needed articles, prepositions, and other linking words. Once speech becomes fully developed and students are generating their own sentences and paragraphs, basic rules of grammar can be introduced.

Parts of Speech

Nouns are words that indicate a person, place, thing, or idea. They may be either common (*student, teacher, room, school*) or proper (*Blanca, Ms. Robinson, Idaho, Frederick Douglass Elementary School*). **Common nouns** are not capitalized, but **proper nouns** must be capitalized. Nouns may also be singular or plural, and students will need practice in forming the plural form of nouns by adding either *–s* or *–es*.

Pronouns are words that take the place of nouns. They may either serve as subjects (*I, you, he, she, it, we, they*) or as objects (*me, you, her, him, it, us, them*) and are known as **subject pronouns** or **object pronouns,** respectively. Pronouns should always have an **antecedent,** or noun to which they refer.

Pronouns must agree in number, person, and gender with their antecedents. Pronoun errors are frequent in developmental writers, and ambiguous pronoun references, lack of pronoun-antecedent agreement, and incorrect use of subject and object pronouns are all common mistakes.

As discussed above, pronouns generally also indicate the perspective or person in which a piece is written. First-person writing generally uses pronouns such as *I*, *me*, *we*, and *our*, and second-person writing uses the pronoun *you*. Third-person texts use a variety of pronoun such as *he*, *she*, *it*, and *them*. Shifts in pronoun person are common in student writing, and teachers need to provide help to students who unnecessarily change point of view in a writing assignment.

Verbs describe an action or state of being or occurrence. They can be action verbs, which like their name implies, describe actions such as *walk*, *eat*, and *speak*, or linking verbs, which describe states of being or link a subject to additional information (*is*, *become*, *seem*). Some verbs may be action verbs or linking verbs depending upon their specific use. If verbs are merely linking a subject to further information, they are considered linking verbs, but if they are expressing an action, they are considered action verbs.

Examples:

This soup tastes bad.

In this sentence, the verb *tastes* links the subject *soup* to its predicate adjective *bad*, so *tastes* is being used as a linking verb.

I taste the soup.

In this sentence, *taste* is describing an action, so it is an action verb.

Helping verbs always appear alongside another main verb and show the tense (*will* be, *had* eaten) or possibility (*may* be, *could* last, *might* enjoy) of another verb. Helping verbs are used to **conjugate**, or change, many verbs to different **tenses**. Unnecessary shifts in tense from present to past or future are prevalent in student writing, and English language learners and native speakers alike will need lots of practice with forming challenging tenses such as the present and past perfect and challenging irregular past tenses with verbs such as *to lie*.

Adjectives modify and describe nouns, and their use is essential to descriptive writing. Student errors with adjectives generally include using an incorrect comparative or superlative form ("He is tallest than me!") or confusing adjectives and adverbs ("She eats hungry/She eats hungrily.").

Adverbs modify adjectives, verbs, or other adverbs and frequently end in *–ly*. Student errors with adverbs are similar to those with adjectives and generally involve the incorrect use of comparatives and superlatives or using adjectives and adverbs interchangeably.

A **preposition** is a word that expresses a relationship between words, and it usually comes before a noun or pronoun. Prepositions help form links in speech and writing, and student errors most frequently involve their omission. Additionally, English language learners may find using prepositions challenging, particularly when they are part of colloquial expressions (e.g., driving me *up* the wall, a pig *in* a poke).

A **conjunction** joins words or sentence parts together. There are both coordinating conjunctions (*and*, *but*, *or*, *nor*, *for*, *yet*, *so*), which join together two independent clauses to form compound sentences, and subordinate conjunctions (*before*, *while*, *because*, *as*), which join dependent clauses to independent clauses to form complex and compound-complex sentences.

Determiners are not parts of speech in themselves but have a similar function: explaining what a noun refers to. They may be adjectives that are used as articles such as *a*, *an*, and *the*; possessive adjectives and pronouns (*my*, *his*, *ours*, *your*); demonstrative pronouns such as *this*, *that*, *these*, and *those*; or any other words that quantify, distribute, or show a difference (*a little*, *half*, *other*, *such*, *quite*).

Like prepositions, determiners are challenging for English language learners. In some languages, determiners are used in only some situations and not others, and some languages lack certain types of English determiners entirely. English language learners who struggle with determiners might benefit from being paired with a native speaker for peer review to help insert needed articles into a piece.

Additionally, variations exist across all parts of speech in different languages. American Sign Language, as just one example, does not use what we might think of as conjugated verbs to show tense; rather, a sign indicating now, next, before, and so on is inserted into the beginning of the sentence to show the intended meaning. It is important for teachers to understand that grammatical knowledge will be more challenging for some students, and they should strive to ensure the classroom is a place where all students are being supported in their learning.

Practice Question

9) A third-grade teacher plans a lesson where students will write a letter to a person they have not seen in a while. How can the teacher encourage students to use detailed, descriptive language in the letter?

A. give students a list of helping verbs to include
B. ask students to include several adjectives and adverbs
C. encourage students to write in a second-person point of view
D. ensure students understand the difference between prepositions and determiners

Sentence Structure

Good writers use a variety of sentence structures to convey their meaning. While young students will generally start with **simple sentences** consisting of a single, independent clause, students should be encouraged to write more advanced sentences as appropriate. **Compound sentences** are made when two independent clauses are joined together using a comma and coordinating conjunction; a semicolon, either alone or with a transitional expression such as *however* or *moreover*; or a colon. Generally, a semicolon alone is only used to join two closely related independent clauses ("My mother likes chocolate; she is a chocoholic."). A colon is generally only used to introduce a second independent clause which is an example or elaboration upon the first ("I have only one thing to say to you: I am very disappointed.").

Complex sentences are formed when a dependent clause is joined to an independent clause with a subordinating conjunction, relative pronoun, or other word. A **dependent clause** is so called because it cannot stand on its own as a sentence, unlike an **independent clause**. The dependent clause may be added anywhere: the beginning, the middle, or the end of the sentence.

Examples:

My mother, *who is a gardener*, likes to spend most of her time outdoors.

In this sentence, the dependent clause is "who is a gardener," beginning with the relative pronoun *who*.

Because she likes to spend most of her time outdoors, my mother is a gardener.

Here, the dependent clause is "[b]ecause she likes to spend most of her time outdoors," beginning with the subordinating conjunction *because*.

My mother is a gardener *as she likes to spend most of her time outdoors*.

In the sentence above, the dependent clause is "as she likes to spend most of her time outdoors," beginning with the subordinating conjunction *as*.

Compound-complex sentences are merely compound sentences with one or more dependent clauses ("My mother is a gardener, but she does not like to spend time outdoors because she has allergies.").

Sentence Structure	Independent Clauses	Dependent Clauses
Simple	1	0
Compound	2 +	0
Complex	1	1 +
Compound-complex	2 +	1 +

Practice Question

10) A fourth-grade teacher reads the following sentence in a student's essay:

Chris has three cats I have two dogs.

How can the teacher help the student revise this sentence?

A. by helping the student differentiate between compound and compound-complex sentence constructions
B. by helping the student identify the dependent clause in the sentence
C. by helping the student identify the two independent clauses in the sentence
D. by helping the student differentiate between active and passive voice

Conventions of Language

Many of the mechanical choices writers must make relate to **punctuation**. While creative writers have liberty to play with punctuation to achieve their desired ends, academic and technical writers must adhere to stricter conventions.

The **period** is the most common **terminal punctuation** mark, used to end declarative (statement) and imperative (command) sentences.

Examples:

Sarah and I are attending a concert.

Meet me outside the concert hall one hour before the show.

The **question mark**, another common terminal punctuation mark, is used to end interrogative sentences (questions).

Example:

How many people are attending the concert?

While the difference between the period and the question mark is usually obvious, confusion sometimes occurs when questions are stated indirectly. In such cases, the period is usually preferable.

Example:

I wonder how many people are attending the concert.

> **Helpful Hint**
>
> The exclamation point has impact only in contrast to its frequency of usage. That is, if the exclamation point is used frequently, each exclamation will be less impactful. On the other hand, if the exclamation point is used sparingly, its use will draw the reader's attention and emphasize the information contained in the sentence.

Exclamation points end exclamatory sentences, in which the writer or speaker is exhibiting intense emotion or energy; thus, writers should carefully consider their use of exclamations. In fact, the exclamation point should be used reservedly or not at all in academic writing unless the exclamation point is within a quotation that a writer incorporates into the text; however, the emphatic usage of *what* or *how* without asking a question demands the usage of the exclamation point.

Example:

What a great show that was!

The **colon** and the **semicolon**, though often confused, each have a unique set of rules surrounding their use. While both punctuation marks are used to join clauses, the construction of the clauses and the relationship between them varies.

The **semicolon** is used to show a general relationship between two independent clauses (IC; IC).

Example:

The disgruntled customer tapped angrily on the counter; she had to wait nearly ten minutes to speak to the manager.

When using the semicolon with a conjunctive adverb to join two independent clauses, the pattern is as follows: independent clause, semicolon, conjunctive adverb, comma, independent clause. Example: *She may not have to take the course this year; however, she eventually will have to sign up for that specific course.*

The **colon**, somewhat less limited than the semicolon in its usage, is used to show a relationship between two clauses and, moreover, to highlight the information contained in the second clause—usually a list, definition, or clarification. While the clause preceding the colon must be an independent clause, the clause that follows does not have to be.

Examples:

Incorrect. The buffet offers three choices that include: ham, turkey, or roast beef.

Correct. The buffet offers three choices: ham, turkey, or roast beef.

Correct. The buffet offers three choices that include the following: ham, turkey, or roast beef.

A writer should also use the colon to separate a title from a subtitle (Title: Subtitle), to separate the hour and the minutes (9:30 a.m.), to follow certain parts of a letter or memo (To:, From:, Date:, RE:), and to follow a formal salutation (To whom it may concern:).

Neither the semicolon nor the colon should be used to set off an introductory phrase from the rest of the sentence.

Examples:

Incorrect. After the trip to the raceway; we realized that we should have brought ear plugs.

Incorrect. After the trip to the raceway: we realized that we should have brought ear plugs.

Correct. After the trip to the raceway, we realized that we should have brought ear plugs.

Many people are taught that, when reading, a comma represents a pause for breath. While this trick may be useful as a way of helping young readers build fluency, it is not a helpful guide for comma usage when writing. Rather, proper comma usage is guided by a set of specific rules.

Helpful Hint

"Let's eat Grandma," OR "Let's eat, Grandma": While this well-known example is humorous, it also demonstrates the need for accurate comma placement.

The following list summarizes the most important comma usage rules:

- Commas are used to separate two independent clauses along with a coordinating conjunction.
    - *George ordered the steak, but Bruce preferred the ham.*
- Commas are used to separate coordinate adjectives.
    - *The shiny, regal horse ran majestically through the wide, open field.*
- Commas are used to separate items in a series.
    - *The list of groceries included cream, coffee, doughnuts, and tea.*
- Commas are used to separate introductory words and phrases from the rest of the sentence.
    - *Slowly, Nathan became aware of his surroundings after the concussion.*
    - *For example, we have thirty students who demand a change.*
- Commas are used to set off nonessential information and appositives.
    - *Estelle, our newly elected chairperson, will be in attendance.*
- Commas are used to set off introductory words from quoted words if the introductory words are not an independent clause.
    - *Elizabeth said sadly, "I want to go home right now for spring break."*
- Commas are used to set off the day and month of a date within a text.
    - *My birthday makes me feel quite old because I was born on February 16, 1958, in Minnesota.*
- Commas are used to set up numbers in a text of more than four digits.
    - *We expect 25,000 visitors to the new museum.*

Quotation marks are used for many purposes, the most common of which are related to academic writing and citation. First, quotation marks enclose titles of short, or relatively short, literary works such as short stories, chapters, and poems. (The titles of longer works, like novels and anthologies, are italicized.) Additionally, quotation marks are used to enclose direct quotations within the text of a document where the quotation is integrated into the text. If a quotation is within another quotation, then the inner quotation uses single quotation marks.

Writers also use quotation marks to set off dialogue. Occasionally, quotation marks are used to enclose words used in a special sense or for a non-literary purpose. (*The shady dealings of his Ponzi scheme earned him his ironic name "Honest Abe."*)

When considering quotation marks versus italics in notating a title, the question of short versus long is a useful guide. A chapter title is written in quotation marks, while the book title itself is italicized. Short poetry titles are written in quotation marks; long epic poem titles are italicized. An article title is written in quotation marks, while the name of the newspaper is italicized.

Apostrophes, sometimes referred to as single quotation marks, have several different purposes:

- to show possession: *boy's watch, John and Mary's house*
- to replace missing letters, numerals, and signs: *do not* = *don't*, 1989 = '89
- to form plurals of letters, numerals, and signs—but only when adding the apostrophe would add clarity: *cross your t's and dot your i's*

Other marks of punctuation include the **en dash** (to indicate a range of dates, for example), the **em dash** (to indicate an abrupt break in a sentence and emphasize the words within the em dashes), the **parentheses** (to enclose insignificant information), the **brackets** (to enclose added words to a quotation and to add insignificant information within parentheses), the **slash** (to separate lines of poetry within a text or to indicate interchangeable terminology), and the **ellipses** (to indicate information removed from a quotation, to indicate a missing line of poetry, or to create a reflective pause).

Practice Question

11) A third-grade teacher reads the following sentence in a student essay. Which punctuation should be added to the sentence?

Freds brother wanted the following items for Christmas a red car a condo and a puppy.

A. Fred's / Christmas; / car, /condo,
B. Fred's / Christmas: / car, / condo,
C. Fred's / Christmas: / car,
D. Fred's / items' / Christmas: / car, / condo,

Spelling

The mechanics of writing will generally involve explicit spelling instruction, and this will likely be part of a program's curriculum. It is important to view spelling as part of a developmental continuum and not overemphasize correct spelling too early when preschool students are still forming mock letters or letter strings. Initially, most children will go through a phase of **inventive spelling**. Inventive spelling or phonetic spelling involves children writing words based solely on the sounds they hear. It generally does not equate with conventional spelling rules. For example, a child may spell the word *cups* as "kpz." Inventive spelling is a normal part of the language development of young children.

Children should be explicitly taught spelling because **orthographic processing**, or the ability to use visual memory of the spelling of the word, is linked to decoding capabilities. Students with weak orthographic processing may have strong letter-sound knowledge, but without the ability to internalize and make a mental "picture" of the way sounds look in print, they will struggle to become fluent readers.

Orthographic processing and its connection to reading is part of the reciprocal relationship between **decoding** (sounding out words) and **encoding** (translating sounds into letter symbols). Generally students who struggle to decode will struggle to encode and students who struggle to encode will struggle to decode. In fact, some programs use an approach called **phonics through spelling** where children write letters for phonemes to spell and break words into phonemes to read.

Spelling instruction may also involve teaching syllabication and syllable patterns (see phonics section) and teaching morphology (see vocabulary section).

A standard **continuum of spelling** can be referenced to tailor spelling instruction appropriate to grade level while always keeping in mind the differing developmental levels within the classroom.

Table 3.4. Continuum of Spelling	
By the end of first grade, most students should be able to correctly spell short words with . . .	• short vowel sounds with a consonant-verb-consonant (*cat*, *dog*, *pin*) pattern [CVC]; • vowel-consonant pattern (*up*, *egg*) and [VC]; • simple consonant-vowel pattern (*go*, *no*) [CV]; and • consonant blends and digraphs in simple and high-frequency words (*chat*, *that*) [CCVC].
By the end of second grade, most students should be spelling words with . . .	• final consonant blends (*rant*, *fast*, *bend*, *link*) [CVCC]; • regular long vowel patterns (*ride*, *tube*) [CVC]; • double consonant endings (*lick*, *fuss*); • more complex long vowel patterns (*suit*, *fail*); and • *r*-controlled vowels (*near*, *bear*, *hair*, *are*).
By the end of third grade, most students should be able to spell words with . . .	• non-*r*-controlled but other consonants that influence vowels (*stall*, *draw*); • diphthongs (*coil*, *soon*, *enjoy*, *wow*); • soft *g*'s and *c*'s (*dice*, *hedge*); • short vowel patterns (*head*, *sought*); • silent consonants (*tomb*, *known*, *gnaw*, *wrote*); • advanced digraphs and blends (*phase*, *character*, *whose*); • contractions; • two-syllable words; • compound words;

Table 3.4. Continuum of Spelling	
	• words with suffixes that show number or degree (*fastest, foxes*); and • special spelling rules such as doubling the final letter on CVC words when adding certain suffixes (*napping, saddest*).

Explicit spelling instruction will generally begin with simple consonant-vowel-consonant (CVC) patterns and progress as students learn new phonics structures. Practice with homophones, or words that have the same pronunciation but a different spelling and meaning, should begin in third grade, or sooner for some students. Common homophones include *there/their/they're*, *to/two/too*, and so on. It is important to point out to students that software applications that might detect spelling errors in other words often fail to pick up on spelling errors with homophones, so students should be extra vigilant when editing and revising writing containing these words.

Did You Know?

Diphthongs are sounds created by two vowels together.

Knowledge of spelling rules or patterns is also important. Some of these are **position-based patterns,** such as

- *i* before *e* (except when a long a sound is present);
- when there is a vowel blend (e.g., /ee/ea/ai/oa), the sound made is typically a long vowel sound based on the first letter; and
- when there is a vowel-consonant-*e* pattern (e.g., *take* or *rate*), the vowel is usually long.

Other spelling rules are based on suffixes:

- Drop a silent *e* before adding any suffix that begins with a vowel (give/giving).
- Keep the *e* when the suffix starts with a consonant (use/useful).
- Drop the *y* when adding a suffix (baby/babies).

Other common spelling rules can be learned and taught with word families, such as words that end in -*ion* (*vacation*, *station*, *decision*) or words that end in -*ck* such as *luck*, *duck*, and *struck*.

It is also important to balance more explicit spelling practice with time to allow students to practice a crucial part of emergent writing: generative knowledge. In this domain students learn to write for a purpose that goes beyond simply forming a word and other mechanical concerns. While preschool students may not be able to write their own stories, teachers at this level can still give students practice by having them dictate a story that the teacher writes for them and perhaps even reads back to the class.

As students master more of the procedural knowledge of writing, they can begin generating more pieces on their own. Students generally progress from writing letter strings and word-like structures under a picture they have drawn to writing and spelling simple words, to constructing sentences and constructing stories.

As students begin to generate more written text, it is also important to emphasize the distinctions between spoken and written text. In speech, meaning can be conveyed in part through tone, pitch, and volume. In writing, punctuation is used to achieve meaning, but it is not always as easy to understand as speech. For example, though an exclamation point is used for emphasis, without context, it might not be clear if the sentence is to be read excitedly or angrily.

Spoken language also tends to be less formal than written language. Slang, for example, is almost always more appropriate in speech than in written communication.

Practice Question

12) A second-grade teacher is planning a unit on plural nouns. Which spelling rule would be MOST appropriate to introduce?

A. drop the *y* when adding a suffix
B. double the final consonant when adding *-ing*
C. keep a silent *e* when a suffix begins with a consonant
D. consider the phonemes in a word before writing it

Writing

As students develop skills in using academic language, they should begin to write their own pieces. When writing expository texts, students should develop an overall **thesis**, or main or controlling idea, that guides their writing. Each paragraph should present support for this idea by having its own **topic sentence** that states the focus of that paragraph. Evidence in each paragraph, such as expert opinions, examples, statistics, and reasons should support the topic sentence.

Students should understand that writing is a process and that even professional writers go through several phases before their finished product is released. This **authoring cycle** generally includes several phases in which ideas are transformed into written form to effectively communicate meaning. Students first need to **brainstorm** ideas. This can take many forms, and teachers might have the entire class generate ideas for writing topics and record them on the board or screen as an initial step.

Students can then create their own **webs** or **outlines** to organize their ideas. This initial planning can help students organize their overall point and supporting details. These activities can be based on a book they have read, where they take a stance on the work (e.g., "I liked the book," "I did not like the book," "My favorite/least favorite part was...") and then list the reasons why or why not. Brainstorming or prewriting activities, including those that leverage **graphic organizers,** can also help students organize the events they wish to recount when writing narratives to ensure their story has a clear beginning, middle, and end.

As students begin to draft, they should consider **cohesion**, or how their work sticks together. Strategies like the use of transitional expressions (e.g. ,first, next, further, therefore) can aid in developing cohesive sentences and paragraphs. Students should also consider whether they have included enough detail to support their overall topic as well as each paragraph's topic sentence.

Writing style is another consideration, especially as students begin writing longer and more complex pieces. Each piece of writing has a unique **style**, or approach. Style can describe the author's choice of words. Similar to style is **voice,** which is comprised of diction, detail, imagery, syntax, and tone. Academic writing generally employs varied sentence structures to drive interest, so students should be encouraged to use a mix of simple, complex, compound, and even compound-complex sentences.

Both word choice and structure can make a piece formal, informal, or somewhere in between. One part of selecting a style is the intended **purpose**, or **task**, and **audience**. Depending on the assignment specifics, students may write in a formal or informal tone, though many writing assignments may ask students to show proficiency with academic language.

With appropriate scaffolding, students must then go through a **revision** and **editing** process in which they strengthen their piece through the addition of more supporting details and connecting words (*because*, *also*, *then*) and proofread for capitalization, end marks, and spelling.

Students should have practice with both peer revision and self-revision. In **peer revision**, classmates aid in putting a second set of eyes on a text to offer feedback for improvements. Receiving feedback helps reinforce the concept that the overarching purpose of writing is to communicate ideas, so the perceptions and suggestions of multiple readers must be taken into account when revising a piece. In **self-revision**, students revise their own writing. Self-revision can be challenging, but one useful strategy is to have students read their piece aloud to catch potential errors.

> **Check Your Understanding**
>
> Which type of rubric or checklist could students use for self and peer revisions?

Teachers may aid students in the revision process by providing a simple checklist to help students ensure they have met certain criteria. One simple revision checklist is the **COPS** mnemonic. This stands for **c**apitalization, **o**rganization, **p**unctuation, and **s**pelling and is used with success in many elementary classrooms.

Students should also **publish** their work after the final copy is created, particularly if the writing project was significant in scope. Having students read their work aloud is one simple and immediate way to publish a piece, as is posting it on a classroom or school bulletin board. Teachers may have students organize and bind their work into a simple book with string or brads, or collect student work into a class-wide literary sampler.

If a teacher uses student portfolios in the classroom, he may have students prepare their pieces for inclusion into a digital or physical folder. This may involve transcribing the piece digitally, adding illustrations, or matting it on construction paper. Teachers should also emphasize to students that, seminal to the idea of publishing, is sharing the work with others. This is a great way to build a home–school connection while encouraging students to share their work with parents. Teachers should also show student work samples or portfolios at parent conferences to further build the home–school connection.

Practice Question

13) As part of a unit in which students write a letter to a family member describing what they did in school yesterday, a second grader struggles to begin. What should the teacher recommend?

A. organizing things the student likes and dislikes about school into a t-chart
B. thinking about the audience and what that person would want to know
C. deciding on a style and voice to convey a degree of formality
D. reviewing the mechanics of forming the greeting and the closing of a friendly letter

Research

Research and library skills are an important part of developing overall student literacy. Generally, there are seven steps in the research process:

1. **Identifying and focusing on the topic:** This might be as simple as having students pick a topic they want to learn more about or develop a research question they wish to answer—before searching online.

2. **Finding background information and conducting a preliminary search:** This involves getting a general overview of a topic and possible subtopics. During this stage students may research a topic using an online search engine or read an online encyclopedia page devoted to a particular topic.

3. **Locating materials:** This could involve working at the library and online. Teachers should encourage students to explore a wide variety of possible resources. As appropriate per the research topic, students should also be encouraged to seek out **primary sources**, or firsthand accounts. Primary sources may be speeches or diaries, surveys or census data, photographs of an event, and several other media that give eyewitness accounts of an event. Many primary sources are available online, and many sites organize these sources into an accessible format for students. Of course, many materials that students find will also be **secondary sources**, or non-firsthand accounts. These include the majority of books, articles, and web pages devoted to a topic.

4. **Evaluating sources:** Students need to determine if certain sources are useful and accessible to them. For example, a library database may generate results for articles in publications to which the library does not have a subscription. Some resources may be inaccessible to students as they may be overly technical or written for an older audience. Students should also make sure they have **credible sources** written by experts. This stage in the research process might be a good time to introduce the different types of information available on the internet and the qualities that help increase reliability (e.g., listed author, .edu or .org domain, publication date).

5. **Note taking:** Note taking may involve the use of formal note cards or simply jotting down main ideas. As developmentally appropriate per student age, teachers should ensure students understand the idea of **paraphrasing**, or changing the author's words into their own, as they take notes. Paraphrasing can help students prevent **plagiarizing**, or presenting someone else's words as their own work.

6. **Writing:** This includes organizing all the notes into sentences and paragraphs. Students need to be cognizant of the overall organization of their work as they introduce a focused topic, provide support, and write a conclusion. Depending on the age group with which teachers work, they may have students make a poster or use another outlet to present their research instead of a formal paper.

7. **Citing sources:** This may include in-text **citations** and preparing a bibliography. To simplify these elements for young students, teachers might use a simpler works cited/bibliography page where students simply list titles of books and authors. Students in the upper elementary grades may work to develop more sophisticated bibliographies in MLA style, as it is generally regarded as the simplest citation style and the one to which students are first introduced.

Of course, these steps may be greatly simplified for very young students and per the scope of the research project; however, even kindergartners can gather information from sources to answer a simple research question, and first-grade students can contribute to a simple class-wide research project with teacher support. The key is introducing students to the various parts of the research process while providing scaffolding as needed to support students as they explore new outlets for their developing literacy.

After students conduct research, they may present their findings to others. The use of varied media often makes a message clearer and more engaging.

Teachers should help students learn to create high-quality and engaging **multimedia projects** to present their research findings. Effective presentations should

- contain an appropriate balance of media elements;
- use sound, images, and video aligned with the overall message of the presentation;
- offer opportunities for audience participation, if possible; and
- be aligned with the project purpose and audience.

Think About It

How can UDL be incorporated into research projects?

Students should strive to use media in their work for a specific purpose—often to elaborate on a point or help the audience visualize something. The use of media elements as "decoration" or "fluff" is generally not a best practice. Students should therefore be taught to recognize and evaluate effective presentations, both those they make themselves and those made by others. Rubrics customized for specific types of media can be very helpful for both teacher and student evaluation of media.

Practice Question

14) During a unit on flags, kindergarten students asked many questions about flags from other states and countries. Which research activity might be MOST appropriate for the teacher to plan for her students to further explore flags?

A. direct them to conduct an online search for three primary sources on flags
B. take them to the library and have them use the database to find flag-related articles
C. have them write a paper on state flags citing two secondary sources
D. help students find pictures of different flags online and then talk about each one

Listening and Speaking

Because communication happens in myriad ways, students should be taught that spoken English is not the only (or even preferred or best manner) of human interaction. Some people speak via sign language or use assistive communication devices. Others speak orally in languages other than English. Further, even oral communication is not limited to spoken words alone. **Facial expressions** and **body language** are important parts of human communication. These types of **nonverbal communication** are essential for students to understand and recognize as part of their overall language and social-emotional development.

Young children develop oral language in a predictable pattern (see "Early Language Development" section in this chapter). In the classroom, this is generally observed with very young students reciting rhymes and songs and then advancing to the use of more complex vocabulary and sentence structures in their speech. As part of typical development, most prekindergarten students (age four) will be able to initiate speech with others and respond in simple conversations with adults and peers; however, the ability to speak clearly and intelligibly develops with time, and it is not unusual for young children to speak with sub-optimal **volume** and **intonation** (rising and falling patterns in speech).

There will be times when students must employ **passive listening** where they listen to a speaker or presentation without conversing. These occasions might be while listening to classroom directions and books or stories being read aloud. Passive listening, so long as it is done intently, is not necessarily bad; it just implies a lack of two-way communication. In fact, some occasions, such as being a respectful audience member, will require students to employ passive listening skills.

Active listening, on the other hand, should be employed whenever there is two-way communication. Active listening is used in many positive behavioral support programs, so if a school or program employs one of these, active listening may become a skill about which teachers are reminding students daily. The goal of active listening is to ensure that the listener has correctly understood the speaker. This is often extended to include an understanding of and empathy with this speaker. Generally, active listening involves making appropriate **eye contact** with the speaker, waiting for the speaker to finish, and then responding in a way that shows understanding. Active listening will be required when students are working together or holding conversations with peers and adults.

Not only should teachers be active listeners to ensure they understand what students are thinking and feeling, but they should also encourage students to employ these techniques whenever they are listening to directions or holding conversations. Active listening can also help students avoid conflict with each other as they refrain from interrupting and practice valuing the thoughts and opinions of others.

Part of listening and responding may involve different **types of questioning** as listeners check for understanding. Speakers generally employ either open-ended questions ("What does your house look like?"), which require a significant response, or closed-ended questions ("Do you like fried chicken?"), which generally require only a simple one-word answer. Speakers may even ask rhetorical questions, which do not require a response but are designed to make the listener think.

An even deeper type of questioning comes from **metacognition**, or an awareness of one's own thinking. Teachers can help students think from a metacognitive perspective by teaching them to ask themselves questions both about their content knowledge ("Have I seen this before?" "Do I know this or need more practice?") and from a socioemotional perspective ("Am I feeling cranky because I am tired or hungry?" "How would I feel if that happened to me?").

During more formal speaking situations, especially those in which the audience is primarily involved in passive listening, several other measures must also be considered. **Audience awareness** involves being aware of those to whom one is speaking and their level of engagement and interest. One way to increase engagement both in formal and informal speaking situations is through appropriate volume and **articulation**, or clarity of speech. It may help teachers to periodically self-assess their own classroom speaking and listening by asking themselves questions such as "Am I keeping an appropriate volume or raising my voice frequently?" and "Am I asking students enough open-ended questions and using active-listening techniques?" Modeling effective communication for students is an important way to help teach these skills.

Practice Question

15) Which of the following is an active listening strategy that can be taught to prekindergarten students?

A. emphasizing proper articulation
B. maintaining eye contact
C. using open-ended questioning
D. practicing oral presentations

Answer Key

1) D: In the holophrastic stage, children use one word to denote a broader desire or meaning. This is the stage after babbling.

2) B: Knowing the difference between a letter, word, and sentence is an important component of print awareness.

3) A: This would help students to practice identifying both letter sounds and the initial sounds of words.

4) A: The pattern is *g* (consonant), *a* (vowel), and *p* (consonant).

5) D: Having students act out a play from a script would give students practice reading expressively.

6) C: The phrase "look just like photographs" explains what realism means and is thus the best strategy.

7) A: Students will likely need background information in terms of what myths and legends are and certain unfamiliar words or ideas that may be included in these stories.

8) A: The theme refers to the general, overarching message about life that is presented in a text.

9) B: Adjectives and adverbs are parts of speech that are tied with detailed descriptions of nouns or verbs.

10) C: This is a fused compound sentence. The teacher can helps the student recognize the two independent clauses: "Chris has three cats"; "I have two dogs." From there, the student can create two simple sentences or, ideally, a compound sentence such as "Chris has three cats, and I have two dogs."

11) B: To be possessive, *Fred's* requires an apostrophe before the *s*. *Christmas* needs a colon to indicate the upcoming list, and *car* and *condo* should be followed by commas since they are items in a series.

12) A: This would apply to many plural words (e.g., ladies, babies).

13) B: Determining audience and purpose is the first phase in any writing assignment.

14) D: Helping students find pictures of different flags online and then talking about each one is an activity that scaffolds students learning and helps them begin to develop research skills. The other activities are not developmentally appropriate for a kindergarten class.

15) B: Maintaining eye contact is a core part of active listening and can help prekindergarten students focus on a speaker. The other activities are not a part of active listening.

4. Social Studies

Foundations of Social Studies Instruction

Social studies instruction generally involves introducing students to several key themes:

- time
- the role of the physical environment
- continuity and change
- cultural exchange
- global connections
- power and governance

The school and classroom are unique environments in that students are united in a common goal to grow and learn in a structured setting and are also somewhat separate in their own cultural experiences. All social groups and cultures share basic needs and wants like food, clothing, housing, and security, and they have some method for addressing the concerns of their members; however, what food, clothing, housing, and security look like may vary greatly among groups. A teacher might use the example of a Mongolian reindeer herder to illustrate this. While many Americans may find security in a stable home in one place, nomadic peoples, such as those who pick up their yurts to follow their herds of reindeer, may find security in a portable home that can adapt to the herd's migration.

A teacher might also show various examples of food and clothing that, while different from each other, still meet the physical needs of a community. Differences in a group of people's **physical environments** (part of the human environment that includes purely physical factors such as climate and vegetation) may dictate food, clothing, and housing choices, as people tend to use the resources most readily available. A teacher may point out the differences in clothing between those living in different climates and how housing and food may also vary based on a location's proximity to the equator. These discussions are easily integrated into science themes as well, and appreciation for differences while maintaining an understanding of unity in purpose to meet basic needs is essential.

Regardless of the physical environment in which a culture lives, there will inevitably be some power structure or governance. This might be a tribal chief in an American Indian culture or a monarch or prime minister in a European nation.

Of course, the way in which different social groups are organized can vary greatly. This may manifest itself on a microlevel within a student's family, whereby certain gender roles are adhered to, or on a macro-level, in which there is a social custom in the community for neighbors to collaborate in providing after-school childcare. Additionally, the **social conditions**, or situations in society based on income, job, or education level, in which one finds oneself may vary across a larger group. For example, all residents of a certain American city may have some shared culture, but this may vary based on socioeconomic status. Higher-income individuals may frequent different stores and restaurants and live in and attend school in different communities.

Teachers will want to model respect and tolerance for people across a broad social strata and various cultural backgrounds and avoid making direct comparisons that might imply a value judgment. Additionally, every effort should be made to make the classroom environment one in which many different cultural experiences and expressions are valued as part of the shared experience of the classroom. Strategies for this may involve inclusion of diverse cultural artwork in the classroom decor and reading stories from many different cultural and social perspectives.

Few individuals or cultures can provide for all of their needs without help. This leads to **interdependence,** whereby groups or individuals are dependent upon others to meet certain needs. Young children can best grasp this concept by understanding their own dependence on farmers and ranchers to produce the food they eat and on manufacturers to make the clothing and products they use.

Elementary-aged students may begin to understand broader ideas of one nation's interdependence upon another. For example, some products not available in one country (like grain in some Middle Eastern countries) must be imported from other countries (like the United States). In exchange, the country with the desired resource receives a payment of cash or a necessary product. This example shows how interdependence leads to the import of grain to some Middle Eastern countries and to the export of grain by the United States. In return, the United States might receive petroleum from a Middle Eastern country.

All parts of the world have different **natural resources** and thus access to some goods but not others. In some parts of the world and even in some desert regions in the United States, it is impossible to grow food, making these areas dependent on others for their very survival. This makes trade relationships and alliances crucial to meet the most basic needs of a community.

Cultural communities that are **intradependent** are not reliant on outsiders to meet the needs of their members and are able to produce resources within their own communities; however, this does not mean that these communities do not have specialists who provide specific goods and services. For example, the relationship between a farrier (a person who shoes horses) and the Amish community is one of intradependence. The farrier is able to meet the needs of other community members whose horses need shoes, but he is likely not able to meet all of his own needs. He might rely on a carpenter within his community to make furniture for his home and a roofer to repair his roof.

Intradependence is not very common in today's world. It is much more common for even developed countries like the United States to rely on other nations like China to produce certain manufactured goods, even though we have the capability to do so. Labor costs are lower in China, so the goods can be produced at a lower price.

Cultures may experience both **unity** and **diversity** simultaneously. For example, in the United States, people are unified under a common system of government and laws. However, there exists great diversity in ethnicity, religion, and language. One common idea is that of unity *in* diversity. That is, certain cultural groups are unified under some common purposes but have a diverse body. Some say that this is the case in the United States.

Some cultures are more heterogeneous, like many parts of the United States, where people of diverse cultural backgrounds can be found. Others are more homogenous and have a single and very dominant

Study Tips

The prefix *intra–* means "within." The prefix *inter–* means "between or among." Intradependence happens within a group, and interdependence happens among different groups.

culture. Since early childhood programs are found in both more and less diverse parts of the nation, and because some schools have a very homogenous student population, it is vitally important to ensure all students have experiences that allow them to appreciate the different cultures throughout the nation and world.

Globalization, the process by which businesses and organizations operate on an international scale, is rapidly increasing. This increase has led to a **global culture** in which certain norms and values are shared across a global scale. The development of a global culture has both negative and positive impacts, as shared understandings lead to more interconnectedness. But sometimes more dominant cultural constructs, such as American consumerism, may spread to the detriment of local culture. While the opening of American fast-food restaurants throughout the world may unite people in their love of french fries or a certain brand of coffee, it might do so at the expense of small local restaurants that preserve traditional cooking methods and foods. It is important for students to understand this dichotomy, as is age appropriate.

Practice Question

1) Which of the following images would be MOST useful for a first-grade teacher to show students to help them understand that housing is different in different environments?

A. an image of a New York City apartment building and an igloo
B. a drawing of a sprawling suburban home and a simple ranch house
C. a picture of a Native American woman and man
D. a photo of the White House and the Pentagon

Civics

A well-managed classroom will introduce students to many different civics concepts through explicit teaching and everyday interactions. Basic concepts of **justice**, or fair treatment, will likely come up quite frequently when young children are involved. In the classroom, this more often involves ensuring each child gets her needs met versus treating each child in the exact same way. This often plays out in assessing the reason for, or antecedent, of a child's behavior. A teacher ignoring a child's inappropriate behavior might be acceptable if the reason for the behavior was a desire for attention, but if attention-seeking was not the likely antecedent of the behavior and if there is a social lesson to be taught, ignoring the behavior may not be the best approach.

Unlike the concept of **equality**, in which all people are treated the same, the concept of **equity** involves giving individuals what they need to be successful. Classrooms are places where equality exists in some cases, and equity exists in others. For example, a teacher might promote equality by giving all her first-grade students ten spelling words each week. She might promote equity by giving her English-language learners a list of ten different words that are more appropriate to their current skill level.

There may be other parts of educational equity within a school or classroom as well. Many schools, realizing that hungry children cannot learn at the same rate as children who get enough to eat, offer free lunches to students who cannot afford to bring or purchase their own lunches. Students with individualized education programs (IEPs) may have accommodations within the classroom, such as scribes, interpreters, or educational aides to promote equity. Federal programs, like Title I and the Every Student Succeeds Act (ESSA), are designed to promote equity in educational environments by ensuring that students with special needs or from disadvantaged backgrounds receive the support they need to take full advantage of educational opportunities. It is important that teachers take the tenets of these programs seriously and familiarize themselves with all of the resources available to their students and help students and their families obtain the resources they need. This will help promote an equitable educational environment.

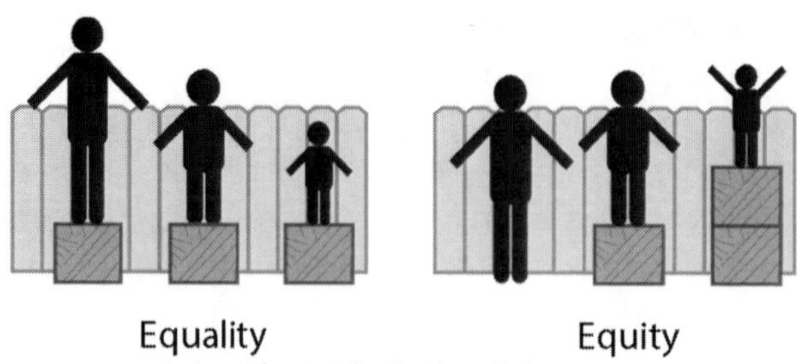

Figure 4.1. Equality Versus Equity

In helping students to understand the concept of **justice**, it is important to equate justice, as much as is possible, with a fitting consequence for an action. It might be just, for example, for Stephanie to be selected as the second-grade Pledge of Allegiance leader because of her excellent classroom conduct and high rates of homework completion. It might also be just for third grader Max to clean up the mess he made in the cafeteria after lunch, causing him to miss classwork and have extra homework. These are natural consequences for actions that represent the truest idea of justice.

Teachers should also promote **tolerance**, or the acceptance of beliefs or behaviors that one does not necessarily agree with, as appropriate in the classroom and help students understand the need for tolerance in pluralistic American society. Freedom of religion is a core tenet of the United States, and many classrooms will have students with different belief systems. Helping students to be understanding and tolerant of the beliefs of others starts with accepting differences. While some students might not understand why certain dietary or dress restrictions are observed by their peers, part of promoting tolerance includes helping students understand that there are many different ways of doing things. The nonprofit organization Learning for Justice (www.learningforjustice.org) created a list of standards appropriate for each K – 12 grade level that can be used as a reference to guide explicit instruction to help students develop tolerance.

Civic participation, or participating in issues of public concern, is important, but it is not practiced in many communities. Low turnouts, particularly at local elections, are evidence of this trend; however, this trend can be reversed by educating young people about how individuals in a society can help in the **decision-making** that affects their communities.

To participate in civic life, individuals must first be informed of the **issues**. Teachers can help their students keep up with current events on a local, national, and global scale through social studies lessons on contemporary issues. Teachers can point out that there are often different **points of view** on any given issue and that different groups bring different backgrounds and desires to any issue. A teacher may illustrate this by proposing an increase in social studies time and a decrease in math time. The teacher might then ask the class to weigh in on the issue: Is everyone in favor? Why are some groups against this? Students are likely to have different points of view based on their ease with or interest in either subject. Often in civic matters, one must **compromise**, or meet those with a different point of view, in the middle on an issue. This give-and-take is part of what makes democracy work.

A representative democracy, such as that of the United States, is based on **democratic ideals**, such as the idea that power and authority in decision-making rest with elected officials who have been designated by the people. The process of electing officials and raising issues of public concern to these officials brings many different viewpoints, as illustrated by the example of students weighing in on the issue of more social studies and less math time. In this example, students approach the issue from an individual perspective: those who like social studies and dislike math would be in favor of more social studies time, while those who like math more may not be in favor. This perspective represents the individual needs of students; however, students must consider many perspectives on the issue. Would a decrease in math time leave students ill-prepared for state tests? Would students who need more math practice be at a disadvantage? These considerations might then lead to making a decision based on the overall needs of the group, which must be balanced with individual needs and preferences. This is a key part of the democratic process.

Students should understand their roles as members of many different communities. They must be advocates in their local community to ensure their schools, hospitals, roads, and local services are operating smoothly and efficiently. They should also appreciate their roles in the larger city, state, and nation regarding their future ability to vote, organize, and have their voices heard.

Did You Know?

Only around 55 percent of eligible Americans voted in the 2016 national election; by 2020, nearly 67 percent of eligible Americans voted, marking the highest turnout for a presidential election in the twenty-first century.

Part of civic engagement is participating in **service projects** that help the community. Such projects could involve anything from canned food drives to help a local food bank, fundraising initiatives for nonprofits, or direct volunteering with a community or social service agency. Teachers may also consider encouraging students to take on leadership roles both in and out of school, as appropriate.

Students should also understand their role as global citizens who must protect the natural resources and biodiversity of the planet. The topic of global **citizenship**, or actions taken to promote social, political, or environmental issues on a global scale, is easily integrated with science topics such as recycling, conservation, and environmental advocacy. Environmental protection is necessary for keeping the plant and animal life on Earth diverse. It is also vital since all living things, their environment, and the economy are interdependent. A teacher might discuss this concept broadly with younger students by explaining that we must protect the earth in order to continue using its resources, such as food and water.

Older students might delve more deeply into this issue and examine the cause-and-effect relationship between the lack of environmental resource protection and the local economy. For example, a community reliant on the shrimping industry might be severely impacted by pollution in the Gulf of Mexico. This action by humans on the environment impacts the shrimp in the Gulf, whose populations may die out or dwindle. This, in turn, impacts the local economy, as shrimping may no longer be possible. This can have all sorts of further consequences, as shrimpers may leave the community, forcing the businesses that served the shrimpers (grocery and clothing stores, restaurants, and so on) to also go out of business. In this way, the environment and the economy are interdependent, and an action on one will impact the other.

Did You Know?

The United Nations Educational, Scientific and Cultural Organization (UNESCO) has created learning tools and objectives for each grade level to promote global citizenship and education.

Practice Question

2) A first-grade teacher wants to help the class develop global citizenship. Which project is MOST developmentally appropriate?

A. The class conducts research on the war in Ukraine.
B. The class identifies the exchange rate for the US dollar in other nations.
C. The class communicates with a first-grade class in another country via teacher-moderated Zoom.
D. The class interviews the school principal about a problem at the school and forms a plan to take action.

Geography

Humans have long been fascinated with geography and their place on the planet. Today, a person's geographic **location**, or exact position on the earth, is typically defined by latitude and longitude coordinates; however, even before the invention of these systems of measurement, explorers and cartographers made attempts to track location. Early **maps** and **globes** featured known land alongside *terra incognita*, or unknown land, which sparked interest in future maritime exploration. Today's maps and globes, both digital and physical, are far more complex and can help travelers navigate to very exact locations.

This precision is made possible by the geographical reference system of latitude and longitude. **Latitude** refers to the coordinates that specify the north-south position of a given point on the surface of the earth. These horizontal lines are usually marked and labeled on globes and include the **equator**—the line representing an angle of 0°—and four other named lines: the Arctic Circle at 66° north, the Antarctic Circle at 66° south, the Tropic of Cancer at 23° north, and the Tropic of Capricorn at 23° south. The climate of locations closer to the equator tends to be hotter because these areas receive more direct sunlight, while the climate of locations farther from it is colder because of the slant of the earth.

Longitude refers to the geographic coordinates that provide an east-west position on the earth's surface. This measurement far postdated the ability to calculate latitude, which could easily be calculated based on the position of the sun and stars. English clockmaker John Harrison invented a device in 1773 that calculated longitude, thereby ushering in a new wave of maritime navigation and exploration. Like latitude, lines of longitude have a central line at 0°, which is known as the **prime meridian**. While there was some initial controversy over where to designate the exact location of this line, it has now been firmly established at the Royal Observatory in Greenwich, United Kingdom. This is the origin of the term *Greenwich Mean Time* (GMT), or the solar time at this point.

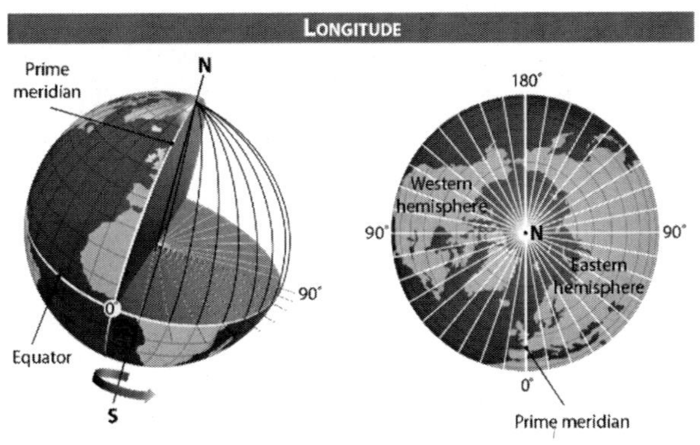

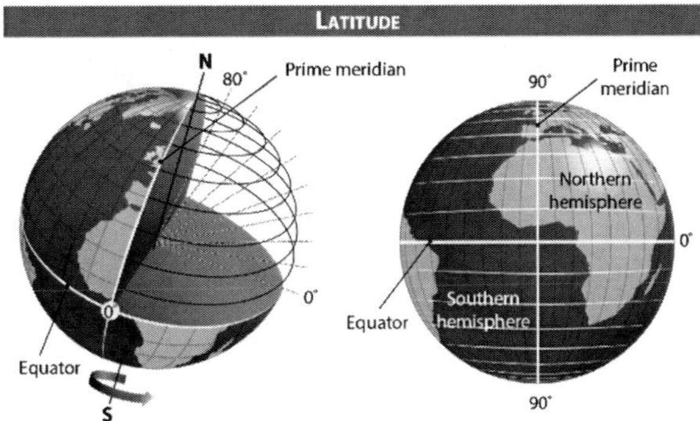

Figure 4.2. Longitude and Latitude

Globes are not practical to use when traveling, so students must be able to read and understand information on maps. Kindergarten students should be introduced to basic **directional terms** such as *left*, *right*, *over*, and *under* and should be able to locate basic locations in familiar environments like their school. They should also begin to recognize other major **landmarks**, or easily recognizable places, in their community. By first grade, students should be able to use the cardinal directions as illustrated by the **compass rose** with some fluency to find the location of objects and places. By second grade, students should start to use maps and globes to identify various locations, including being able to identify the map **title**, using the map's **legend** to understand what symbols or colors represent, using the **scale** to measure distances, and using a map's **grid** reference system to identify the coordinates of locations.

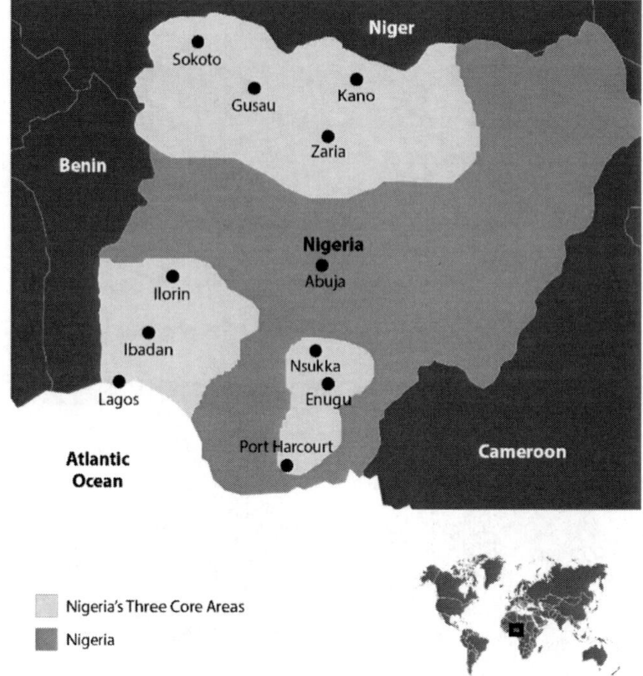

Figure 4.3. Parts of the Map

Students should be afforded plenty of practice with maps and be given opportunities to use and make simple maps. This might take the form of a class-wide project to draw a map of the school in the second or third grade, or even a simple sketch of the classroom layout for kindergartners and first graders. The key is making the map-focused activities as purposeful and relevant as possible to keep student engagement high and help them recognize and practice using and creating maps with purpose.

Maps and globes are not the only part of geographic study. **Regions** are the basic units of geography and describe areas of land that have common features. Regions can be based on political or cultural similarities but are often defined in terms of climate and vegetation. These regional differences affect human behavior and interaction with the environment. The major climate regions are as follows:

- **polar**: cold and dry year-round
- **temperate**: cold winters, mild summers, some forests and plains/prairies
- **arid**: hot and dry year-round and include some deserts (also found to an extent in cold tundra regions)
- **tropical**: always hot and wet, rain forests
- **Mediterranean**: mild winters and hot, dry summers
- **tundra**: cold year-round with three subtypes:
    - Arctic tundra is found in the far Northern Hemisphere and features a very desolate landscape. The ground is frozen in these cold desert regions, making it impossible for most plants to grow.

- Antarctic tundra is found in Antarctica and features some desolate landscape and desert; however, some areas support plant life.
- Alpine tundra is a mountainous region that also does not have significant plant life.

These environmental conditions impact people in a variety of ways. People living on plains and prairies where there are few trees, for example, often have to build houses out of materials other than lumber. People living in mountain and desert regions may have to import food from other areas since the landscape makes farming difficult. People who live in particularly fragile environments, such as the rain forest, often use the intense biodiversity around them to develop innovative solutions to meet their needs, such as growing small batches of crops in the limited ground space and hunting a wide variety of animals. One challenge facing many of the world's geographic regions is the desire for economic development balanced with the preservation of natural environments. Destroying rain forests, for example, not only displaces animals but also forces their inhabitants to change their very ways of life.

> **Check Your Understanding**
>
> What is the climate of your local community? How does this impact your daily life and the lives of your students?

In addition to the six populated **continents** of North and South America, Asia, Europe, Africa, and Australia, there are two other large formations that account for the solid surface area of the planet. The North Pole is the northernmost point on the globe and is sometimes referred to as the Arctic. It is not a landform in the strictest sense because it is really a large sheet of ice that expands and contracts based on temperature; however, some definitions of "the Arctic" cover the entire region of the Arctic Ocean and inhabited areas such as parts of Canada and Greenland. The South Pole, on the other hand, is located on the continent of Antarctica and represents the southernmost point on the globe. Antarctica boasts no permanent residents, but it is, like the North Pole, an important location for research stations.

The surface of the earth is 71 percent water, and its continents are surrounded by five **oceans:** the Atlantic, Pacific, Indian, Arctic, and Antarctic. The Antarctic Ocean is also sometimes referred to as the Southern Ocean or the Antarctic Sea. These saltwater bodies are connected by **seas**, which are generally smaller than oceans, often surrounded partly or wholly by land, saltwater, and usually connect with their larger counterparts.

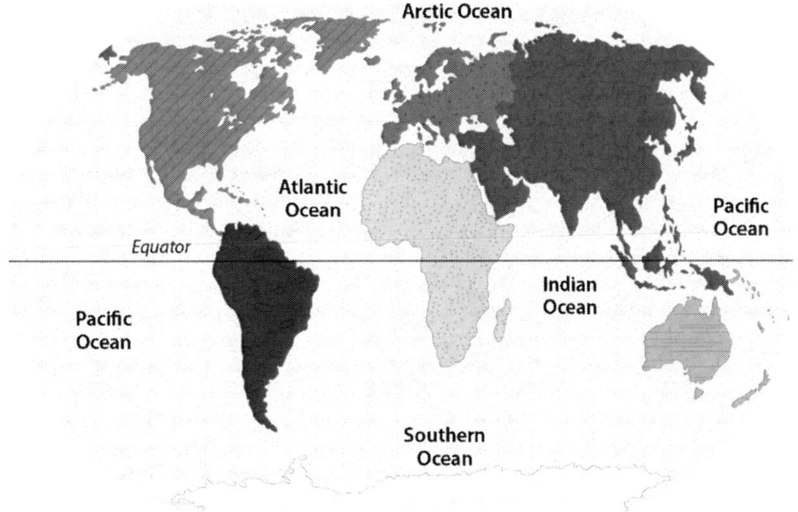

Figure 4.4. The Continents and Oceans

Rivers and their smaller cousins, **streams**, are flowing bodies of water that empty into seas and oceans and are generally freshwater. **Lakes,** like seas, are large bodies of water that are surrounded by land; though unlike seas, they are usually freshwater. While some lakes are natural, many are artificial and constructed for recreation. Most other bodies of water are naturally occurring and impact those in their vicinity. People who live near large bodies of water use the water source for food and transportation. Teachers whose programs are located near a body of water can ask students to consider the ways in which the body of water impacts the life of the community. Is fishing a popular local industry? Does the beach or lake promote tourism to the area?

Study Tips

Can you come up with a mnemonic device that would help students remember the names and locations of the oceans?

In addition to the **physical characteristics** of places and regions, such as climate, landforms, natural resources, and bodies of water, are **human characteristics** of regions. These include religion, clothing, housing, transportation, language, and common foods, among others.

Instruction in physical and human characteristics of places should include a discussion of how the physical characteristic of places impact the human characteristics, such as the natural resources of the area being used for food and home construction.

Practice Question

3) A first-grade teacher wants to assess students' mastery of identifying the continents. Which type of assessment would be MOST appropriate?

A. having students get a blank map and label the continents
B. having students create their own multimedia map with labeled continents
C. having students point to the continent that matches the name read orally
D. having students use modeling clay to form a continent of their choosing

History

World History

Students should be exposed to major themes in world history as appropriate and dictated by the standards. Such general themes include

- examining historic documents in world history, such as the Magna Carta and the Declaration of Independence;
- identifying artifacts and sites of major events in world history;
- comparing and contrasting world cultures; and
- identifying conflict and cooperation among world cultures.

These themes can be illustrated using a variety of different cultures and civilizations. Common global cultures and themes used for PK – 4instruction follow.

Ancient Egypt

Students of all ages typically enjoy studying about Ancient Egypt. The fertile land on the banks of the Nile River allowed the early Egyptians to develop settled communities thanks to agriculture and irrigation. Known for their pyramids, art, use of papyrus as paper, and pictorial writing (**hieroglyphs**), the ancient Egyptians emerged as early as 5000 BCE and were united under one monarch, or **pharaoh**.

Figure 4.5. Hieroglyphs

Around 250 BCE, Egypt's civilizational institutions, administrative structure, written language, art, and architecture were becoming well developed. In addition, the religious framework of ancient Egypt had become established, with a complex mythology of various gods. The ancient Egyptians also developed astronomy and the twenty-four-hour system of measuring time. It was during this period that the famous **pyramids** were erected at Giza; these structures were actually burial tombs for pharaohs. Major pharaohs included Hatshepsut, Thutmose III, Akhenaten, and Ramesses II.

This civilization can be used to illustrate for students different religious beliefs, different architectural styles, different ways of communicating, and the ways in which agriculture relate to human settlement.

Ancient Greece

Ancient Greece is another popular civilization to help students understand major social studies themes and ideas.

Ancient Greece was composed of small **city-states** like **Athens**, the first known **democracy**, and the military state **Sparta**. Around 460 BCE, Athens became a revolutionary democracy controlled by the poor and working classes. In fact, the term *democracy* comes from the Greek word *demokratia*—"people power." It was participatory rather than representative; officials were chosen by groups rather than elected. Athenian ideals have influenced politics and governance throughout history.

Athens was the strongest of the many small political bodies; in fact, the word *political* comes from the Greek word ***polis*** meaning "city-state" or "community," and much of Greece became unified under Athens following the Peloponnesian war between Athens and Sparta. It was during this period, the **Golden Age** of Greek civilization, that much of the Hellenic art, architecture, and philosophy known today emerged, including the **Parthenon** and other masterpieces of ancient Greek sculpture and architecture.

The Greeks established numerous colonies across the Black Sea, southern Italy, Sicily, and the eastern Mediterranean, spreading Greek culture throughout the Mediterranean world; it was eventually conquered by the rising Mediterranean power, Rome.

When students study Ancient Greek civilization, they can make comparisons and contrasts to American democracy as well as think about how celebrations like the Olympics have changed over time. This civilization is also useful for ELA integration as many myths from ancient Greece are available in modified form to be accessible to students of all ages.

Rome

One of the most powerful civilizations the world has ever known is that of Rome.

Originally a kingdom, Rome became a republic in 509 BCE, and as such, Romans elected lawmakers (senators) to the **Senate**. The Romans developed highly advanced infrastructure, including aqueducts and roads, some of which are still in use today. Economically powerful, Rome began conquering areas around the Mediterranean with its increasingly powerful military, including Greece, expanding westward to North Africa. With conquest of territory and expansion of trade came increased slavery, and working-class Romans were displaced; at the same time, the wealthy ruling class became more powerful and corrupt.

The people, or *Populare*, wanted a more democratic republic. As the Senate weakened due to its own corruption, **Julius Caesar**, a popular military leader widely supported by the *Populare*, emerged. Forcing the corrupt Senate to give him control, Caesar began to transition Rome from a republic to what would become an empire. Caesar was assassinated in 44 BCE; however, in that short time he had been able to consolidate and centralize imperial control. His nephew Octavian eventually gained control of Rome in 27 BCE, taking the name **Augustus Caesar** and becoming the first Roman emperor.

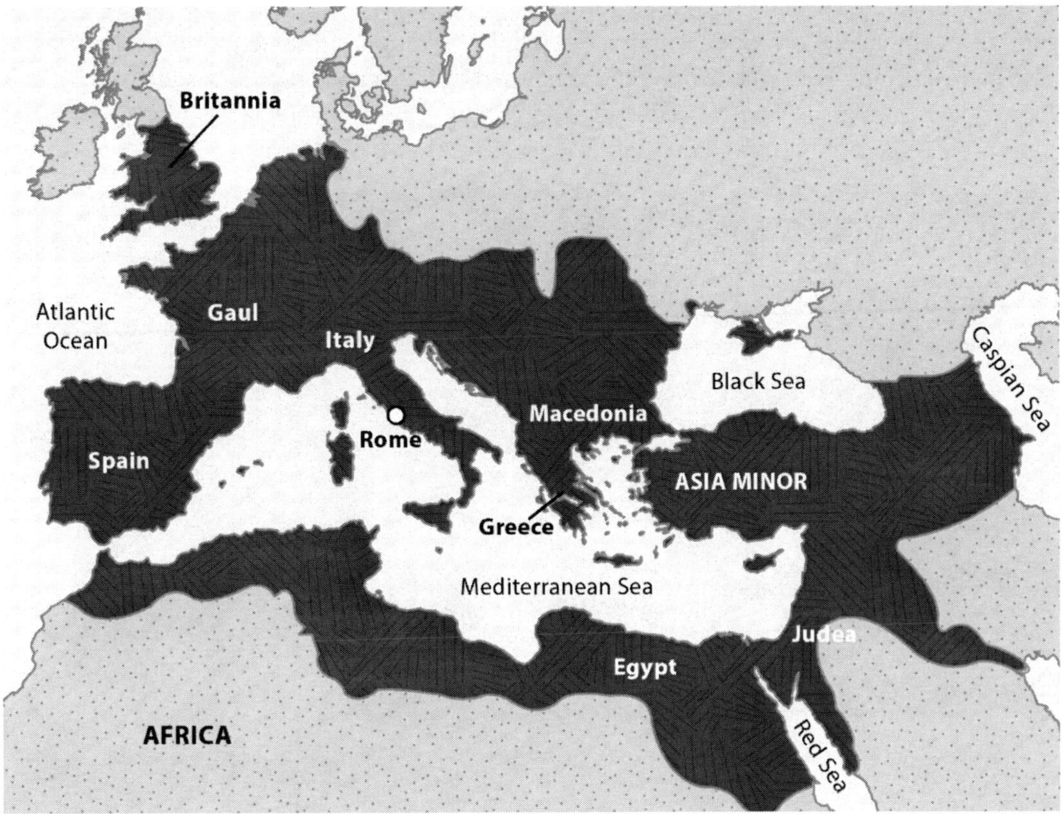

Figure 4.7. Pax Romana

At this time, Rome reached the height of its power, and the Mediterranean region enjoyed a period of stability known as the ***Pax Romana***. Rome controlled the entire Mediterranean region, Europe, and much of the Middle East and North Africa. Latin literature flourished, as did art, architecture, philosophy, mathematics, science, and international trade throughout Rome and beyond into Asia and Africa.

Check Your Understanding

What were similarities among ancient civilizations that allowed societies to grow and flourish?

A series of Barbarian invasions led to an empire already in decline splitting into an East and West in 395 CE. After the western empire was pillaged by Visigoths in 410, the fall of Rome was in full force with the date of its end cited as 476 CE by many scholars. The eastern empire, or Byzantium, would continue for many years to come.

Themes of power and governance are a key part of both the Roman Republic and the Roman Empire and thus appropriate topics for elementary students. Students can also learn about how Roman society was organized and the various cultural and artistic achievements of this civilization.

The Silk Road

In helping students understand cultural exchange, there is perhaps no better example than the Silk Road, which was at its height between 500 and 800 CE. Uniting East and West, the Silk Road was perhaps the first step in what we know today as globalization.

The Silk Road reflected the transnational nature of Central Asia: the nomadic culture of Central Asia lent itself to trade among the major civilizations of China, Persia, the Near East, and Europe. Buddhism and Islam spread into China. Chinese, Islamic, and European art, pottery, and goods were interchanged—essentially, early globalization. The Islamic tradition of the **hajj**, or the pilgrimage to Mecca, also spurred cultural interaction. Islam had spread from Spain throughout North Africa, the Sahel, the Middle East, Persia, Central Asia, India, and China; peoples from all these regions traveled and met in Arabia as part of their religious pilgrimage.

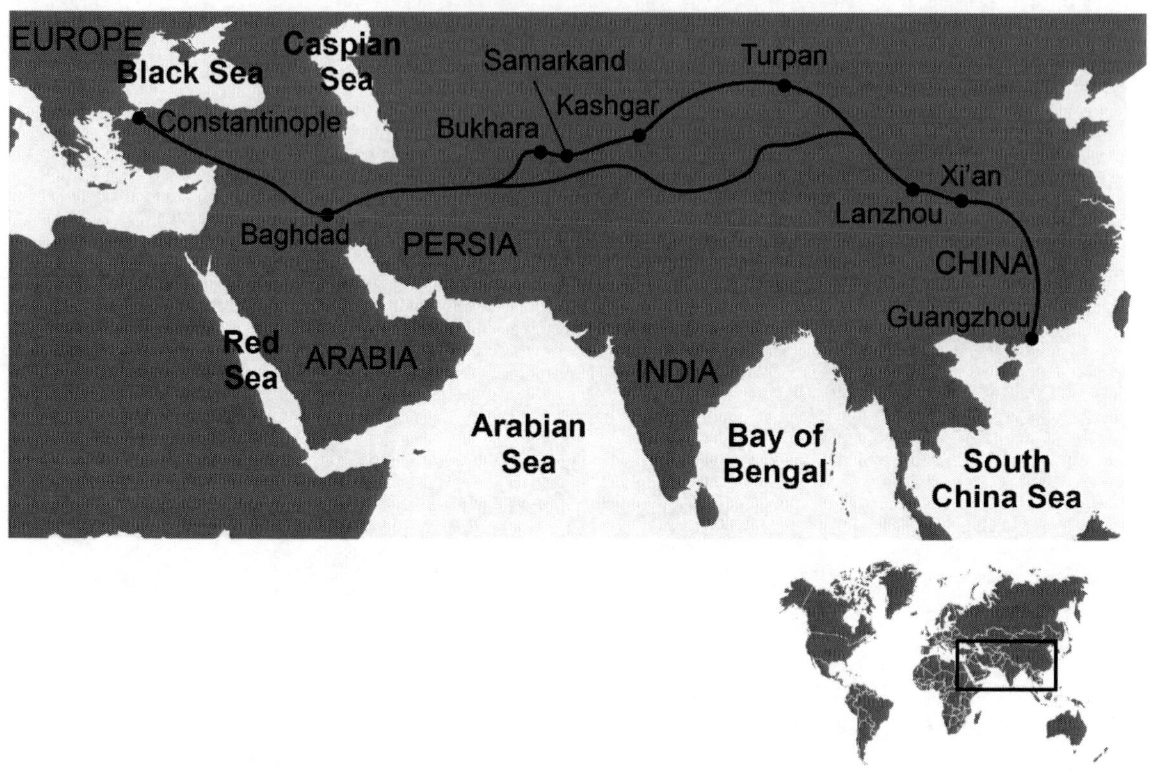

Figure 4.8. Silk Road

The European Middle Ages

Themes of change (with some continuity) can be illustrated with examples from the Middle Ages. In Europe, the early **Middle Ages** (or Dark Ages) from the fall of Rome to about the tenth century, was a chaotic, unstable, and unsafe time. What protection and stability existed were represented and maintained by the Catholic Church and the feudal system.

Society and economics were characterized by decentralization, local governance, or **feudalism**, a hierarchy where land and protection were offered in exchange for loyalty. In exchange for protection, **vassals** would pledge fealty, or pay homage to **lords**, landowners who would reward their vassals' loyalty with land, or **fiefs**. Economic and social organization consisted of manors, self-sustaining areas possessed by lords but worked by peasants. The peasants were **serfs**, not slaves but not entirely free. Tied to the land, they worked for the lord in exchange for protection; however they were not obligated to fight. Usually they were also granted some land for their own use. While not true slaves, their lives were effectively controlled by the lord.

Warriors who fought for lords, called **knights**, were rewarded with land and could become minor lords in their own right. Lords themselves could be vassals of other lords; that hierarchy extended upward to kings or the Catholic Church. The Catholic Church itself was a major landowner and political power. In a Europe not yet dominated by sovereign states, the **pope** was not only a religious leader, but also a political one.

There were, however, limits on sovereign power. In 1215, long before the revolution, English barons forced King John to sign the **Magna Carta**, which protected their property and rights from the king and was the basis for today's parliamentary system in that country. The Magna Carta also established what was known as the **rule of law**, which established equality before the law of all citizens, including the monarch.
Studying life in the Middle Ages can further develop students' awareness of power and governance and a rigid social hierarchy. The role of religion in society as well as the conflict between religion and other elements of society is also apparent when studying this time period.

The Americas

Studying native cultures in the Americas can help students understand the ways in which people interact with their physical environment as well as the role of cultural exchange. The two primary civilizations were the Maya and the Inca, whose civilizations are somewhat well-known because they were still in existence at the time that the Europeans came to the Americas.

The **Maya**, who preceded the Aztecs in Mesoamerica, had dominated the Yucatan peninsula around 300 CE. They developed a complex spiritual belief system accompanied by relief art, a detailed calendar, a written language, and pyramidal temples that still stand today. In addition, they studied astronomy and mathematics. Maya political administration was organized under monarchial city-states from around 300 until around 900, when the civilization began to decline.

> **Helpful Hint**
>
> Quetzalcoatl was an Aztec God involved in many rites and rituals.

As smaller Mesoamerican civilizations had weakened and collapsed, the **Aztecs** had come to dominate Mexico and much of Mesoamerica. Their military power and militaristic culture allowed the Aztecs to dominate the region and regional trade. The main city of the Aztec empire, **Tenochtitlan**, was founded in 1325 and, at its height, was a major world city home to several million people.

Meanwhile, in the Andean highlands, the **Incas** had emerged. Based in Cuzco, the Incas had consolidated their power and strengthened in the area, likely due to a surplus of their staple crop maize from their highly effective terrace irrigation system, around 1300. Inca engineers built the citadel of **Machu Picchu** and imperial infrastructure, including roads throughout the Andes. In order to subdue local peoples, they moved conquered groups elsewhere in the empire and repopulated conquered areas with Incas.

Practice Questions

4) A third-grade teacher is planning instruction on democratic ideals. Which civilization could the teacher reference as being one origin of American democracy?

A. Egypt
B. Greece
C. Byzantium
D. Persia

5) A first-grade teacher wants to help students understand the connection between physical features of the earth and human civilizations. Which example BEST illustrates this point?

A. Ancient Romans built a sewer system.
B. Ancient Greeks built temples to their gods.
C. Ancient Americans conquered other civilizations.
D. Ancient Egyptians settled near a river.

United States History

Students should be exposed to major themes in United States history. Common topics are discussed below.

Native Americans

When European settlers came to North America in the 1600s, they found an already populated continent. An estimated 60,000 Native Americans lived in the area that would become the first New England colonies.

Major civilizations that would play an important and ongoing role in North American history included the **Iroquois** in the Northeast, known for longhouses and farming in the Three Sisters tradition; they consisted of a confederation of six tribes. The **Algonquin** were another important northeastern civilization; rivals of the Iroquois, the Algonquin were important in the fur trade. Algonquin languages were spoken throughout the Great Lakes region.

Farther west, the **Shawnee** were an Algonquin-speaking people based in the Ohio Valley; however their presence extended as far south and east as the present-day Carolinas and Georgia. The **Lenape** were considered by the Shawnee to be their "grandfathers" and thus accorded respect. Another Algonquin-speaking tribe, the **Kickapoo** were originally from the Great Lakes region and moved west. The Algonquin-speaking **Miami** moved from Wisconsin to the Ohio Valley region, forming settled societies and farming maize. They too took part in the fur trade as it developed during European colonial times. These tribes later formed the Northwest Confederacy to fight US westward expansion.

The War for Independence

European powers had begun colonizing North America in the sixteenth century to access fur and agricultural resources; by the eighteenth century, Britain controlled most of the east coast of the continent, including the Thirteen Colonies, which became the original United States. France and Britain battled for control of northeastern North America, and following the **French and Indian War**, Great Britain consolidated its control over much of the continent.

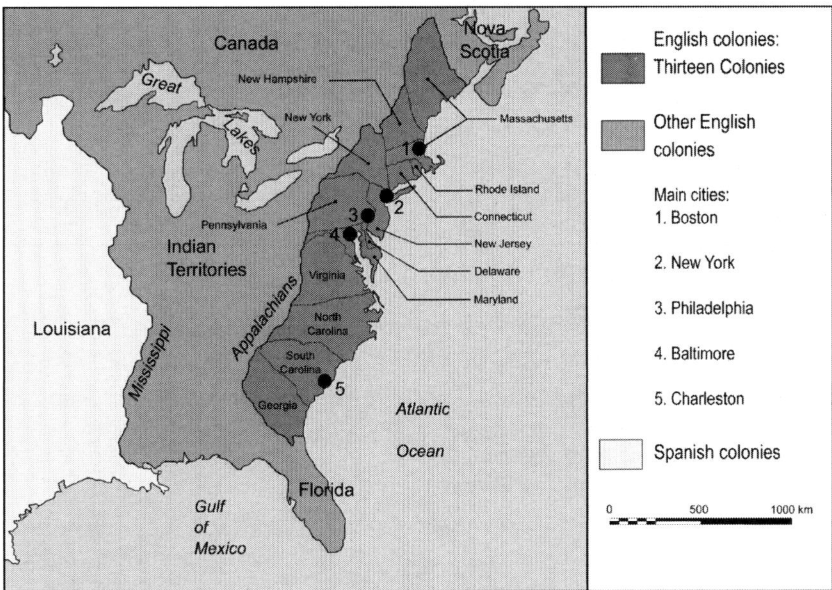

Figure 4.11. The Thirteen Colonies

Despite British victory in the French and Indian War, it had gone greatly into debt. Furthermore, there were concerns that the colonies required a stronger military presence following Native American attacks and uprisings like **Pontiac's Rebellion** in 1763. Consequently, **King George III** signed the **Proclamation of 1763**, an agreement not to settle land west of the Appalachians, in an effort to make peace; however much settlement continued in practice.

King George III enforced heavy taxes and restrictive acts in the colonies to generate income for the Crown and eventually to punish disobedience. England expanded the **Molasses Act** of 1733, passing the **Sugar Act** in 1764 to raise revenue by taxing sugar and molasses, which were widely consumed in the colonies. In 1765, Britain enforced the **Quartering Act**, forcing colonists to provide shelter to British troops stationed in the region.

The 1765 **Stamp Act**, the first direct tax on the colonists, triggered more tensions. Any document required a costly stamp, the revenue reverting to the British government. Colonists felt the tax violated their rights, given that they did not have direct representation in British Parliament. As a result, they began boycotting British goods and engaging in violent protest. **Samuel Adams** led the **Sons and Daughters of Liberty** in violent acts against tax collectors and stirred up rebellion with his **Committees of Correspondence**, which distributed anti-British propaganda.

Protests against the Quartering Act in Boston led to the **Boston Massacre** in 1770, when British troops fired on a crowd of protestors. By 1773, in a climate of continued unrest driven by the Committees of Correspondence, colonists protested the latest taxes on tea levied by the **Tea Act** in the famous **Boston Tea Party** by dressing as Native Americans and tossing tea off a ship in Boston Harbor. In response, the government passed the **Intolerable Acts**, closing Boston Harbor and bringing Massachusetts back under direct royal control.

In response to the Intolerable Acts, colonial leaders met in Philadelphia at the **First Continental Congress** in 1774 and presented colonial concerns to the king, who ignored them; however, violent conflict began in 1775 at **Lexington and Concord**, when American militiamen (**minutemen**) gathered to resist British efforts to seize weapons and arrest rebels in Concord. On June 17, 1775, the Americans fought the British at the **Battle of Bunker Hill**; despite American losses, the number of casualties the rebels inflicted caused the king to declare that the colonies were in rebellion. Troops were deployed to the colonies, and the Siege of Boston began.

In May 1775, the **Second Continental Congress** met at Philadelphia to debate the way forward. Debate among leaders like Benjamin Franklin, John Adams, Thomas Jefferson, and James Madison centered between the wisdom of continued efforts at compromise and negotiations, and declaring independence. Again, the king ignored them. By the summer of 1776, the Continental Congress agreed on the need to break from Britain; on July 4, 1776, it declared the independence of the United States of America and issued the **Declaration of Independence**.

Americans were still divided over independence: **Patriots** favored independence while those still loyal to Britain were known as **Tories**. **George Washington** had been appointed head of the Continental Army and led a largely unpaid and unprofessional army; despite early losses, Washington gained ground due to strong leadership, superior knowledge of the land, and support from France.

Initially, the British seemed to have many advantages in the war, including more resources and troops. Britain won the **Battle of Brooklyn** (Battle of Long Island) in August 1776 and captured New York City. The tide turned in 1777 at **Valley Forge**, when Washington and his army survived the bitterly cold winter and managed to overcome British military forces.

A victory at **Saratoga** led the French to help the rebels in 1778. France was an important player in the Revolutionary War, sending supplies and troops to aid the Continental Army from 1778 – 1782. Its assistance is viewed by some scholars as crucial to the ultimate success of Patriot forces.

After Saratoga, fighting shifted south. Britain captured Georgia and Charleston, South Carolina; however, British forces could not adequately control the country as they proceeded to Yorktown, Virginia in 1781. At the **Battle of Yorktown**, British forces were defeated by the Continental Army with support from France and were forced to surrender.

Meanwhile, the British people did not favor the war and voted the Tories out of Parliament; the incoming Whig party sought to end the war. After troops fought for two more years, the **Treaty of Paris** ended the revolution in September 1783. In 1787, the first draft of the Constitution was written, and George Washington became the first president of the United States two years later. The American Revolution would go on to inspire revolutions around the world.

> **Helpful Hint**
>
> Teaching about **Sacagawea**, the Lemhi Shoshone woman who joined the Lewis and Clark expedition, is one way to bring diverse historical actors into classroom instruction.

The Revolutionary War also had impacts on the new nation. In the spirit of freedom and liberty sparked by popular rhetoric, movements for the abolition of slavery began to grow. Other groups began to argue for expanded rights for women. The Anglican Church, or the Church of England in the colonies, largely ceased to exist as its head was the British monarch. Other traditions of the mother country, such as laws dictating land inheritance, were abolished. New markets beyond England were also opened for the goods of American farmers and merchants. Additionally, new land in the western territories became "open" for conquest and settlement by Americans.

Westward Expansion

In the nineteenth century, the idea of **Manifest Destiny**, or the sense that it was the fate of the United States to expand westward and settle the continent, pervaded. In 1803 President Thomas Jefferson oversaw the **Louisiana Purchase**, which nearly doubled the size of the United States. **Meriwether Lewis** and **William Clark** were dispatched to explore the western frontier of the territory: Jefferson hoped to find an all-water route to the Pacific Ocean (via the Missouri River). While this route did not exist, Lewis and Clark returned with a deeper knowledge of the territory the US had come to control.

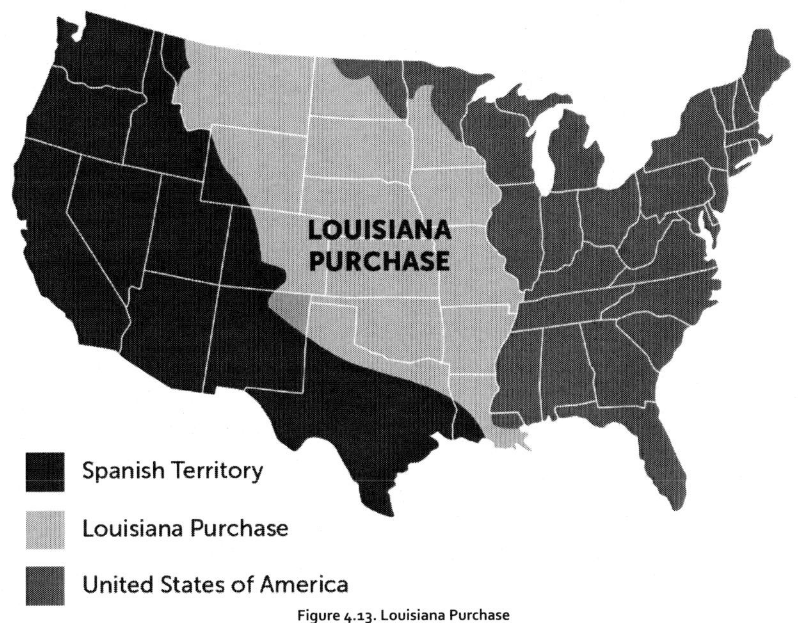

Figure 4.13. Louisiana Purchase

Slavery and Civil War

The country was increasingly divided over slavery; **sectionalism** grew, strengthening disunity between the North and the South. Reform movements continued to include **abolitionism**, the ending of slavery. The former slave **Frederick Douglass** advocated abolition. An activist leader and writer, Douglass publicized the movement along with the American Anti-Slavery Society and publications like Harriet Beecher Stowe's *Uncle Tom's Cabin*. He and other activists, like **Harriet Tubman**, helped free slaves using the **Underground Railroad**. An estimated 100,000 slaves escaped the South between 1810 and 1850 through a system of safe houses, even though these actions violated state laws. The radical abolitionist **John Brown** led violent protests against slavery. Abolitionism became a key social and political issue in the mid-nineteenth century; slavery was the main cause of the **Civil War**.

Following Lincoln's election, South Carolina immediately seceded, followed by Mississippi, Alabama, Florida, Louisiana, Georgia, and Texas. They formed the Confederate States of America, or the **Confederacy**, on February 1, 1861, under the leadership of **Jefferson Davis**, a senator from Mississippi. Shortly after the South's secession, Confederate forces attacked Union troops in Sumter, South Carolina; the **Battle of Fort Sumter** sparked the Civil War. As a result, Virginia, Tennessee, North Carolina, and Arkansas seceded and joined the Confederacy. West Virginia was formed when the western part of Virginia refused to join the Confederacy.

The reasons for the Civil War were both complex and simple. On the one hand, slavery was the central issue; however, slavery was part of deeper divisions related to notions of states' rights. Though states' rights are seemingly a political issue, they reflect the different economic interests of northern and southern states. Slavery was central to the cash-crop economy of the South but much less central to the more industrialized North that relied on non-forced labor. At the outset of conflict, each side had distinct advantages and disadvantages:

- The North had a larger population of 21 million versus the South's 9 million.
- The North had almost ten times as many manufacturing plants as the South.
- The North had 70 percent of all rail lines.
- The South had a "home field" advantage.
- The South had a long coastline that made blockade a challenge.
- Some historians also believe the southern states had better military leadership.

Both sides believed the conflict would be short-lived; however, after the First **Battle of Bull Run**, when the Union failed to route the Confederacy, it became clear that the war would not end quickly. Realizing how difficult it would be to defeat the Confederacy, the Union developed the **Anaconda Plan**, a plan to "squeeze" the Confederacy, including creating a naval blockade and taking control of the Mississippi River. Since the South depended on international trade in cotton for much of its income, a naval blockade would have serious economic ramifications for the Confederacy.

The Second Battle of Bull Run was a tactical Confederate victory led by General Robert E. Lee and Stonewall Jackson. The Union army remained intact, but the loss was a heavy blow to morale. The Battle of Antietam was the first battle to be fought on Union soil. Union General George B. McClellan halted General Lee's invasion of Maryland but failed to defeat Confederate forces. Undaunted, on January 1, 1863, President Lincoln decreed the end of slavery in the rebel states with the **Emancipation Proclamation**. The **Battle of Gettysburg** was a major Union victory. It was the bloodiest battle in American history up to this point; the Confederate army would not recover.

Meanwhile, following the **Siege of Vicksburg**, Mississippi, Union forces led by General Ulysses S. Grant gained control over the Mississippi River, completing the Anaconda Plan. The Battle of Atlanta was the final major battle of the Civil War. Victorious, the Union proceeded into the South, and the Confederacy fell. In April 1865, General Lee surrendered to General Grant at Appomattox, Virginia, and the war ended.

Practice Questions

6) A fourth-grade teacher wants to plan an activity to help students better understand the Emancipation Proclamation, even though it includes somewhat archaic vernacular. Which strategy is likely to be MOST effective?

A. having students use a dictionary to look up unknown words in the document as they read it silently
B. having students and teacher work together in a guided reading of the document
C. having students take turns reading the document aloud to the class while the teacher assists with pronunciation
D. having students watch a video about Abraham Lincoln's contributions to the United States

7) A teacher wants students to see the connection between geography and military strategy during the Civil War. Which question could *start* a discussion about the purpose of the Anaconda Plan?

A. How was the population of the nation spread out?
B. Why did textile production begin in the North?
C. What climate made the South ideal for growing cotton?
D. How were goods transported during this time period?

Pennsylvania History

Nobleman **William Penn** was granted a charter to colonize Pennsylvania by King Charles II in 1681. His father had lent money to the Crown, and the charter was a reward to the Penn family. The colony would be a space for **Quakers**, who faced discrimination in Europe, to live and worship freely. Land was purchased by the king from the Native Americans living in the majority of Pennsylvania, though the colony was not free of conflict between settlers and Native Peoples. By the late eighteenth century, most Native Americans migrated westward after the defeat of the French in the French and Indian War and many failed attempts at diplomacy and resistance.

Most English settlers were Quakers, but Anglicans were also a large demographic. In addition to settlers from England, immigrants from Wales, Ireland, Scotland, and Germany were also drawn to the colony. Enslaved Africans were also brought to Pennsylvania even though Quakers opposed the practice.

The colony was based on what was called the **Great Law**, which guaranteed freedom of conscience; however, there was conflict throughout the colonial period among various factions. Lieutenant governors, who were non-quakers, were constantly at odds with the Assembly, which was usually majority Quaker.

Nevertheless, the colony, and its shining star, the city of Philadelphia, were often hailed as centers of commerce and culture. **Benjamin Franklin** was perhaps one of the best known Pennsylvanians. He is credited with establishing newspapers, a library, hospital, and post office, among other accomplishments.

The city of Philadelphia served as the center of government during the Revolutionary War. In fact, the *Declaration of Independence* was signed in Independence Hall in Philadelphia. Soldiers from the colony also fought in great numbers in the Revolutionary War. Pennsylvania factories and farms also produced materials needed for the war effort.

Did You Know?

The city of Philadelphia was once known as the Athens of America because of its myriad cultural offerings.

While the war for independence was in progress, controversy over the government of the colony raged. Like other colonies, some Pennsylvanians wanted to remain loyal to the British crown while others did not; however the colonial government was still quite active. In 1779, the government took back public lands claimed by the Penn family, and in 1780, the commonwealth of Pennsylvania enacted a law to gradually abolish slavery—the first such law in the New England.

The city of Philadelphia was also the place where the new federal government would be debated and organized. The delegation from Pennsylvania to the **Constitutional Convention** included Benjamin Franklin and seven other men who supported the new stronger federal government. Pennsylvania was the second state to ratify the Constitution on December 12, 1787.

Factional disputes within the commonwealth were settled after independence, and in 1790, a state constitution was adopted. The document provided for two legislative bodies and a governor with broad powers. In 1791, the Pennsylvania State Supreme Court established its right to overturn legislative acts deemed unconstitutional—a principle that remains to the present.

In the years following the founding of the new nation, the state grew and flourished through immigration, urbanization, and economic development. Large numbers of Irish immigrants fleeing the potato famine of the 1840s were a significant immigrant population. Factories, particularly those related to textiles, grew and produced more and more due to mechanization. By 1860, there were more than 200 **textile** mills in the state, but **iron** and **steel** were also very important industries. The Cambria Iron Works became the largest mill in the United States. **Railroads,** of which Pennsylvania had more than any other state by 1860, allowed goods to be shipped throughout the nation.

The Gradual Emancipation Act of 1780 meant that by 1850, all African Americans in the state were free (except those who had escaped from other states); however, the issue of slavery, particularly in new Western territories, continued to plague the nation. A large **abolition** movement grew in Pennsylvania, and the state was an important part of what would become known as the Underground Railroad, where enslaved people were aided in efforts to escape to Canada.

When Civil War broke out, some 350,000 Pennsylvanians served in the Union Army. Pennsylvania was also the site of the Battle of Gettysburg (July 1 – 3, 1863), the bloodiest battle of the Civil War, with more than 50,000 casualties. In spite of the large losses, the battle, which ended in a Union victory, is often cited as an important turning point in the war and a significant blow to the Confederacy.

In the years after the Civil War, the state continued to grow. Government and social services expanded as the progressive agenda of the early twentieth century spread. When the United States entered **World War I** in 1917, the state was once again seminal to the war effort. Mills, factories, and shipyards supplied the American war machine. As in the Revolutionary War and the Civil War, Pennsylvanians also answered the call to serve and more than 300,000 Pennsylvanians performed military service during the war.

Unfortunately, just at the war's end, Philadelphia became the center of the **influenza epidemic of 1918**. A lack of understanding of the disease coupled with panic and confusion led to large loss of life; however, immigration to the state continued. These new immigrants were different from those of past eras and contained large numbers of Scandinavians, Jews, Slavs, and Italians. Additionally, large numbers of African Americans from the South came to Pennsylvania in the Great Migration. By 1940, Pennsylvania was the second most populous state in the nation.

When the **Great Depression** hit following the market crash of 1929, Pennsylvania was impacted greatly because of the numbers of citizens working as industrial laborers. **World War II**, however, reinvigorated Pennsylvania industry, which was once again crucial to the war effort. The state became known as the "arsenal of America," producing guns, planes, tanks, and ships in droves. Over a million Pennsylvanians also served in the armed forces during the war.

After the Second World War, the state began to diversify its economy as steel production began to decline and demand for coal was supplanted by other energy sources. Though raw acreage used for agriculture has also declined in recent years, thirty percent of the state's land is still used for farming, and production has increased due to new technologies.

Pennsylvania today is the fifth largest American state in population with over 13 million residents. It is known as the birthplace of American democracy.

Practice Questions

8) Which of the following activities would BEST help third graders recognize the significance of farming in Pennsylvania?

A. watching a video about an Amish community that uses non-mechanical farming methods
B. creating a map showing how much of the Commonwealth's land is farmland
C. doing an activity where students plan and maintain a school garden
D. using a multimedia tool to prepare a timeline of legislation impacting the Commonwealth's farmers

9) A teacher could use the example of the Gradual Emancipation Act of 1780 to illustrate which of the following?

A. the challenges freed African Americans faced after emancipation
B. the role of women in the American abolition movement
C. the different views about slavery in different parts of the US
D. the question of how slavery would be handled in new US territories

Government

Government is the basic institution that makes and enforces laws to keep order, provide security, and provide public services. Understanding the basics of government will help children to grow up to be responsible citizens who select leaders fit for their office. The United States government is composed of three branches: the executive, legislative, and judicial. A system of **checks and balances** keeps each branch from having too much power.

The **executive branch** of government is made up of the **president, vice president**, and fifteen **executive departments,** including the Departments of Defense, Commerce, State, Justice, and Labor. The executive branch enforces the laws. The president and vice president are elected members of the executive branch, but officials in other executive branch departments and agencies are appointed.

The legislative branch includes both houses of **Congress:** the Senate and the House of Representatives. The legislative branch makes the laws. Members of both the House and the Senate are elected, with each state electing two senators per state, and the number of representatives totaling 435 but varying in number based on state population. California and Texas have the most representatives at fifty-three and thirty-six, respectively, while Pennsylvania has seventeen.

The judicial branch comprises the federal court system, including the **Supreme Court**. The Supreme Court is made up of nine justices who are nominated by the president and approved by the Senate. The judicial branch interprets the meaning of the laws.

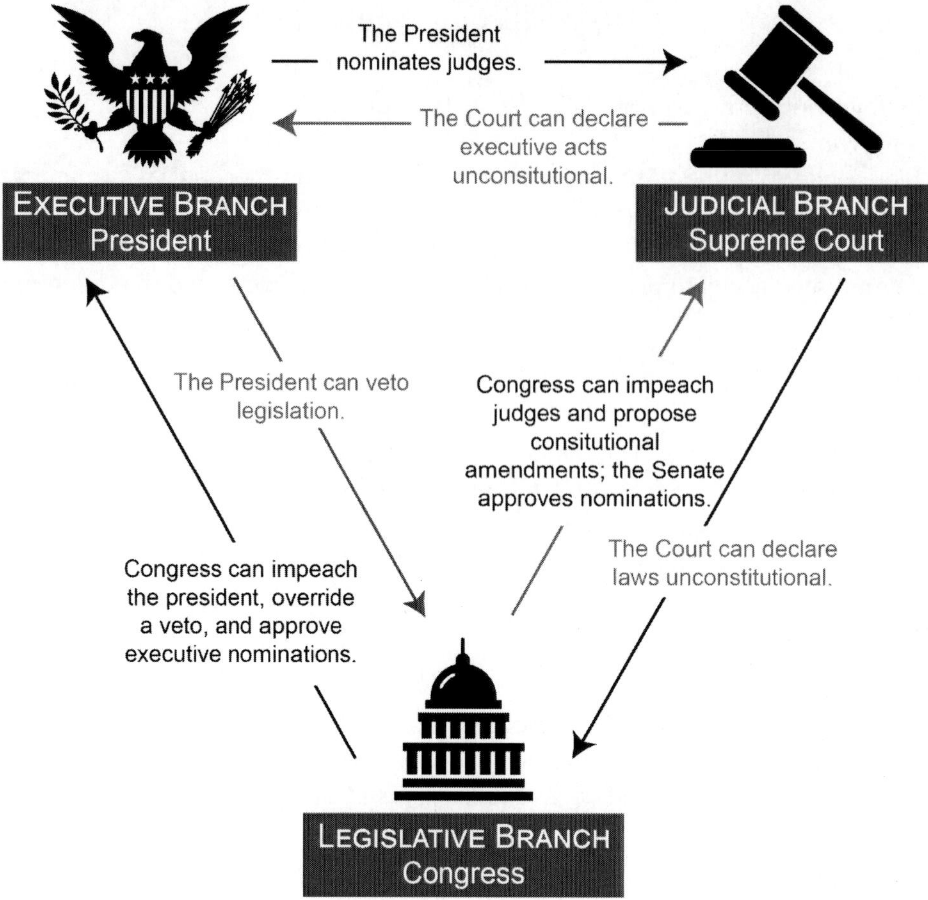
The President nominates judges.
The Court can declare executive acts unconsitutional.
EXECUTIVE BRANCH
President
JUDICIAL BRANCH
Supreme Court
The President can veto legislation.
Congress can impeach judges and propose consitutional amendments; the Senate approves nominations.
The Court can declare laws unconstitutional.
Congress can impeach the president, override a veto, and approve executive nominations.
LEGISLATIVE BRANCH
Congress

Figure 4.15. Checks and Balances

The federal government was formed by and operates based on the outline set out in the **Constitution**. In its interpretation of the laws made by Congress, the Supreme Court frequently examines whether legislation is in line with this document. While the basic governmental framework has been laid out, the political actors are selected through citizens who **vote** in **elections**.

Beyond the federal government is **state government**. State governments are modeled after federal governments. In Pennsylvania, there is an executive branch including a governor, lieutenant governor, attorney general, auditor general, and state treasurer as well as the governor's cabinet and many commonwealth agencies.

The legislative branch is made up of the **House of Representatives**, with 203 members and a state senate with 50 members. Like the federal legislative branch, these bodies make laws for the commonwealth. The judicial branch is made up of many courts as well as the Supreme Court of Pennsylvania. Unlike federal Supreme Court justices, these judges are elected for ten-year terms. At the end of their terms, if they wish to continue serving, they must be re-elected in a yes/no retention election.

> **Study Tips**
>
> The names of the different branches of government tell what they do: The executive branch is like the executive of a company—it ensures the "execution" of the company's objectives (e.g., laws). The legislative branch "legislates," or deals in making laws. The judicial branch "judges," or interprets the laws.

State government is important, but it cannot handle each, single everyday matter. That is where **local government** comes in. The Pennsylvania Constitution provides for six types of local government: county, township, borough, town, city, and school district. The state has sixty-seven counties divided into 2,560 municipalities. County government is headed by a board of commissioners with three members. Other county government includes sheriffs, district attorneys, treasurers, and various clerks.

Each county is then divided into municipalities called townships, boroughs, or cities. Townships generally involve an heir of William Penn and a sparse population. Townships are governed by a board of governors serving six-year terms, a board of commissioners serving five-year terms, or a board of supervisors serving six-year terms. Boroughs are smaller than cities. They elect a mayor and council and may also have a borough manager, who is hired to assist in administrative duties. Cities have a mayor and a city charter, which outlines laws that are distinct from state control.

The 500 school districts in the state are responsible for educating school-aged children. School districts may cross county lines.

Classrooms are excellent places to encourage an understanding of representative democracy. Teachers might have the class vote on classroom issues, such as which type of class pet to get. The early childhood classroom is also an appropriate environment for students to learn the role of government officials as servants of the public. Having special "classroom helpers" assigned to complete key housekeeping or administrative tasks can help students understand service to the classroom community. Assigning a student the responsibility of emptying out the pencil sharpener each day or collecting assignments, for example, can help students to appreciate the value in service to community, the foundation upon which all public service should rest.

Practice Questions

10) Lessons based on checks and balances could be used to broaden student understanding of which of the following?

A. community formation
B. global connections
C. democratic ideals
D. historical trends

11) A fourth-grade teacher wants to help students understand continuity and change in the context of American history. Which activity would BEST promote this understanding?

A. creating a map of major battles of the Revolutionary War and Civil War
B. making a poster explaining the reasons for which the Union had advantages during the Civil War
C. using a Venn diagram to compare and contrast the Articles of Confederation and the Constitution
D. holding a class-wide debate over whether the Articles of Confederation were effective

Economics

Elementary-level students should understand the basic concepts of supply and demand, scarcity, opportunity cost, how and why people generate wealth, how technology affects the economy, and the government's role in the economy.

The study of economics is the study of the production, distribution, and consumption of products as well as how people produce and obtain these goods. It explains how people interact with the market; studying economics usually explains the behavior of people or the government.

One of the most important concepts in economics is **supply and demand**. Supply refers to how much the market can actually offer, and demand is how much desire there is for a product or service. The demand is the relationship between price and quantity, which is how much people are willing to pay for the product. The supply simply means how much product producers are willing to supply at a certain price. This relationship between price and how much product is offered to the market is known as the supply relationship.

Price is used to show the relationship between supply and demand. When the demand is high for a product, the price generally goes up. When the demand is low, price falls; however, if the price is considered too high by the public, there may be excess supply because people will purchase less. Causes of excess supply include other price changes, including the price of alternative goods and public preferences. Likewise, there might be excess demand if the price is set too low and many people want the product, but there may not be enough supply. This might happen if there is a

Helpful Hint

Supply, demand, and equilibrium prices are a great way to integrate graphs and mathematics skills into social studies.

government ban on the product, the government imposes a price ceiling, or suppliers decide to not raise prices.

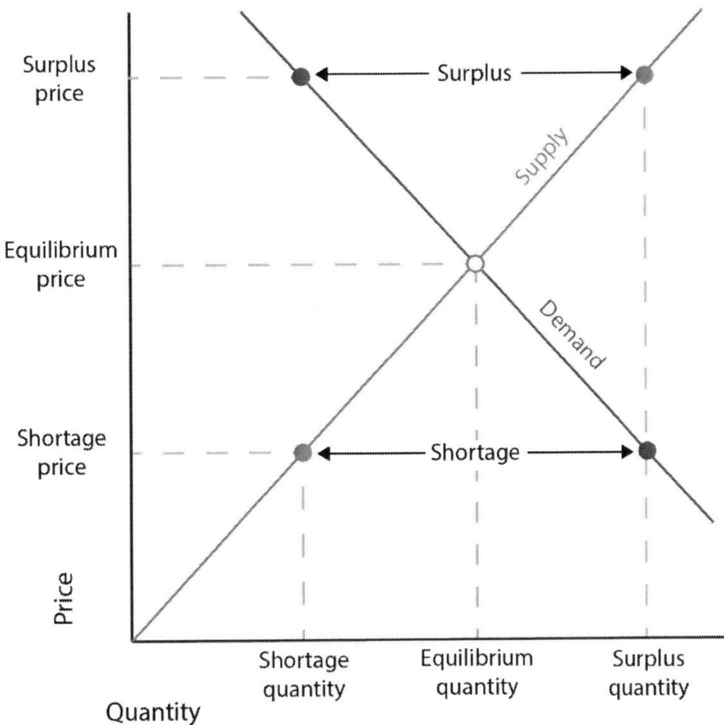

Figure 4.16. Equilibrium Price

For example, before Halloween, prices of Halloween candy are high because consumers are willing to pay high prices. They want to purchase enough candy to celebrate the holiday at parties and to distribute to trick-or-treaters, even if it is expensive. After Halloween, leftover candy is usually on sale. This is because demand for candy is low: the holiday is over and so people do not need it. That leftover candy represents excess supply. In order to get rid of it, suppliers drop prices to entice consumers with a sweet tooth to buy it even though Halloween has passed.

When supply and demand are equal, the economy is at equilibrium; however, that is not always the case. When there is insufficient supply to meet demand, the result is **scarcity**. People need to choose which want to satisfy. For example, if there is a low supply of chocolate, chocolate prices will be high. Consequently, a consumer must decide whether to spend more money than usual on chocolate or not to buy any at all.

Every choice has a value. **Opportunity cost** is when a consumer makes a choice at the cost of another choice or the value of an opportunity. For example, imagine that someone must choose between eating chocolate cake or apple pie. If that person chooses the chocolate cake, she gives up the opportunity to eat the apple pie. The opportunity cost is the apple pie. Decisions made by an individual or the government based on opportunity cost are driven by needs, wants, income, and time.

When making economic choices both parts of the value (costs and benefits) should be considered. The ideal choice will have the greatest benefits at the lowest cost. For example, there are two stores that sell chocolate, but the first store sells it at $35 a box and the second store sells it at $40 a box; however, it takes an hour to drive to the first store and it will cost about $10 in gas to get there and back, while it takes 15 minutes and $2.50 in gas to reach the second store. Economically speaking, it is not worthwhile to drive to the first store. Choosing to pay more for the chocolate at the second store is the cost, and the benefit is the time and cost of gas saved by rejecting the first store.

People use resources in order to create **wealth** and enhance their lives. These resources are either goods or services people provide in exchange for money. People provide labor, creating goods and services available for purchase. Labor refers to people who work in almost any job (e.g., on farms, in factories, or as computer programmers). The goods and services produced enhance people's lives. For example, not everyone owns a farm or can grow a variety of produce, so consumers depend on farmers around the world to grow various agricultural products in order to obtain them. Those farmers use resources such as water and land in order to generate wealth. Likewise, not everyone can fix a computer, so a consumer can bring his computer to an expert to be repaired. The owner of a computer repair service would be compensated with cash and be able to build that wealth by using that cash to invest in the business, buy property, invest in the stock market, or for other purposes.

Technological innovation is also driven by the economy (and vice versa). For example, more efficient transportation has increased trade and the exchange of wealth. Railroads enabled US businesses to transport raw materials to their production facilities, thereby increasing the production of goods. These areas then will need more people to provide labor, helping companies and individuals generate more wealth and providing jobs and salaries to workers, who themselves were thus able to generate more wealth in cash. More recently, computers and the internet have sped up communication and commerce, opening new ways of doing business.

When population increases, people consume more resources, generating more demand for products to meet their needs. In addition, as companies generate more wealth, they can invest in innovation and even more new technology.

The federal government helps to regulate the economy. **Government regulation** falls into either economic regulation or social regulation. Economic regulation controls prices directly or indirectly. The government works to prevent monopolies—the control of a market for a good or service by one company or group. For example, the government may prohibit utility companies from raising their prices beyond a certain point. Antitrust law is another type of economic regulation. It strengthens market forces to protect consumers from businesses and to eliminate or minimize the need for direct regulation. These laws are intended to ensure fair competition in the US economy.

Social regulation encourages businesses to behave responsibly and prohibits harmful behavior. For example, the US Occupational Safety and Health Administration (OSHA) enforces workplace regulations to protect worker safety, and the Environmental Protection Agency (EPA) regulates industry by upholding environmental standards for emissions and waste.

Finally, the government collects **taxes** not only to cover its expenses but also to help fuel the economy. Federal taxes pay for costs like federal employee salaries and retirement programs, government programs, and the military. Other government programs that are financed through taxes include veterans' benefits and NASA. Payroll taxes help **finance** the Medicare and Social Security programs which provide assistance for the elderly and those with low incomes. Government spending helps to increase the wealth of businesses and individuals. For example, if the government spends money to build bridges and highways, construction businesses generate more income. If an individual is retired or cannot work for health reasons, Social Security will provide assistance.

Practice Question

12) Teachers could BEST use an economics unit on opportunity cost to promote student understanding of which of the following themes?

A. decision making
B. compromise
C. point of view
D. rights and responsibilities

Answer Key

1) A: An image of a New York City apartment building and an igloo would show students how housing is different based on environmental conditions.

2) C: Communicating with a first-grade class in another country via teacher-moderated Zoom is developmentally appropriate and will help students learn about the way of life in another part of the world.

3) C: Having students use modeling clay to form a continent of their choosing is the best assessment method because it evaluates students' abilities to identify the continents but does not require students to spell the names of the continents, which would likely prove challenging for first graders.

4) B: The word *democracy* comes from the Greek word meaning "people power."

5) D: The example of ancient Egyptians settling near a river shows the interconnection between human civilizations and physical features that meet the needs of humans.

6) B: Since this is a key historical document that contains advanced vocabulary, it is best presented to students with teacher guidance and scaffolding.

7) D: Asking students about how goods were transported during the Civil War will help them understand that goods were moved by either train or water during this time. Since most rail lines were in the North, cutting off coastal routes for Southern trade was an effective military strategy.

8) B: Because 30 percent of the state's land is farmland, creating a map showing how much of the Commonwealth's land is farmland would help students see how significant this activity is.

9) C: The fact that Pennsylvania passed an emancipation act in 1780 while slavery continued in the South illustrates the disparate views about slavery in different parts of the US.

10) C: Checks and balances prevent any one entity from having too much power. Having the power rest with the people and not within individuals or institutions is a part of the American democratic ideals.

11) C: Using a Venn diagram to compare and contrast the Articles of Confederation and the Constitution would allow students to see what stayed the same (individual state governments with certain powers) and what changed (stronger federal government).

12) A: Because there is an opportunity cost associated with a certain action, people must make responsible decisions based on their assessment of that opportunity cost.

5. Arts and Humanities

Dance

Dance is typically defined as rhythmic body movements in sequence. Dance comes in many forms, sometimes called styles or genres. Style of dance is often associated with a certain culture, but all dance is similar in its existence as a medium for human **artistic expression**. All dances also contain what is often referred to as **elements of dance:** movements of the body using time, space, and energy. Dance elements are distinct from **dance techniques**, which are the particular skills required for a style or genre of dance (e.g., a plié in ballet).

A dance performance may be a **dance study** (a short performance made up of different **phrases**, or sequences of related movements) or a **dance work**, which is typically a longer performance with a clear beginning, middle or development, and end.

Some dances are **choreographed**, or planned phrases. Choreographed dance involves the intentional use of space, time/tempo, repetition, and energy. Other dances are improvised, such as getting up to dance at a friend's wedding. Students can plan or improvise dance in response to different types of **stimuli** designed to inspire feelings, thoughts, and actions. These stimuli may include

- music,
- literary or nonfiction texts,
- objects,
- print or video images,
- symbols,
- past experiences, and
- dances they have observed others perform.

When dancing, students employ both **locomotor** movements, or those where the body travels in space (e.g., skips and leaps) and **non-locomotor** movements, or those where the body does not travel in space (e.g., twists and bends).

Students will learn many technical dance skills, such as **coordination**, or the ability to control or execute movements; **balance**, or the ability to establish and maintain the body's equilibrium; **rhythm**, or the ability to move the body in sync with music; and **tempo**, or the ability to dance at the appropriate rate of speed. Dancers will also develop **kinesthetic awareness**, or an awareness of how different parts of the body are moving while in motion.

Some dance performances will be solos; others will be done in a group. Either way, dancers must maintain **spatial awareness**, or an understanding about the space around them. Dancers in groups must maintain appropriate **spatial relationships** with other dancers as they perform in a shared or **negative space**,

Did You Know?

Though *Swan Lake* is now regarded as one of the most famous ballets ever, its first performance in 1877 was judged harshly by critics, who called it "too noisy."

which is the area between dancers. Negative space exists in contrast with **personal space**, or the area as far as the individual dancer can reach.

Students receiving dance instruction will also be tasked with interpreting dance they see their peers or professionals perform. In interpreting or analyzing dance performances, students should consider the following:

- genre or style
- movement patterns and characteristics
- the time period and/or location from which the dance originates
- what the dance reveals about the time and/or location represented

Analyzing dance in this way will help students develop **dance literacy**, or general knowledge of dance. Students should also become familiar with basic dance styles such as **ballroom dance**, which began in France in the 1500s and includes styles like the waltz, tango, and quickstep; **performance dance**, which includes ballet, modern, and contemporary dance; **jazz dance**, including tap, swing, the Charleston, and disco; **Latin dance** like salsa, flamenco, and lambada; other **global dances** like polka and belly dance; and **hip-hop dance** like breakdance, locking, and popping.

Students should also be aware of the intersection between dance and human culture, how dance has changed over time, and how certain dance styles have influenced other dance styles in a process of blending and borrowing.

Practice Question

1) A third-grade student is struggling to complete a full turn and sometimes stumbles or has to put his hands down. Which technical dance skill should this student's teacher help him practice?

A. tempo
B. rhythm
C. spatial awareness
D. balance

Music

Teaching music is important to help students enhance skills that they can transfer to other subject areas. Students who are exposed to music education tend to do better in language development (e.g., reading tests) than students who are not. Music education helps to develop the left side of the brain, which is critical to processing language. Music also engages numerous parts of the brain, including the cognitive, hedonic, planning, and sensory systems. Furthermore, research has shown links between spatial intelligence and music studies, which means that students learn to visualize the different elements that are working together and recognize patterns, which corresponds with the problem-solving skills needed in mathematics.

As a music teacher, it is also important to help students make connections between music across other disciplines and the real world. To do so, teachers must vary lessons. For example, listening to music can teach students about different musical genres and expose students to the history of these. Music can also be connected to literature: students may learn to conduct research for a music-related project and in the process draw upon knowledge learned in different classes. Lessons on music culture may also tie into social studies.

To make real-world connections, teachers help students recognize the impact of music in their everyday lives. Teachers expose students to music from popular culture, such as commercials, movies and television shows. Teachers can also help students understand the emotional aspects of music (e.g., by using songs to remember significant events). Providing and studying informational texts is another way for students to understand music in real-world contexts.

Teaching music requires that the teacher has a sound knowledge of music notation, music-making, and **music terminology**. Students should understand that music **notation** is a method of writing down music so that anyone can play it. It helps composers create music by clearly indicating how they want it to sound; anyone who can read music will be able to play or sing the song accurately. Teachers can start helping students understand music notation by presenting it and breaking down the different elements of the modern system of notation.

The main system of notation currently used is writing musical notes on a **stave**, which is composed of a five-line **staff** with four spaces in between. The music is read from left to right, and there is usually a **clef** in front of a staff of written music. This helps to show exactly which notes are played, such as the treble clef or the bass clef. The location of the note on the staff indicates the **pitch**, or the position of a sound within the range of sounds; sharps or flats may be in front of the note. Notes that are very high or low can be placed on ledger lines above or below the stave.

The key signature is found after the clef, which indicates which sharps or flats will be used regularly. The time signature, placed afterwards, divides the music into regular groupings of beats using bars or measures. There are usually words that show the tempo, or the speed of music. There may also be dynamic marks to indicate how loud or soft to play the music at certain points.

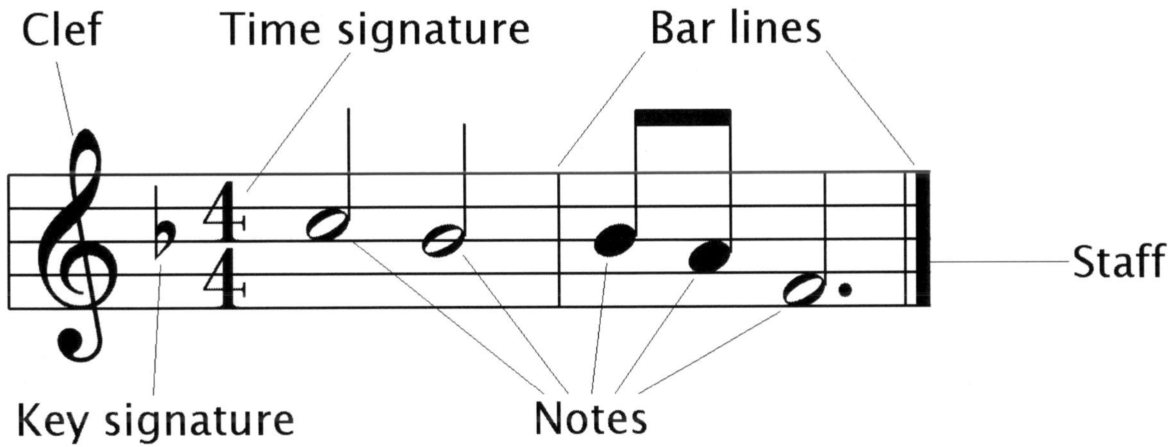

Figure 5.1. Musical Notation

Understanding music terminology can help students develop a better understanding of the elements of music. Teachers must explain what pitch, rhythm, melody, texture, timbre, and dynamics are and how they apply to music. Teachers should help students develop these concepts by reading musical notation, listening to music, and carrying out practical exercises.

Pitch can be high or low; scales are created by organizing patterns of pitches with intervals in between. Types of **scales** include chromatic, gapped, pentatonic, and major/minor. Having students listen to many pitches and practice the different types of scales offers them a more practical approach to learning. Teachers typically start by using a number system to help younger students learn the notes and then move on to *solfeggio* (*do, re, me, fa, so, la, ti, do*) as they progress.

Rhythm governs time in music. It is a specific pattern in time—a tempo—much like a steady pulse. These are organized into **meter**, which arranges these pulses into groups. These then can be further divided into two, three, or four smaller units. To help students develop an understanding of rhythm, teachers begin by using familiar songs or nursery rhymes and have the students clap along. The students feel and count the beats in a song, learning to distinguish when notes should start and end. Students can then understand the rhythmic patterns of the song. Students can progress to recognizing rhythm just by listening to a song or creating it by playing a musical instrument.

A combination of pitch and rhythm is called a **melody**. Melody describes the size of the intervals of the contour (rising or falling)—the tune of a song. As such, it is the main focus of a song and a way for a composer to communicate with her audience. **Harmony** relies on the melody, and is the use of pitches or chords simultaneously—the notes that support melodies. To develop the concept of melody, teachers should have students listen to and consider how a melody rises and falls, or compare melodic contours. These actions develop melodic personality. Teachers can also introduce the names and sounds of notes first to help children develop a sense of melody and understand how to read music. Having students learn a five-note scale and the different clefs can teach them how different pitches affect the melody. As students progress through the grades, teachers can even create lessons that help students see how different melodies can imply different emotions.

The **timbre**, or **tone**, is the musical characteristic that distinguishes between different instruments. When discussing timbre, students should be exposed to as many sounds as possible. Students can describe the sound by naming the instrument (once they have learned it), or using different terms. Words can include *brassy*, *bright*, *raspy*, *shrill*, *dark*, or *buzzy*. As students become more advanced, they can group different timbres according to instrument type, whether it be woodwind, brass, string, or percussion. Students should be taught to understand that the timbre is the same even if the same instrument is played at different pitches and volumes.

Dynamics refers to the loud or soft parts of a piece of music. They can change gradually or suddenly (crescendo or decrescendo), or have a large dynamic range if there are very soft and incredibly loud passages in the composition.

Combining melody, rhythm, and harmony is what makes up the **texture** in a composition, as these all determine the overall quality of the sound. Texture includes the number of layers and how these relate to one another. There are different types of musical textures. Monophonic is made of one voice or line with no accompaniment. Polyphonic includes many musical voices that imitate or counter one another, including the rhythm or melody. An example of this would be songs popular during the Renaissance or Baroque periods. Homophonic consists of a main melody which is accompanied by harmonic chords. An example of this would be a singer with a piano accompaniment. The texture would be considered homorhythmic if all parts have a similar rhythm. Teachers should introduce one texture at a time so students have time to listen to and develop their understanding of how to accurately

Helpful Hint

Each instrument differs in high and low pitches. The instruments with the highest pitch tend to be in the woodwind family, with the piccolo being the highest. The lowest-pitched instruments tend to be in the brass or string family, with the double bass being the lowest.

identify textures. Students can also preform different songs to get a feel for how different textures work.

At the elementary level, students may learn to play simple instruments as they develop their understanding of the elements of music. At the early elementary level (up to the third grade), students may not have developed the fine muscle control that would allow them to play more complicated instruments. Teachers should select items, such as Orff and other simple percussion instruments, that are easier to play and help students visualize pitch and rhythm while they develop their motor skills. Later, recorders are introduced when students are able to physically play them. This simple instrument helps students develop the skills, such as breathing techniques, that are necessary for more advanced instruments and allows them to gain experience reading sheet music, which is simplified with recorders since there is only one tone. Teachers can also use the recorder to teach a wide variety of songs and ensembles using one instrument.

In the upper elementary grades, students should have developed the motor skills to play the types of instruments used in band programs. Since students should have learned how to read basic sheet music and utilize the breathing techniques appropriate for woodwind instruments, teachers can help students advance by applying their knowledge of other elements of music, such as harmony and timbre.

As in dance, music is a way for human artistic expression, and music is entwined with human culture. Students should be exposed to multiple musical styles and genres, understand the context of each, and recognize what is being communicated about a given culture or group. Students should be further encouraged to pursue their own musical interests and develop their own music based on their interests and experiences.

Practice Question

2) A second-grade teacher plays students two recordings of the same song: One is a piccolo solo of the song, and one is a double bass solo. Which musical element could the teacher ask the students to contrast?

A. notation
B. pitch
C. harmony
D. dynamics

Drama

Drama is an expression that tells a story to an audience through the actions and dialogue of characters, which are brought to life by actors who play the roles on stage. Dramatic works, called **plays,** are written in poetic or lyrical verses, or in regular prose. Along with the dialogue between the characters, authors rely on **stage directions** to describe the sets and to give instructions to the actors about what they are to do.

In some plays, actors perform long speeches in which the characters explain their thinking about philosophical ideas or social issues. These **monologues** can be directed toward another character. A monologue delivered as if nobody were listening is called a **soliloquy** (as in Shakespeare's famous "To be or not to be" soliloquy from *Hamlet*).

Sometimes characters in drama (or fiction) have very unique attributes, such as a manner of speech, dress, or a catchphrase. Such devices make characters memorable to readers and are known as **character tags**.

Dramatic interpretations may be based on **scripted dramas** or **improvised** (i.e., spontaneous) scenes and monologues. Younger students may participate in **guided drama experiences**, where a leader supports student actors via side-coaching and prompting without stopping the action of the play.

Students should also be given opportunities to learn about the **technical elements** of theatre, such as the integration of **lighting**, and **sound** elements, such as music or sound effects. Other elements include props, which can be **representational materials**—actual objects like silk flowers or trees— or **non-representational materials**, which can be made into props via imagination (e.g., a beam in the cafeteria that becomes a magic tree).

Materials for students to use to create their own props, scenery, puppets, and costumes should be part of the supplies of the theatre classroom. These supplies need not be elaborate and can be recycled materials, such as plastic bottles and cans (useful for sound effects); old boxes (useful for scenery); and scraps of fabric or discarded clothing (useful for costumes).

Large group performances are not the only activities in which students will participate. They might be given opportunities to tell stories, sing songs, or perform **spoken word poetry**, an oral performance of poetry with a certain beat or rhythm.

Did You Know?

The Ancient Greeks were the first to put on theatrical performances, which date back to the sixth century BCE.

Students should also have opportunities to connect English language arts skills with theatre as they consider the plot, characterization, setting, character motivations, and dialogue in dramas they read and perform. As with dance and music, dramatic interpretations from various cultures should be explored and analyzed for how they express important themes and ideas.

Practice Question

3) In an improvised duet scene, a fourth-grade student runs away from a desk in the classroom, screaming "Snake! Snake!" What does this exemplify?

A. guided drama experience
B. character tags
C. stage directions
D. non-representational materials

Visual Arts

The **visual arts** include drawing, painting, sculpting, and photography. While the tools and techniques used in these art forms can be very different, they all rely on the same foundational elements and principles.

A good understanding of the elements and principles of art is necessary for the creation and analysis of art. Teachers should show children that artists use these elements and principles to make decisions when creating their own art, and that students should apply this knowledge to their own works.

Art is created through the use of line, shape, form, value, texture, space, and color. Together, these are known as the **elements of art**.

Line in art is called a moving dot: it can control the viewer's eye, indicate form and movement, describe edges, and point out a light source in a drawing. Artists use different line qualities and contours to suggest form. To indicate value or a light source, artists use cross-hatching lines in varying degrees.

A closed contour is what creates **shape**, which is two-dimensional. A shape can create balance and affect the composition, establishing positive and negative spaces. Different types of shapes include regular (i.e., geometric) and organic (i.e., free-form) shapes. When students understand the basics of shapes, they can create complex forms by combining simple organic and regular shapes.

Form is like shape except that it is three-dimensional. Creating form requires an understanding of how light reflects upon an object, or its **value**. Teachers should help students understand where the highlight, the reflected light, the mid-tone, the core shadow, and the cast shadows are in order to create an illusion of form. Having students create a value scale and understand how it applies to objects they see is also helpful. Value also helps to create **texture**, which refers to how an object would feel if someone were to touch it. Students can develop their sense of texture through exposure to a wide variety of objects and by understanding how light reflects off rough, smooth, matte, and shiny surfaces.

> **Helpful Hint**
>
> To engage young children, have them create and analyze art that relates to topics that are familiar to them, such as family, friends, sports, holidays, and animals.

Creating an illusion of **space** can help students in creating an artwork on a two-dimensional surface. Students should experiment with different techniques such as overlapping shapes, shape placement, sizes of shapes, and perspective to see how objects can appear closer or farther away.

The color wheel is primarily used to teach students the theories of **color**. There are different types of colors:

- **Primary colors** (red, yellow, and blue) cannot be made using other colors.
- **Secondary colors** are made by mixing primary colors.
    - yellow + blue = green
    - red + blue = purple
    - red + yellow = orange
- **Tertiary colors** are made by mixing one primary color with half the saturation of a second primary color (e.g., blue + 1/2 red = violet).

The color wheel also shows **complementary colors,** which appear opposite each other on the wheel. When paired together, complementary colors offer a stark contrast that is pleasing to the eye.

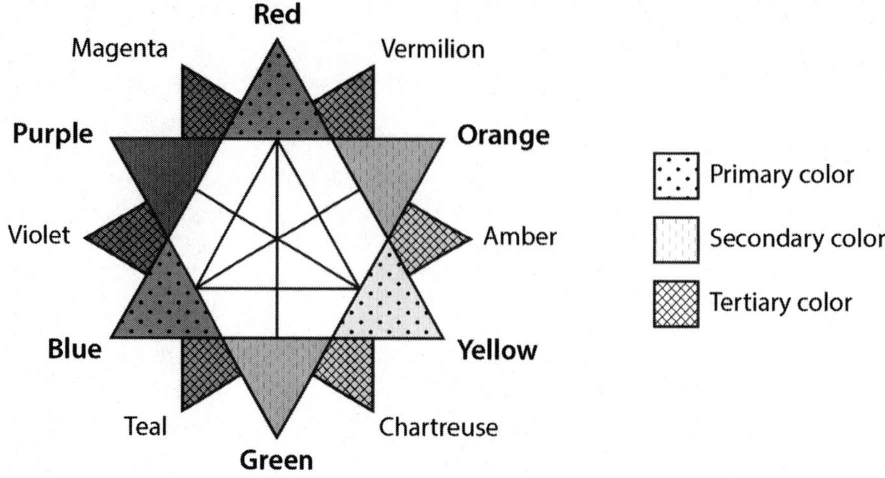

Figure 5.2. The RGB Color Wheel

The **principles of art** refer to the composition of the elements of art within a piece of work. These principles include

- balance,
- unity,
- contrast,
- movement,
- emphasis,
- pattern, and
- proportion.

In order to create **balance** in an artwork, colors, forms, shapes, or textures need to be combined in harmony. Harmony also helps to create **unity** in a piece of work by creating a sense of wholeness.

Artists generate **contrast** by using various elements of art (e.g., shapes, form, colors, or lines) to capture the viewer's attention and draw it toward a certain part of the work. **Movement** guides the viewer's eye through a composition, usually to highlight areas of contrast or emphasis. Repeating occurrences of a design element (e.g., shapes, forms, or textures in an art piece) are called **patterns**.

Finally, **proportion** describes the way in which the sizes of objects appear. For example, objects that are farther away appear smaller and have less detail than objects that are closer.

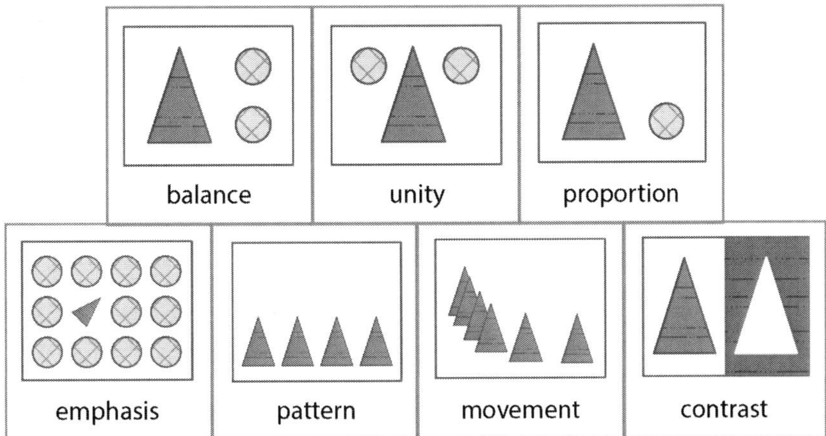

Figure 5.3. Principles of Art

Art history should also be taught so that students can gain an understanding of how artists and art made contributions to culture and society and how art reflects what is important in a society at a certain time. In studying art history, students learn how artists interact with their contemporaneous cultures, respond to historical events and social change, and address other artistic movements. Art history lessons should encourage students to ask why an artist created a certain piece of art, how it was used, and what its purpose was.

As students study individual artists and their bodies of work, they should be encouraged to consider the mind of the artist as she created the work, and how the artwork relates to its time period. Teachers should provide as much relevant background as possible so that students can use that knowledge to view and discuss the artwork. Even young children can benefit from exposure to the art and music of the different civilizations throughout human history.

Teachers can also use art history to help students explore world history and other cultures. Students can be taught about art from ancient civilizations such as ancient Egypt, the ancient Mayans, ancient Ethiopia, classical Greece and Rome, and more. They can also be introduced to modern art from various cultures around the world.

Helpful Hint

Students should be encouraged to think about works of art as stories about life. One way to do this is by asking students to consider and articulate the "story" they see in a work of art.

Teachers can also engage students with art history by having them create art from different cultures and time periods. Students can use supplies like pipe cleaners, wood craft sticks, cardboard, and construction paper to build their own versions of ancient pyramids and temples. To help build motor skills, children can use modeling clay to make their own sculptures during a lesson on classical civilization. Watercolors, tempera paints, and pastels are also great tools for young students who may be inspired by Claude Monet or Jackson Pollock to make their own impressionist- and modern-style artworks.

Practice Question

4) A kindergarten teacher has his students paint a picture that includes animals of different sizes. Which principle of art is the teacher introducing to his students?

A. pattern
B. movement
C. proportion
D. unity

Answer Key

1) D: Balance refers to the ability to retain the body's equilibrium and avoid stumbling or falling.

2) B: These two instruments have the highest (piccolo) and lowest (double bass) pitches, so asking students to contrast the pitches is the best exercise.

3) D: The student is using imagination to turn the desk into a snake.

4) C: Having students draw animals of different sizes introduces them to proportion, or the way the sizes of the elements in an artwork relate to each other.

6. Mathematics

Mathematics Instruction and Assessment

Teaching math requires knowledge of research-based or evidence-based math instructional techniques. These techniques include the following:

- **Introducing the language of math:** Just like any discipline, mathematics has its own language, or system of symbols that represent ideas. Students must be taught this language in order to perform math operations successfully.
- **Explicit, systematic instruction:** Systematic math instruction involves **modeling** in a step-by-step process, which may include **think-alouds,** where the teacher describes his thought process while solving an example problem. After the demonstration, the teacher should offer **guided practice** where the students and teacher work a problem together, followed by **independent practice,** where students work alone or with other students to solve a problem. The teacher should then assess understanding and offer feedback and clarification as needed.
- **Visual representations:** Sometimes called schematic diagrams or representations, these are visual tools (e.g., fraction strips, models, or multiplication arrays) that help students correctly solve problems. Research suggests these tools lead to greater accuracy in problem solving, especially for young students who are still developing procedural knowledge.
- **Word problem instruction:** This involves helping students understand math vocabulary and translating the problem into an algorithm or visual representation.
- **Problem-solving strategies:** Students should be taught to plan or **decide** how to approach a problem, and then select an appropriate strategy from their existing knowledge base. As they work, they should **monitor** how things are going and employ estimation or rounding skills to see if their answers makes sense. If their approach is not working, they should **modify** their approach accordingly.
- **Talking about math:** Another research-based strategy is discussing multiple ways of solving a problem and comparing different approaches, and perhaps even different answers. This helps students further develop their overall math understanding, including recognizing errors made by others.
- **Using a CRA methodology:** The abbreviation *CRA* stands for concrete-representational-abstract. In the first phase, students learn a math concept through the **concrete,** meaning that students and teachers first use tangible materials, or **manipulatives**. For example, the class might use an abacus, counting chips, or base ten blocks. In the **representational** stage, the concrete is transformed to the pictorial. Teachers and students might draw pictures or use dots or tallies. In the final **abstract,** or symbolic stage, numbers and standard algorithms are used.
- **Technology to enhance, not replace:** Technology can be particularly useful in classrooms with students at multiple points in their math journey, as well as students with various levels of English language proficiency. In balanced math instruction, tech tools can help students extend

understanding and think about problems with greater depth of thought; however, these tools should not replace computational capabilities.

At times, math teaching will involve both whole-group, small-group, and even individual help or instruction. Using small-group instruction can be particularly useful when some students are in need of reteaching while others may be ready to explore more with an extension activity.

High-quality math teaching involves frequent assessments, including both ongoing formative assessments and summative assessments at the end of units or concepts. While written assessments are common, other tools can also be used:

- Individual student whiteboards can show each student's answer to a problem.
- One-problem exit tickets at the end of a class can easily determine students who understand the concepts that were taught and those who may need reteaching.
- Short interactive quizzes via Google Forms, Kahoot, or platforms can also quickly identify the level of student understanding.
- Reflection journals or notes can also be useful in encouraging students to employ metacognitive strategies and monitor their own learning.

Students who are English language learners (ELLs) will also benefit from specific and targeted instructional strategies, particularly when working with word problems. To help these students, the teacher should provide explicit math vocabulary instruction as well as math banks or glossaries for students. Teachers can also help students break down word problems with the aid of sentence frames as appropriate. Manipulatives can also be very useful with ELLs as can simplified assessment strategies that limit the need for long oral explanation on the part of the student. For example, instead of asking "How did you solve that problem?" students could be asked, "Did you add or subtract first?"

Effective math teachers are also aware of common student mistakes and misconceptions. Common misconceptions include the following:

- adding instead of subtracting (after subtraction is first introduced)
- believing that subtraction is commutative
- believing subtraction should always be from the "bigger number," which creates a problem when subtracting two or three-digit numbers with regrouping
- believing that .10 is more than .4
- believing that multiplication always makes numbers bigger, which is not true of decimals and fractions
- believing that division should aways involve dividing the larger number by the smaller number, which creates a problem when working with fractions
- thinking that any multiplication by 10 involves simply "adding a 0," which is not true with decimals

Helpful Hint

If students are always taught to erase all their work and start again, they may never be able to recognize their own mistakes. Students should practice finding the error in their calculations and erasing only the part after the error.

Practice Question

1) When teaching students subtraction, which of the following represents the concrete stage?
   A. The teacher draws three circles and crosses one out.
   B. The teacher holds three blocks and takes one away.
   C. The teacher writes 3 - 1 on the board.
   D. The teacher asks students to write 3 – 1 = 2.

Early Math Skills

Skills such as **counting** and skip counting, which involve rote memorization of numeric words in a proper order, are some of the most important math concepts introduced to young children. **Skip counting** is a form of counting where numbers are not consecutively recited by one. Skip counting can occur in twos, threes, or any fixed pattern. As children learn counting, they may not quite understand the concept of one-to-one correspondence in **numeration**.

One-to one correspondence is the ability to say one number for each object pointed to or touched consecutively. For instance, when counting out "one, two, three, four" using **counters** or other objects, children who have not developed the concept of one-to-one correspondence may skip an object or count it more than once. Placing objects in a line and using counting motions, like pointing or clapping while saying each number out loud, helps correlate each number to an object.

Which group has more counters?

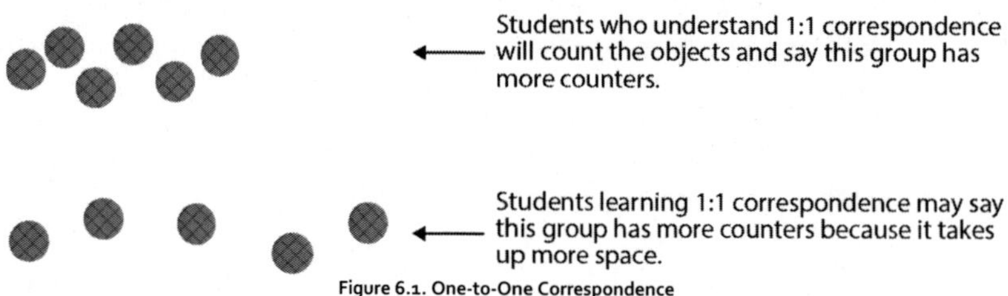

Students who understand 1:1 correspondence will count the objects and say this group has more counters.
Students learning 1:1 correspondence may say this group has more counters because it takes up more space.

Figure 6.1. One-to-One Correspondence

Pattern matching, **grouping**, **sorting**, and **sequencing** are concepts in early math development that aid in understanding numeration. As children begin to **categorize** objects in their environment by how they are alike or different, a natural sense of order occurs. Since many fundamental math skills cannot be directly taught at a young age, **manipulatives** in the form of toys, puzzles, games, or even general household items provide excellent practice material. Toy blocks can be grouped or sorted by color, shape or size; clothes can be arranged or sequenced by **pattern**; toys can be put away while counting each one.

> **Helpful Hint**
>
> Help students connect counting to cardinality: When counting objects in a set, the last word said is the number of objects in that set.

Number conservation refers to the understanding that a number of objects remains the same even when the objects are rearranged. A child putting away five stuffed animals will recognize that the quantity does not change regardless of which animal is put away first.

Over time, a child maturing in age and cognitive development will have the ability to mentally conduct numeration in various ways. One such way is by **subitizing**—the capacity to view a small number of objects and immediately recognize how many there are without counting. Another numeric skill involves mastering one-to-one correspondence, which leads to an understanding of **cardinality**—finding out how many objects are in a group or set.

Practice Question

2) A preschooler walks over to a classmate flipping through a board book and immediately exclaims that there are five cookies in the picture. Which of the following skills is the student demonstrating?

A. sequencing
B. sorting
C. skip counting
D. subitizing

Number Sense

Place Value

A **digit** (0 to 9) is a symbol used to make numbers. For instance, the number *5,182* is made up of the digits *5*, *1*, *8*, and *2*. The value of the position of each digit in a number is called its **place value**. In the number *5,182*, the digit *5* is in the **thousands** place; the digit *1* is in the **hundreds** place; the digit *8* is in the **tens** place, and the digit *2* is in the **ones** place.

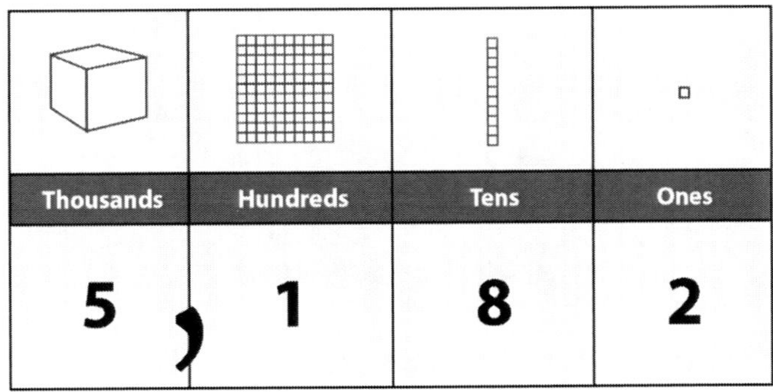

5000 + 100 + 80 + 2 = 5,182

Figure 6.2. Place Value Chart

A **place value chart** is a good visual aid to show children how to understand the value of digits using pictures or objects, such as base-ten blocks. The chart has place values listed right to left in the way numbers are typically formed. The chart also aids in reading and writing multi-digit numbers accurately, as each digit is placed in a column that correlates to its value.

Common Student Errors

Misunderstanding how to expand numbers ($306 = 30 + 6$)

Decreasing the number in the specified place when rounding down ($163 > 150$)

Another way to express a number is by decomposing it. **Decomposing** a number breaks it down into individual parts. For instance, the number *6,417* can be decomposed to 6,000 + 400 + 10 + 7. Similarly, **composing** a number involves adding the individual parts. For example, 9,000 + 400 + 30 + 1 can be written as 9,431.

> **Study Tip**
>
> The following rhyme can be used to teach rounding rules: Find the number, look next door. Four or less, let it rest. Five or more, raise the score.

Rounding is a useful skill. When working with large figures, it is often easier to work with values rounded to the nearest ten or hundred; it is not always necessary to work with an exact number. **Rounding** a number makes it simpler to work with.

Using whole numbers makes it easier to explain rounding. **Whole numbers** are the numbers *0, 1, 2, 3, 4,* and so on. They do not include negative numbers, decimals, or fractions. Rounding a whole number, such as 83 to the nearest ten gives 80, because 83 is closer to 80 than it is to 90. The number *87*, however, will be rounded up to 90. Similarly, rounding the number *345* to the nearest hundred is 300 since 345 is closer to 300 than it is to 400. Rounding the number *5,782* to the nearest hundred will be 5,800, because the hundreds value of 782 is closer to 800 than it is to 700.

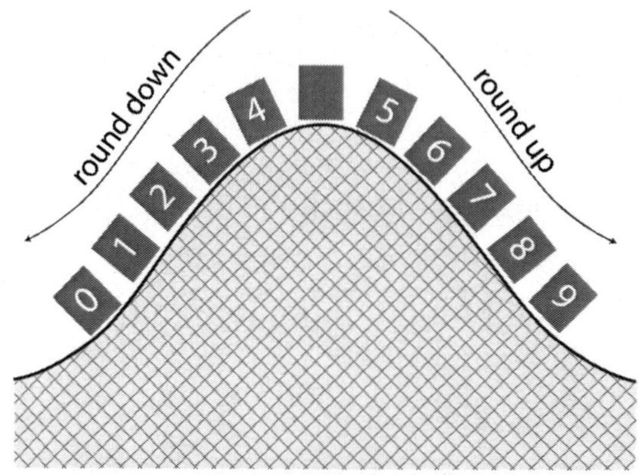

Figure 6.3. Rounding

Practice Question

3) A second-grade teacher wants to give an example of using rounding in an authentic context. In which of the following scenarios would it be appropriate to use rounding?

A. A window repairer measures windows that need glass replacement.
B. A teacher is ordering pizzas for a school party with one hundred students.
C. In a marathon, winners take prizes for first, second, and third place.
D. A man is paying for a shirt at a store and needs to know the amount.

Operations with Whole Numbers

The four basic operations in math are addition, subtraction, multiplication, and division.

The concept of addition can be explained to children through visuals, such as two groups of blocks. Students can count the number of blocks in the first group and then count the number of blocks in the second group. After combining the groups together, the students should count all of the blocks; by doing this, they have just **added** the two sets of blocks together.

There are many ways to introduce addition: using counters or manipulatives, a **number line**, or paper and pencil. Counters provide a hands-on approach to counting out amounts, much like using fingers to count. As children learn to count out each amount before adding, they reinforce one-to-one correspondence.

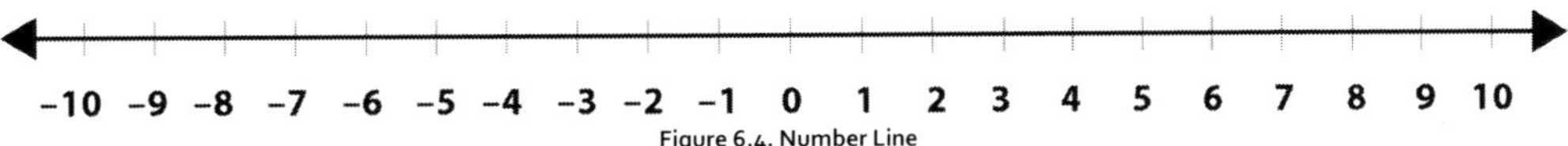

Figure 6.4. Number Line

Number lines help children visualize addition in the form of measurement and help them understand what the answers of addition and subtraction mean. For an addition equation, such as 6 + 3, take the first **addend**, 6, on the number line. Then "jump" three spaces to the right, landing at 9. In a subtraction equation, such as 10 − 4, mark 10 on the number line. Then "jump" four spaces to the left, landing at 6. Eventually students can use the number line with negative numbers, fractions, and decimals.

Helping children solve problems with addition involves familiarizing them with common symbols like the addition and equal signs (+ and =) and words such as *addends*, *plus*, *all together*, *in all*, and *sum*. Once they understand these, they can progress to simple paper-and-pencil exercises with addition sentences or equations, such as 3 + 4 = 7.

After children have achieved a certain level of familiarity with the above, they will be able to learn different strategies for addition, such as counting forward or backward, skip counting, grouping, and using doubles. **Grouping** refers to viewing numbers in a sequence that makes logical sense. For example, there are many ways to group numbers to add up to 10: 1 and 9, 2 and 8, 3 and 7, 4 and 6 all add up to 10. Using **doubles** is a type of grouping where the two numbers used in an addition equation are the same: 2 + 2, 3 + 3, 4 + 4, and so on. Both of these strategies help children strengthen number sense and expand their thinking.

Subtraction can be explained as the inverse, or opposite, of addition because the two operations cancel each other out. Terms such as *minuend*, *minus*, *take away*, *left*, *remaining*, and *difference* should be introduced.

An everyday scenario can help get the concept of subtraction across: "You have ten blocks and you give me three of them. How many blocks do you have left?" Children count out ten blocks and then move three of the blocks away. After they count out the seven remaining blocks, they have **subtracted** three from ten and can now understand a simple subtraction equation, $10 - 3 = 7$.

An extremely useful technique in relating addition and subtraction is a fact family. Just like people, numbers have relationships with each other under certain circumstances. For example, 5 + 2 is the same as 2 + 5—they both add up to 7. Understanding that can help children deduce that 7 − 2 = 5 and 7 − 5 = 2. The same three numbers have an addition and subtraction relationship. This relationship is called a **fact family**. A fact family like this one always gives two addition equations and two subtraction equations.

> **Common Student Errors**
>
> Always subtracting the smaller number from the larger number ($953 - 27 = 934$)
>
> Knowing how to perform an operation, but not when
>
> Thinking that subtraction is commutative ($9 - 4 = 4 - 9$).

Multiplication and division are also inverse operations and are typically introduced at a point when a child can comfortably identify numbers up to 20 and is familiar with addition and subtraction. They can begin to understand terms such as *multiplier*, *factor*, *product*, *multiply*, and *times*.

Multiplication is basically repeated addition, so 5 × 3 is the same as 5 + 5 + 5. A **multiplication chart** can help students learn the multiples of small whole numbers. In the chart, children can just focus on the diagonals (e.g., $2 \times 2, 3 \times 3, 4 \times 4$) and the sections either above or below the diagonals (because of the commutative property of multiplication, which states that 5×3 is equivalent to 3×5).

X	0	1	2	3	4	5	6	7	8	9	10
0	0	0	0	0	0	0	0	0	0	0	0
1	0	1	2	3	4	5	6	7	8	9	10
2	0	2	4	6	8	10	12	14	16	18	20
3	0	3	6	9	12	15	18	21	24	27	30
4	0	4	8	12	16	20	24	28	32	36	40
5	0	5	10	15	20	25	30	35	40	45	50
6	0	6	12	18	24	30	36	42	48	54	60
7	0	7	14	21	28	35	42	49	56	63	70
8	0	8	16	24	32	40	48	56	64	72	80
9	0	9	18	27	36	45	54	63	72	81	90
10	0	10	20	30	40	50	60	70	80	90	100

Figure 6.5. Multiplication Chart

It is no surprise that children develop concrete understanding with the aid of visual representations, such as cookie dough laid out on a baking tray, seats in a movie theatre, or a dozen doughnuts in a box. Such items are commonly arranged in rows and columns, called **arrays**, which can help explain multiplication: the number of rows and columns each refer to the factors used in a multiplication equation.

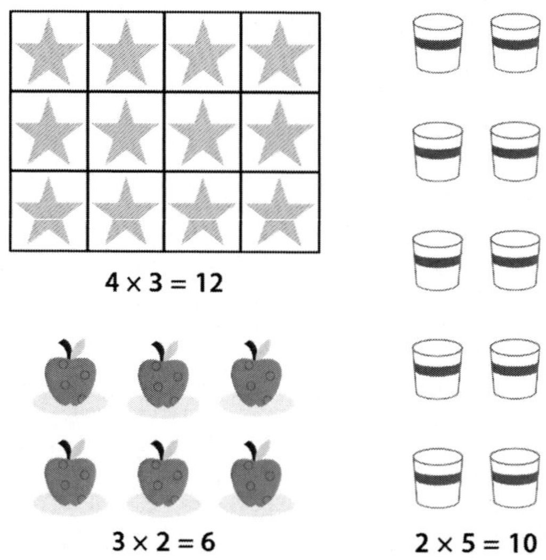

Figure 6.6. Arrays

Just as addition and subtraction are related in fact families, multiplication and division have a relationship too. **Division** is the act of splitting into equal parts or groups. For example, if three friends wish to share a pizza cut into nine slices, how many slices would each friend get? The terms *divisor*, *dividend*, *quotient*, *divided by*, and *remainder* are used in division. In this example, $9/3$ $(or\ 9 \div 3)$ equals three wholes. If a number does not completely divide to give a whole number, the division will result in a **remainder**. For example, sharing twelve cupcakes with five friends ($12/5$ *or* $12 \div 5$) will result in two whole cupcakes per friend with two left over, or a remainder of 2.

Arrays can also be used with division problems. In Figure 6.7., seven people are to share fourteen pizza slices. How many slices will each person get? The division equation is written as $14 \div 7 = 2$. The fourteen pizza slices are split into seven equal groups. That results in two slices per person.

$14 \div 7 = 2$

Figure 6.7. Using Arrays for Division

Check Your Understanding

How could you use manipulatives to teach students about remainders?

Multiplication and division are inverse operations and related through fact families. For instance, 3 × 6 is the same as 6 × 3. They both multiply to give 18. Now, using these same numbers, a child can deduce that 18 ÷ 3 = 6 and 18 ÷ 6 = 3—the three numbers have a multiplication and division relationship. A fact family such as this one always includes two multiplication equations and two division equations.

Practice Question

4) A third-grade student writes the following: 6 ÷ 3 = 2, so 2 ÷ 3 = 6. What could the teacher do to help this student with the misconception?

A. explain that the order of operations does not matter in multiplication but matters in division
B. explain that division can only occur if one number is larger than the other
C. give the student more practice with division fast facts
D. use pictorial representations to show that division is the inverse of multiplication, not the inverse of subtraction

Fractions

A fraction can be described as part of a whole. The top number of a fraction is called the **numerator,** and the bottom number is the **denominator**. The numerator represents how many of the parts are taken, and the denominator represents how many equal parts the object is split into. A fraction is the division of the top number by the bottom number.

For early learners, a **visual fraction model** is a pictorial way of understanding fractions. It could include objects, shapes, or figures divided into fractions.

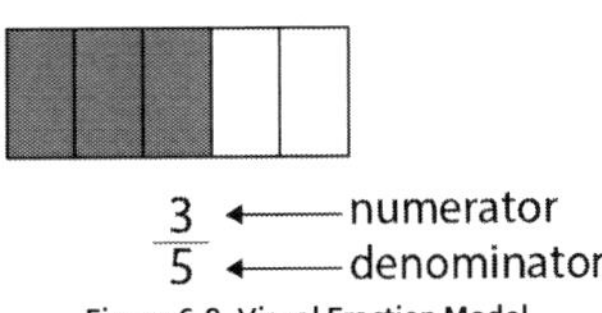

Figure 6.8. Visual Fraction Model

A **unit fraction** is a fraction in which the numerator is 1, such as 1/6 or 1/10. While the numerator stays 1, the denominator is the number that determines whether the value of a unit fraction decreases or increases. Consider Figure 6.9: Rectangle A is divided into four equal parts, and rectangle B is divided into two parts. The unit fraction in A is 1/4 and the unit fraction in B is 1/2. Visually it is clear that 1/4 is smaller than 1/2. Rectangle A has been divided into more equal parts than rectangle B; hence its unit fraction is smaller.

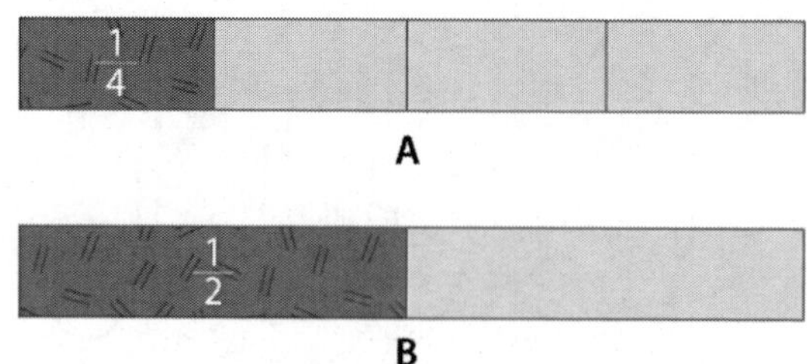

Figure 6.9. Comparing Unit Fractions

The math operations of addition, subtraction, multiplication, and division can be executed on fractions just as on whole numbers, but with a few modifications: When adding or subtracting two fractions, the denominator is important. For fractions with like (same) denominators, simply add or subtract the numerator and write the final answer over the same denominator. For example, $\frac{3}{10} + \frac{5}{10} = \frac{8}{10}$ and $\frac{5}{6} - \frac{1}{6} = \frac{4}{6}$.

For fractions with unlike (different) denominators, a common denominator should be found first. When two or more denominators are the same or brought to the same number, that number is called a **common denominator**. A common denominator can be found by finding the smallest whole number that is divisible by both denominators. Another way to find the common denominator is to simply multiply denominators together to result in a common number.

After finding the common denominator, the two fractions can be rewritten with the new denominator and added as usual. For instance, when adding $\frac{3}{4}$ *to* $\frac{1}{8}$, the denominators 4 and *8* have 8 as a common multiple. The number 4 goes into 8 twice (4 × 2). The number *8* is the smallest whole number divisible by 4 and 8. Therefore, $\frac{3}{4}$ can be brought to the common denominator of 8 by multiplying both the numerator (3) and the denominator (4) by 2. This addition equation can now be expressed as $\frac{6}{8} + \frac{1}{8} = \frac{7}{8}$.

Similarly, in a subtraction equation, such as $\frac{3}{5} - \frac{1}{15}$, the denominators 5 and 15 have 15 as a common multiple. The number 5 goes into 15 three times. So, $\frac{3}{5}$ can be brought to a common denominator of 15 by multiplying the numerator, *3*, and the denominator, *5*, by 3. This subtraction equation can now be written as $\frac{9}{15} - \frac{1}{15} = \frac{8}{15}$.

Common Student Errors

Thinking that the fraction with the larger denominator is larger ($\frac{1}{5} > \frac{1}{3}$)

Adding the numerators and the denominators ($\frac{1}{3} + \frac{2}{5} = \frac{3}{8}$)

Misunderstanding the relationship between the fraction bar and the decimal ($\frac{3}{5} = 3.5$ *or* 0.35)

Multiplying fractions requires the least work: both numerators are multiplied, and both denominators are multiplied. When dividing fractions, the reciprocal of the second fraction needs to be found first. A **reciprocal** is found by swapping the numerator and denominator. After taking the reciprocal of the second fraction, the two fractions can simply be multiplied as usual to arrive at the final answer. Examples for using various equations with fractions are described in Table 6.1.

Table 6.1. Examples of Using Equations with Fractions

Equation Type	Examples with Fractions
Addition	• $\frac{7}{11}+\frac{2}{11}=\frac{9}{11}$ (like denominators) • $\frac{2}{9}+\frac{1}{3}=\frac{2}{9}+\frac{3}{9}=\frac{5}{9}$ (unlike denominators)
Subtraction	• $\frac{9}{12}-\frac{2}{12}=\frac{7}{12}$ (like denominators) • $\frac{5}{6}-\frac{1}{3}=\frac{5}{6}-\frac{2}{6}=\frac{3}{6}$ (unlike denominators)
Multiplication	• $\frac{4}{5}\times\frac{3}{7}=\frac{4\times3}{5\times7}=\frac{12}{35}$
Division	• $\frac{1}{3}\div\frac{2}{5}=\frac{1}{3}\times\frac{5}{2}=\frac{5}{6}$

Multiplication and division can result in large numerators and/or denominators. Fractions should be **simplified**—or **reduced**—for ease of understanding by dividing both the numerator and denominator by their greatest common factor. The **greatest common factor (GCF)** is the highest number that can divide *exactly* into two or more numbers. A **common factor** is a number that can be divided into *two or more* numbers. The factors of the number *6* are 1, 2, 3, 6; the factors of the number *15* are 1, 3, 5, 15. The numbers *6* and *15* both have common factors of 1 and 3. The largest of those common factors is called the greatest common factor.

In the fraction $\frac{8}{12}$, the numerator *8* and the denominator *12* have the number *4* as their greatest common factor (i.e., the number *4* is the highest factor common to both numbers). After dividing both numbers, the reduced fraction is now $\frac{2}{3}$. The fractions $\frac{8}{12}$ and $\frac{2}{3}$ are called **equivalent** fractions because even though they are expressed differently, they represent the same quantity.

Fractions are not always less than 1. There are fractions where the numerator is larger than the denominator. These are called **improper fractions**. In such cases, decomposing a fraction can be useful. **Decomposing** fractions involves splitting them into smaller pieces. Consider the improper fraction $\frac{7}{5}$: this can be decomposed into a part equal to 1 and a part smaller than 1: $\frac{7}{5}=\frac{5}{5}+\frac{2}{5}$.

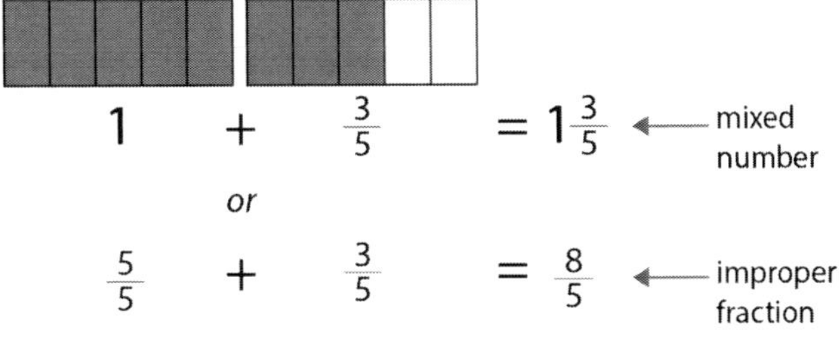

Figure 6.10. Types of Fractions

There are also fractions that contain whole numbers with a fractional part. These are called **mixed numbers**. For instance, $4\frac{2}{3}$ is a mixed number. This number can be decomposed as $4\frac{2}{3} = 1 + 1 + 1 + 1 + \frac{2}{3} = \frac{3}{3} + \frac{3}{3} + \frac{3}{3} + \frac{3}{3} + \frac{1}{3} + \frac{1}{3}$. This results in six fractions with a common denominator of 3. Decomposing fractions can make addition and subtraction of some fractions more straightforward.

Many real-life circumstances involve fractions. For example, if mom buys 5/12 of a pound of chicken, and dad buys $\frac{1}{3}$ of a pound of chicken, who purchased the larger amount?

To solve this, both fractions must first be brought to a common denominator—in this case, 12. So, for dad's chicken that weighs $\frac{1}{3}$ pound, both the numerator and denominator will need to be multiplied by 4 $\left(\frac{1}{3} = \frac{4}{12}\right)$. Upon comparison, $\frac{5}{12}$ is greater than $\frac{4}{12}$ since the numerator 5 is larger than the numerator 4; therefore, mom purchased the larger amount.

Comparing fractions can also be done by using **grid** or **area models**.

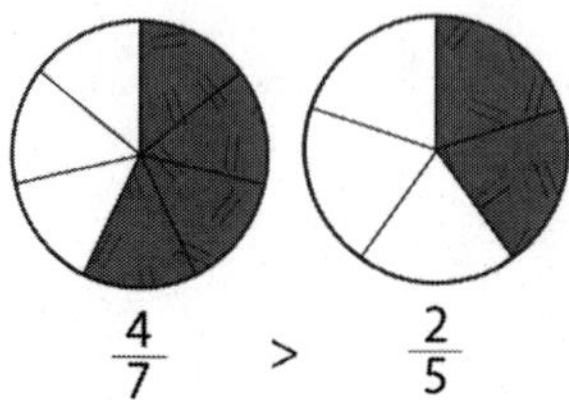

$$\frac{4}{7} > \frac{2}{5}$$

Figure 6.11. Comparing Fractions

Practice Question

5) A second-grade teacher wants to help students understand that some fractions are bigger than others. She has two laminated "pizzas": one is cut into eighths and one is cut into fourths. She takes one piece out of the pizza cut into fourths and one piece out of the pizza cut into eighths. Which question is MOST likely to generate a correct response and help students understand the concept?

A. Which pizza has more, the one where I took 1/8 away or the one where I took 1/4 away?
B. Which pizza has more, the one with 7/8 left or the one with ¾ left?
C. Which pizza needs more to be made whole again?
D. Which pizza needs the least to be made whole again?

Algebraic Thinking

Algebraic thinking involves simplifying mathematical ideas and developing the ability to express reasoning in age-appropriate ways. It requires the ability to identify, extend, describe, create patterns, and manipulate properties and orders of math operations.

Patterns

A pattern is a series or **sequence** that repeats. People's lives are a series of patterns—they wake up, get ready for work or school, make the drive back home, make dinner, and so forth; then the cycle repeats.

Children are known to do well with structure and routine. The predictable nature of what comes next—patterns—in their day-to-day schedules helps them feel secure. Even babies can identify patterns soon after birth. An expectable routine of feeding, playing, and napping is based on patterns of repetition.

Children with a good understanding of patterns are enhancing their problem-solving, number manipulation, and counting skills. Identifying patterns is a vital skill in mathematical reasoning.

In math, patterns are sequences that repeat based on a rule. Common types of patterns in math are number patterns and shape patterns. These involve different numbers or shapes ordered and repeated according to a rule. One game that can help children understand patterns is to use a box of blocks and lay them out using a pattern of colors (e.g., red, blue, yellow, green; red, blue, yellow, green).

> **Helpful Hint**
> Teachers can use paint and paper to teach students about symmetry by painting a picture on the top half of a piece of paper and then folding the paper in half while the paint is still wet. The image created will be a mirror image of the original painting. The painting as a whole is symmetrical, and the fold line is the line of symmetry.

Children can then **predict**, or guess, the pattern that should come next. For variety, the teacher can use different colors, a different number of blocks, or other items like crayons, beads, and beanbags. Sometimes children follow the pattern for a while and then begin to make up their own. They may feel bored or want to use their favorite color. Rather than correcting them, the teacher should reinforce the concept by encouraging them to try different patterns.

Recognizing patterns is not just a visual matching skill. Songs are full of repetition, and children gravitate toward catchy tunes. Many songs have an appealing hook that children love to repeat. Beating rhythmically on a drum or the lid of a container with hands or spoons can give children practice with recurring musical pattern matching.

There are also naturally occurring patterns in nature. Examples include trees, spirals, stripes, waves, and symmetries. **Symmetry** occurs when a shape looks the same when it has been flipped or turned. For example, a sunflower looks the same no matter how it is rotated around its center.

Children can find symmetry outdoors. Many flowers are symmetrical. Teachers should experiment with plucked flowers and encourage the children to find symmetry in them. Figure 6.12. shows some examples of symmetrical patterns found in nature.

Figure 6.12. Examples of Symmetry in Nature

Practice Question

6) A teacher wants to encourage students to think mathematically. Which activity is aligned with the goal of developing a student's mathematical thinking in a constructivist manner?

A. Students are given a written sequence and asked to extend it.
B. Student groups are given pictures of shapes and asked to categorize them.
C. Students are taken on a nature walk and asked to identify something with natural symmetry.
D. Student groups quiz each other on math vocabulary prior to a summative assessment.

Properties and Order of Operations

As children become comfortable with addition, subtraction, multiplication, and division, they initially gain exposure performing these operations between two numbers. But what if an expression requires multiple operations? There are rules that dictate the order in which these operations are to be completed.

A math equation with multiple operations could include a combination of any of the four basic math operations plus parentheses and exponents. **Parentheses,** ( ), are symbols used to group things together. They take precedence in any math expression, and the operation(s) inside them must be performed first.

The next operation that takes precedence is exponents. An **exponent** is a number written as a superscript above a base number that indicates how many times to use that base number in multiplication. For example, $2^4 = 2 \times 2 \times 2 \times 2 = 16$. The exponent is 4 and the base number is 2. Sometimes it is phrased as 2 "to the power of" 4. The general rules for the order of operations can be remembered using the mnemonic device *PEMDAS*:

- Any operation inside **p**arentheses is solved first.
- Any number with an **e**xponent is solved next.
- Then **m**ultiply and **d**ivide from left to right.
- Lastly, **a**dd and **s**ubtract from left to right.

At this point, children can be introduced to "tricks" and properties of math operations that will make problem solving easier. There are four basic properties of math operations.

Common Student Errors

Starting at the wrong end of the ruler or at 1 instead of at 0

Counting the lines instead of the spaces on a ruler.

The **commutative property** (for addition and multiplication) maintains that the order of the numbers in a math expression does not matter. For example, in addition, $5 + 4$ and $4 + 5$ have the same result, 9. In multiplication, 3×7 and 7×3 both equal 21. Switching the two numbers in an addition or multiplication equation does not change the end value. The commutative property does not apply to subtraction or division.

The **associative property** refers to the order in which a single operation (e.g., addition) is done within a group. These groups are typically contained within a parenthesis. An addition equation like $3 + (9 + 5)$ can be written as $(3 + 9) + 5$ to equal 17. In multiplication, $6 \times (2 \times 4)$ can be written as $(6 \times 2) \times 4$ *to yield* 48. This property requires regrouping numbers. The associative property does not apply to subtraction or division.

The **distributive** property refers to distributing through the values within parentheses. For example, $3 \times (6 + 2)$ can be rewritten as $3 \times 6 + 3 \times 2$. (Remember that multiplication and division are performed before addition and subtraction.) Both equations produce an answer of 24.

Check Your Understanding

Which property is described in the statement $8 + 20 = 20 + 8$?

Addition and multiplication have a special property called the identity property. The **additive identity** is zero. This means that any number added to zero remains the same and keeps its identity: $6 + 0 = 6$

or $0 + 2 = 2$. The **multiplicative identity** is one. This means that any number multiplied by one remains the same and retains its identity: $130 \times 1 = 130 \; or \; 1 \times 54 = 54$.

Practice Question

7) Which of the following skills should students master before learning the associative property?

A. order of operations
B. decomposing whole numbers
C. multiplication
D. adding fractions

Geometry and Measurement

Measurement

Measurement refers to numbers that show the size or amount of some characteristic. The numbers can refer to characteristics like length, weight, time, money, or distance and are measured in specific units such as feet, pounds, minutes, dollars, or miles. A **unit of measurement** is the unit or term used to measure a characteristic. These units can be standard or nonstandard.

A **standard unit of measurement** is a defined, universal convention used to quantify the characteristic being measured. Examples include inches, miles, and meters (for distance) or ounces, pounds, and kilograms (for mass). A **nonstandard** unit of measurement refers to items not commonly used for measuring, such as paper clips, popsicle sticks, or an arm length.

Standard units of measurement can be classified into a number of systems. Most countries use the **metric** system, which uses units such as centimeters, kilometers, grams, and kilograms. In the United States, **US customary units** are used, including inches, feet, ounces, and pounds.

Children typically love measuring, especially **length** or **height**. They gain a degree of satisfaction in knowing the longest or tallest object in a group. They can use a nonstandard unit of measurement, like a pencil or a stick, to measure various things around the house or classroom and can use a ruler to measure small items. They can now also understand terms such as *length*, *how long*, *how short*, *width*, *tall*, *height*, and *inches*.

Another way to get students to practice math skills through measurement is by introducing them to metric mass, types of currency (money), and telling time.

People generally use the word *weight* to express how heavy or light something is. Weight is actually the measure of gravity pulling on an object, and **mass** is how much matter is packed into an object. Weight can vary depending on gravitational pull. For instance, the weight of an object on the moon is less than that on Earth because the gravitational pull is weaker on the moon; however, the object's mass remains the same. The standard unit of measurement for mass is kilogram.

Older children should be familiar with money—the denominations of US currency, skip counting, and converting currency. The four most-used coins and their values (penny = one cent, nickel = five cents, dime = ten cents, quarter = twenty-five cents) can be used to show conversions between values, such as the relationships between nickels and dimes, pennies and nickels, and nickels and quarters. Using play money is a great way to practice these types of calculations, which often involve skip counting.

The comfort of knowing what comes next in their day-to-day schedule has been shown to help children understand and manage **time**; however, teaching the concept of time to children can be a challenging undertaking.

Which type of clock is best to start with—analog or digital? The analog clock has moveable parts and can show elapsed time. It is also visually appealing. It can cover most of the concepts a child is expected to know with regard to time. A digital clock may seem easier, but it is less useful for showing elapsed time or future time (e.g., how many hours until dinner and when to wake up in the morning).

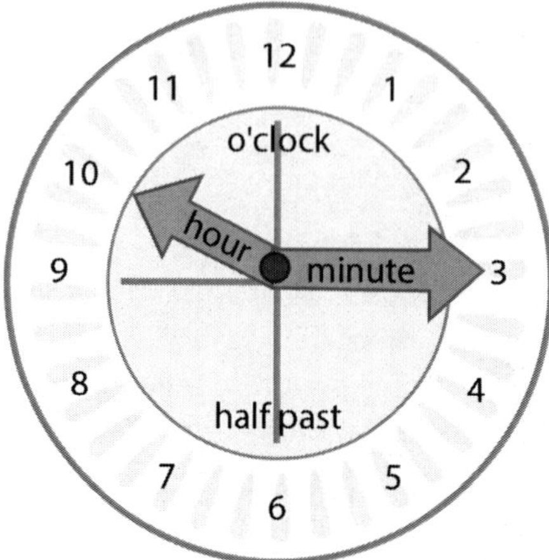

Figure 6.13. Analog Clock Made from a Paper Plate

An analog clock can introduce students to hours and minutes. The ability to count to sixty will benefit students in this exercise. Teachers can slowly introduce skip counting by fives for the minute hand. Terms such as *hour*, *minute*, *o'clock*, *half past*, *quarter past*, and *quarter till* can be introduced concurrently. Once children are comfortable with the ins and outs of an analog clock, they can experiment with a digital clock. A fun activity involves matching time on a digital clock to an analog clock.

Practice Question

8) A kindergarten teacher asks her students to choose a nonstandard unit to measure the length of the classroom. Which of the following is the MOST appropriate nonstandard unit for the students to use?

A. a carpet square
B. paper clips
C. a yardstick
D. popsicle sticks

Two-Dimensional Shapes

Shapes can be described in various dimensions. A one-dimensional (1-D) object is just a point or points on a line. A common 1-D measurement is distance. A two-dimensional (2-D) object is a closed, flat figure with no depth that can be expressed on a **plane** (e.g., a drawing of a triangle, square, or rectangle on a paper); it has length and width. A simple way to describe a three-dimensional (3-D) solid is something that takes up space—a ball, tree, house, or car. It has height, depth, length, surface area, and volume.

Children's first drawings are probably replications of triangles, circles, rectangles, and squares—standard 2-D shapes. By age five, hand-eye coordination improves and drawings become more recognizable. This is a precursor to basic understanding of geometry. At this point, terms like *base*, *height*, *sides*, and many others become relevant.

An easy way to teach children to compose a 2-D shape is by first placing the corners—or vertices. For example, for a triangle, a student should draw three points on paper and join the points with lines. The triangle now has three corners and three **sides**. In more advanced geometry, children are ready to understand that the measure of the space between two lines that connect is called an **angle**. Another term to introduce is the bottom of a triangle, which is called the **base**. The measurement from the top of a triangle to its base is called the **height**.

Shape	Sides Angles	Looks Like
Circle	no flat side no angles	clock
Triangle	3 sides 3 angles	YIELD yield sign
Square	4 sides 4 angles	Q W E R A S keyboard keys
Rectangle	4 sides 4 angles	TV
Hexagon	6 sides 6 angles	white shapes in soccer ball

Figure 6.14. Two-Dimensional Shapes Anchor Chart

Just like a triangle, a rectangle and a square can be composed by first placing the vertices and then connecting the points. Squares and rectangles are classified as **quadrilaterals**—four-sided figures with four straight sides. A square is a type of rectangle. Both have four right angles, but a **square**'s sides are all the same length, while a **rectangle** has two long sides and two short sides. The **length** of a rectangle is typically its longer side, while the **height** (or width) is its shorter side.

A circle is a 2-D shape with equal height and width (which is called the **diameter**). It is worth mentioning that half of a circle's diameter is called its **radius**. The radius is used to find area and circumference (the length of the circle's outline); however, a circle does not contain any corners or vertices, so a child trying to free draw a circle could very well end up with a misshapen circle. Sketching a circle is a challenge for young children as they do not have points or vertices to connect. One suggestion is to draw circles of different sizes on a paper and let the child trace over them. Another tip is to tie a pencil's end to a thread and secure the other end of the thread to a paper clip pierced into the center of a piece of paper.

This will ensure that the thread stays taut as the child attempts to draw the outline of the circle. Advanced tools to draw circles include protractors, compasses, and stencils or templates.

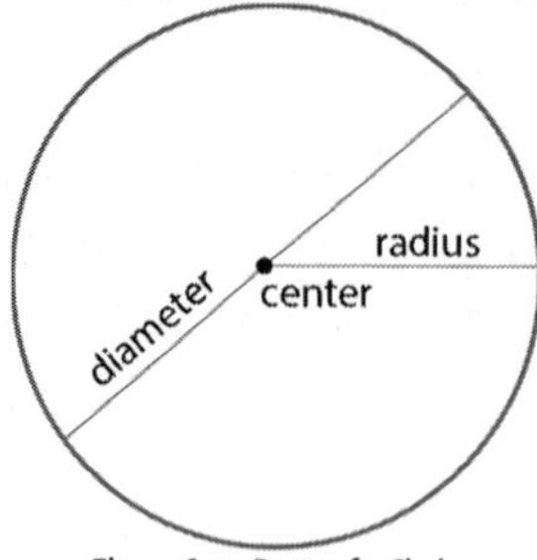

Figure 6.15. Parts of a Circle

A precursor to very advanced math topics like geometry, algebra, trigonometry, and calculus involves understanding the concept of area and perimeter of 2-D shapes. The **perimeter** is the length of the outline of a 2-D shape. The **area** of a 2-D shape is the amount of space inside it. Perimeter can be taught by letting students use nonstandard units of measurement like paper clips or toothpicks to measure the outline of an object, such as a book or piece of paper. Math cubes can be used to fill up the insides of a 2-D shape, introducing students to the concept of area.

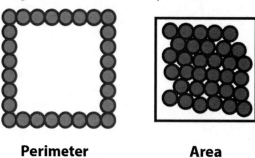

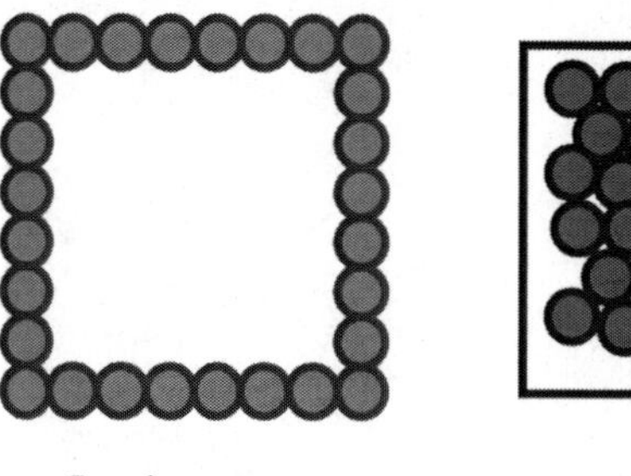

Figure 6.16. Using Nonstandard Units to Measure Perimeter and Area

Practice Question

9) A kindergarten teacher is preparing a unit on shapes. As part of UDL, the teacher should do which of the following?

A. prepare for multiple ways of presenting the shapes, such as visually and haptically
B. omit some of the lesson content for students without well-developed fine motor skills
C. introduce basic shapes to some students and more complex shapes to other students
D. assess student proficiency prior to the lesson with an oral or written diagnostic test

Three-Dimensional Shapes

Three-dimensional (3-D) shapes have distinct attributes and characteristics. The main attribute differentiating 2-D shapes from 3-D shapes is that 2-D shapes are considered "flat," while 3-D shapes take up space—they can be held and are solid.

It is this attribute of 3-D shapes that associates them with objects in everyday life. For example, a beach ball is a **sphere**; sugar cubes are **cubes**; Egyptian pyramids are **pyramids**; a wedge of cheese can be a **prism**. Many of these 3-D solids are human-made. When discussing engineered 3-D solids with

Check Your Understanding

Which attribute is characteristic of a 3-D shape but not of a 2-D shape?

students, teachers should ask how students think engineers or designers created them. What types of measurements would they have to know to create these objects?

The **volume** of a 3-D shape is the amount of space it occupies. There are mathematical formulas for calculating volume depending on the shape. The **surface area** is the total area of every surface of a 3-D shape. The **face** of a 3-D shape is any flat, visible surface. For instance, a cube has six square faces. Its surface area is the area of all of its six faces added together. A visual way for children to find the surface area of a 3-D solid is to flatten it into a 2-D shape on paper. This flattened version is called a **net**.

Shape	Net	Faces Vertices	Looks Like
Sphere 	can't be flattened	1 curved face no vertices	*baseball balloon the moon*
Cube 	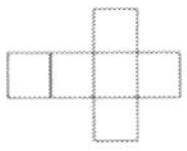	6 faces 8 vertices	*dice ice cube*
Rectangular Prism 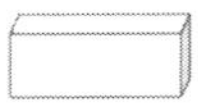	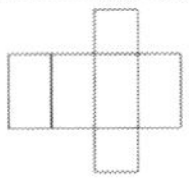	6 faces 8 vertices	*lego book box*
Pyramid 	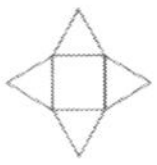	5 faces 5 vertices	*pyramids in Egypt*
Cylinder 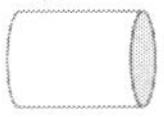	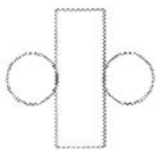	2 flat faces 1 curved face	*cup soda can marker*
Cone 		1 flat face 1 curved face	*ice cream cone party hat*

Figure 6.17. Three-Dimensional Shapes Anchor Chart

Practice Question

10) A first-grade teacher wants to integrate art and a math unit on 3-D shapes. Which activity would be the MOST appropriate?

A. origami
B. fiber art
C. media arts
D. painting

Data Analysis and Probability

Graphs

The world is filled with numerical information that needs to be collected, organized, and deciphered. Some examples of such numerical information are test scores of students in a classroom, income of people in an organization, or costs of airline tickets. Manipulating information or data is the basis for the science of statistical analysis. Data collection is the process of grouping and measuring information on specific topics. This data can be displayed in the form of pictures, charts, or graphs. A **graph** is an illustration of values or data. Graphs are useful because they are visual and can represent the data better than words and numbers alone. Graphs and charts may be considered compact and concise depictions of data.

A **bar graph** is a display of bars of different colors or sizes. The longer the bar, the larger the number represented. For example, the bar graph in Figure 6.18. shows the **comparison** of the number of students who chose red, blue, green, black, or pink as their favorite color. It shows quantitative data and is best used to compare different groups.

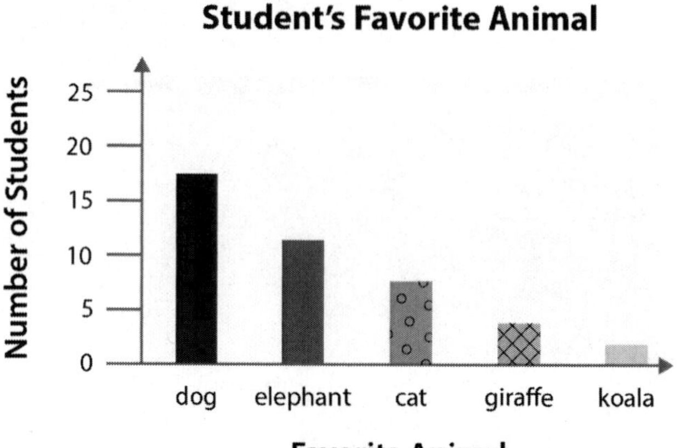

Figure 6.18. Bar Graph

A **line graph** is a type of graph that uses data values as points connected by lines. It is typically used to show how the variable being measured changes in value. The example in Figure 6.19 shows the math test scores of a student through middle school and high school years. A math score is marked for each grade and each point is connected by lines. It is a type of chart used to visualize the changes in the value of a variable over time.

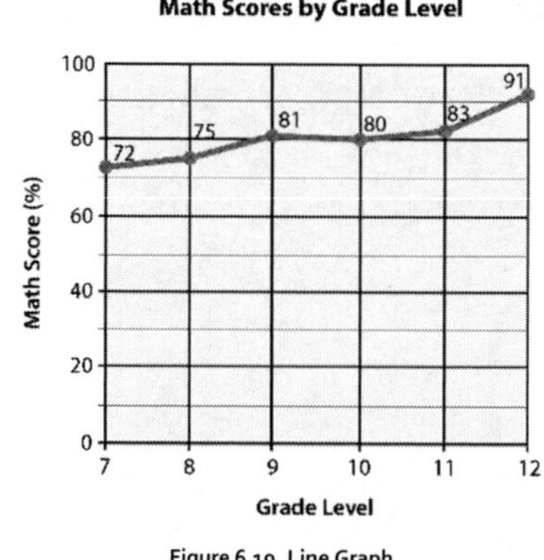

Figure 6.19. Line Graph

Scatter plots are like line graphs, but their purpose is unique. They are used to show how one variable (or set) can be affected by another. In other words, a scatter plot shows the **correlation** between the two variables or sets of data being plotted. In the Figure 6.20., student test scores are plotted against the number of hours spent studying. The more hours spent studying, the better the test scores. Both variables are increasing together, indicating a positive correlation.

Hours of Study vs. Test Scores

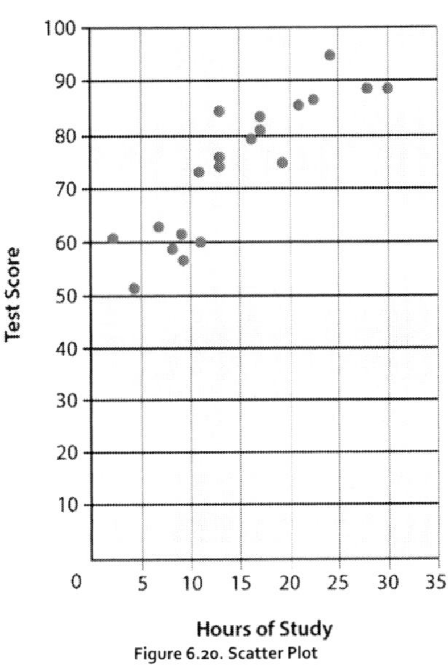

Figure 6.20. Scatter Plot

Pie charts are circular graphs. They look like a pie divided into slices. Pie charts are useful when showing quantities as parts of a whole. They are a common statistical graphic used in the business world that can also be useful in a school environment. For instance, the pie chart in Figure 6.21. shows the number of textbooks classified by genre in a school's library; it shows quantitative data. The largest slice represents the category with the highest number of books. The entire circle represents all books in the library.

Number of Library Books by Topic

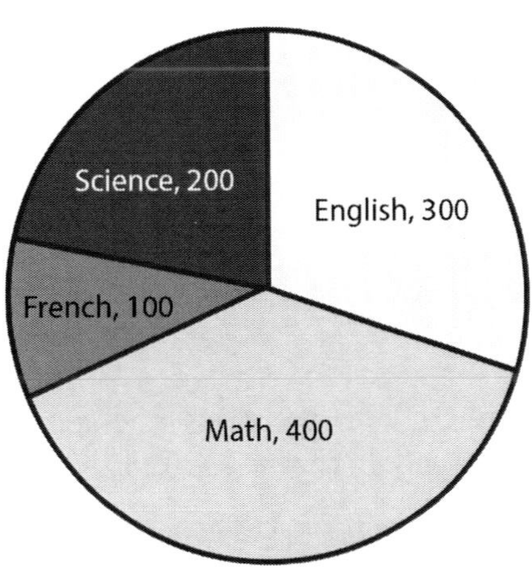

Figure 6.21. Pie Chart

A **line plot** is a type of graph that shows data frequency along a number line. One example is a list of test scores received by twenty students: 86, 84, 87, 81, 84, 89, 81, 87, 92, 91, 92, 88, 81, 86, 85, 84, 88, 82, 83, 86.

To make a line plot, a range that includes all of the data in suitable intervals should first be established. From there, each number can be plotted using a symbol (such as an *X* or an *).

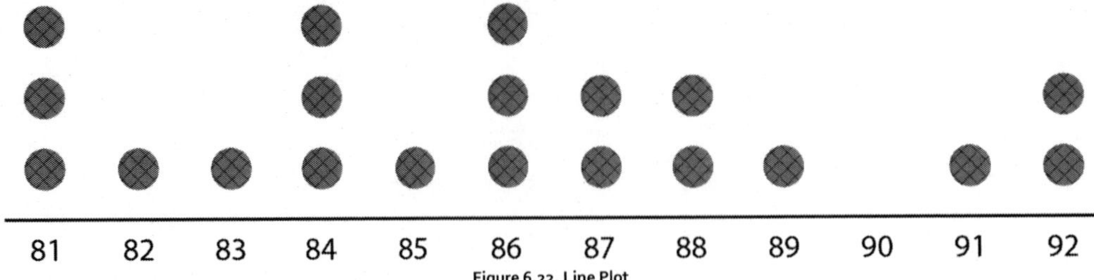

Figure 6.22. Line Plot

A **stem-and-leaf** plot shows data frequency among the categories of values that occur. These plots are useful for presenting the same set of data in the shape of a distribution. Using the same example of the twenty student test scores, the data should first be sorted in ascending order: 81, 81, 81, 82, 83, 84, 84, 84, 85, 86, 86, 86, 87, 87, 88, 88, 89, 91, 92, 92.

The *stem* consists of the highest (or first) place value digit of the data numbers (in this case, tens); the *leaf* consists of all of the other digit(s) (in this case, ones).

Stem	Leaf
8	1 1 1 2 3 4 4 4 5 6 6 6 7 7 8 8 9
9	1 2 2

Figure 6.23. Stem-and-Leaf Plot

To read a stem-and-leaf plot, simply connect the tens (first column) to the ones (second column).

Practice Question

11) A second-grade teacher has her students pick which genre of movie they like best. Which of the following should the students use to present the class-wide data?

A. line plot
B. scatter plot
C. stem-and-leaf plot
D. pie chart

Measures of Central Tendency

How is all this data in the form of graphs, charts, and plots meaningful? Statistical tools such as mean, median, and mode give insight into viewing this data in specific forms.

The **average**—or **mean**—of a group of data refers to the sum of all data divided by the total number of data items. This is a way to measure which value best represents a sample of data. Think of the average as the "spokesperson" for the entire data set. For example, Li, Jess, and Antoine get allowances of $14, $20, and $17, respectively. What amount could serve as the "spokesperson" for the students' allowances? Find the average: $(14 + 20 + 17)/3 = 51/3 = 17$. Take the total amount received ($51), and divide that by the total number of people (3). The average of $17 is one way to describe the data set.

Again take the example of the twenty student test scores. If the scores were redistributed to ensure that each student has the same score, that score is referred to as the mean. Just as in calculating the average, first add up all the test scores: 81 + 84 + 87 + 81 + 84 + 89 + 81 + 87 + 92 + 91 + 92 + 88 + 81 + 86 + 85 + 84 + 88 + 82 + 83 + 86 = 1,712

Divide this by the number of scores (20): 1,712/20 = 85.6, which is the mean score for each student.

When there are extreme values in a data set and the data is very spread out, the average could be skewed high or low due to the wide range of data. In this case, the mean may actually misrepresent the data. The **median**, which is the middle value of a data group, is a good substitute in this instance. Unlike the average or mean, the median is not affected by a very low or very high data value.

Using the same example of the twenty student test scores, here are the scores in ascending order: 81, 81, 81, 82, 83, 84, 84, 84, 85, 86, 86, 86, 87, 87, 88, 88, 89, 91, 92, 92

Since this is an even group of data, the median will be the average of the middle two values (in bold). The median here is (86 + 86)/2 = 86.

Helpful Hint

You can use the following rhyme to teach statistical terms:
Hey diddle diddle,
The median's the middle.
You add and divide the mean.
The mode's the one you find the most,
and the range is the difference between.

Another statistical tool is called the **mode**, which is the number or numbers that occur most frequently in the data. Here is a conceivable scenario for using the mode instead of the average. Say, for instance, a teacher is measuring the height of each of her fifteen fifth-grade students as part of a math unit on measurement. Most students are of similar height, but she has one exceptionally tall student. Finding the average height of the group of fifteen students will result in a skewed number because of the one tall student. So using the mode can be effective, as it will show where most of the student's heights lie. Unlike the average or the median, the mode is not unique. In a data set, there can be several different data values that occur at the same frequency. This will result in more than one mode. In the example of the twenty student test scores, the modes of the data set are 81, 84, and 86. They each occur three times.

The **range** is the difference between the smallest and the largest values.

Practice Question

12) For a school project, a third-grade student contacted an ice cream store owner to collect data on ice cream sales. She wanted to know which flavor customers purchase the most. The owner's response was chocolate. Which of the following statistical measures does chocolate represent?

A. mode
B. mean
C. median
D. range

Probability

Sometimes the goal of quantitative research and data analysis is to determine the chance of something occurring or to make a prediction.

Probability is the likelihood, or chance, that something will happen. Probability is expressed as a fraction with the numerator being the number of successful outcomes and the denominator being the total number of outcomes, or as a decimal. For example, if there are 25 marbles in a bag and 4 marbles are red, the probability of randomly pulling a red marble out of the bag is 425 (also written as 0.16 or 16%).

Another example involves a spinner with 8 sections, with 3 that are choice A, 2 that are choice B, and 3 that are choice C. The probability of landing on choice A would be 38 (also written as 0.375 or 37.5%).

Probabilities are always numbers between 0 and 1, inclusive. If there is no chance of something occurring, its probability is 0; if there's a 100% chance of something occurring, its probability is 1.

Replacement means putting something back the way it was before an event occurred. For example, the probability of drawing 4 red marbles out of 25 marbles twice, with replacement, would be $425 \times 425 = 16625$. The same probability without replacement would be $425 \times 324 = 12600 = 150$, since there would be one less red marble and one less of the total marbles. Note that probabilities are multiplied when the events are independent from each other.

For the probability of something happening at least one time, take the probably of the event not happening at all, and subtract this probability from 1. For example, the probability of rolling a two on at least one of two dice would be *1 minus the probability of not rolling a two on either die*, which would be expressed as follows: $1 - 56 \times 56 = 1 - 2536 = 1136$ = 0.31

Probability can also be **predicted** through a **probability model**. For example, a drawer has 3 green socks, 2 blue socks, 4 yellow socks, 6 red socks, and 5 purple socks. If you pull out 1 sock ten times (replacing the pulled out sock each time), how many times would you expect a sock that is NOT green or blue?

The formula would be the total number of possibilities: P (not green or blue socks) = 15. This number is then divided by the total number of socks: 15/20 (or ¾). Converting this to a decimal, the probability of NOT drawing a green or blue sock is .75. This is the probability model.

The probability model can then be used to make a **prediction**. If there are 10 draws into the sock drawer, we would need to multiply .75 × 10 to make a prediction that 7.5 times, one will NOT draw a green or blue sock.

The prediction can be tested by actually drawing one sock ten times to see how many non-blue or non-green socks were selected. Likely, the actual result will not match the prediction of 7.5 times because the sample size is so small. If the experiment were repeated with a total of 2,0000 socks (300 green, 200 blue, 400 yellow, 600 red, 500 purple), with a prediction of 750, the actual non-green or non-blue socks would probably be far closer to the prediction.

Practice Question

13) A fourth-grade teacher is introducing the class to the concept of probability. Which underlying concept do the students need to master first?

A. fractions and decimals
B. patterns and tessellations
C. order of operations
D. the distributive property

Answer Key

1) B: In the concrete stage, student understanding is built by using concrete objects or manipulatives.

2) D: Subitizing refers to the capacity to identify a small number of objects and immediately recognize how many there are without counting.

3) B: The teacher can estimate how many pizzas she will need by assuming each person will eat a certain amount and multiplying that number by 100.

4) A: Although the commutative property applies to addition and multiplication, it does not apply to division.

5) B: Students can visually see that 7/8 of a pizza is more than ¾ of a pizza.

6) C: Taking students on a nature walk and asking them to identify something with natural symmetry will allow them to construct their own knowledge and think mathematically as they look for objects that are symmetrical.

7) C: The associative property addresses grouping addition or multiplication problems. To understand the associative property, students should know how to add and multiply.

8) A: Students can lay carpet squares end-to-end to measure the length of the room.

9) A: The universal design for learning (UDL) involves multiple means of representation. Students with visual impairments could still access the lesson content if the shapes were also presented in a tactile way that would allow students to touch and feel them.

10) A: Origami is paper folding. Students could use paper to make 3-D shapes.

11) D: A pie chart is best used when comparing part of a whole (in this case genres of movies by percentage of class members).

12) A: The mode is the most frequently occurring data value, which is chocolate.

13) A: Probability is expressed in terms of fractions or decimals of occurrence, so these concepts must be understood first.

7. Science, Health, and Motor Development

Science

Scientific Inquiry

Young children are naturally curious about exploring their world. This innate curiosity should be nurtured and extended to scientific inquiry. Research has established that **scientific thinking**, or the ability to make predictions, gather and analyze evidence, and draw conclusions, is important in child development. The ability to think scientifically helps children effectively problem solve in all sorts of contexts.

Most scientific study, both by professionals and students, is based on the process of investigation or inquiry. Inquiry-based science is guided by the scientific method, which provides a framework for observing, measuring, and drawing conclusions about the world.

The first step in the scientific method is **observation**, often of a problem or an unknown or unexplained situation. From observations, scientists develop questions and research the currently available information about a particular topic. This research helps them formulate a reasonable and testable explanation for their observations, a statement known as a **hypothesis**. Scientists then design and conduct an **experiment** in which they collect data that will demonstrate whether their hypothesis is false or not. It is important to note that a hypothesis can never be proven true—it can be confirmed as false, or enough data can be collected to *infer* that it is true. In order for data to support a hypothesis, it must be consistent and reproducible.

Scientists use a rigorous set of rules to design experiments. The protocols of **experimental design** are meant to ensure that scientists are actually testing what they set out to test. A well-designed experiment will measure the impact of a single factor on a system, thus allowing the experimenter to draw conclusions about that factor.

During the experiment, scientists collect data, which must then be analyzed. As data is analyzed, scientists ask the following types of questions:

- Do the results seem logical? For example, if the experiment studies a new type of fertilizer and all the plants grow to double their size in only a week, scientists might want to recheck measurements as the results seem outside of common logic.
- Do the results match or refute predictions? It is not unusual for the hypothesis to be incorrect or for no change at all to have been observed during an experiment.
- Is there **verifiable evidence**? Scientists do not use terms like "It appears like…." or "The substance kind of changed….." Scientists work with empirical data.

After the data is analyzed, it must be presented appropriately. This can mean running a statistical analysis on the data (e.g., finding the mean) or putting the data in graph form. An analysis allows scientists to see trends in the data and determine if those trends are statistically significant. From the data and its analysis, scientists can draw a **conclusion** about the experiment.

Scientists must describe their data in a way that others can understand but must be cognizant of various factors that may impact results and color the data. **Scale** is one important factor to consider. For example, if the researcher only uses two different fertilizers in a plant growth experiment, the results may not be **generalizable**, or applicable to a broader population (i.e., all fertilizers).

Part of conducting scientific investigations in the classroom is **safety**. Standard safety equipment like goggles, aprons, protective gloves, and a fire extinguisher must be available. In addition to using standard safety equipment, students should be instructed on appropriate apparel. For example, long hair should be tied back and loose clothing and jewelry should be secured. Closed-toe shoes should be worn.

If students are working with chemicals, they should be instructed in the proper handling, use, and disposal of these substances. If students are working with specimens, they should also be instructed in how to handle these specimens appropriately. This is particularly important when working with animal specimens. As living things, such specimens should never be handled in a disrespectful or joking manner.

Emergency procedures should include proactively monitoring students and equipment and wearing safety gear. Plans for emergency first aid for electric shock, poisoning, burns, fire, evacuations, spills, and animal bites should be established.

While scientific inquiry varies based on the research questions at hand, some basic frameworks guide scientific thinking.

One foundation of scientific thinking is the notion of **systems,** defined as two or more parts that make a whole. There are many interconnected systems in our world such as eco*systems*, the solar *system*, and even the human digestive *system*. Within systems are **subsystems**, or self-contained systems within the broader system. On Earth, there are four main subsystems:

- lithosphere (land)
- atmosphere (air)
- hydrosphere (water)
- biosphere (life)

Scientists may focus their inquiries on one or more of these subsystems. For example, climate scientists might study the impacts of changes in atmosphere on the hydrosphere and biosphere.

> **Helpful Hint**
>
> The phrase "Queen Rachel hopes every coward gains courage" can help students remember the scientific method: question, research, hypothesis, experiment, collect data, graph/analyze data, conclusion.

Another basic scientific principle is the **movement of energy and matter** throughout systems. Energy and matter may move through space or time, but they are not destroyed. For example, energy moves through the food chain from producers to consumers to predators. Though it changes form and even involves the death of certain organisms, it is not destroyed—only transferred.

Practice Question

1) A first-grade teacher wants to help students develop their observation skills in a unit on living things. The MOST effective way to achieve this goal would be to have the students do which of the following?

A. watch as the teacher puts drops of food coloring into a beaker of water
B. describe how plants can survive in a desert with little water
C. put a plant in a closet out of the sun and describe how it changes over time
D. create a poster that shows concrete examples of the four interconnected Earth systems

Assessment in Science

The standards require students to participate in many hands-on science activities. These activities should not only be lab-based activities but should also include activities to encourage students' higher-level thinking skills. Students should be asked to analyze, synthesize, evaluate, and problem-solve. Such higher-order thinking should involve students building upon prior knowledge. For example, if students learn about the hydrosphere, they might then gather samples of water from various sources to examine under a microscope to differentiate between different water sources.

Assessment in science will involve various strategies, both formal and informal (see child development, learning, and assessment chapter for more information on assessment types). Informal assessments might include

- observation,
- class discussions,
- end-of-class exit tickets,
- the use of clickers or real-time polls or quizzes with apps like Kahoot!, and
- informal lab journals that describe challenges or observations.

More formal assessments might include

- written or digital lab reports;
- posters or multimedia presentations;
- portfolios;
- student profiles or mastery checklists (for younger students); and
- written assessments, both constructed-response and selected-response.

Both informal and formal assessments and formative and summative assessments should be used to evaluate individual student strengths and needs and to modify instruction. Assessment data might reveal knowledge or skill gaps that need remediation or reteaching. The data might also reveal which students could benefit from extension or enrichment activities.

Practice Question

2) After a lab where student groups use simple machines, a teacher wants to assess student understanding to determine how effective the lab was in helping students see the advantages of these devices. Which assessment is MOST appropriate?

A. having students construct their own simple machine
B. asking students to list the main types of simple machines
C. having students list two tasks that could be done with each type of simple machine
D. asking students to turn to a peer and describe challenges they encountered in the simple machines lab

Life Science

Living Things

Life on Earth is guided by the concept of structure and function. **Structure** refers to the shape or structure of a type of matter or an entire organism and how this relates to its action, behavior, or **function**. For example, a fish with sharp teeth has a body part or form related to the function or chewing its prey.

Helpful Hint

The phrase "**K**ing **P**hillip **c**ame **o**ver **f**rom **g**reat **S**pain" is a way to remember the order of taxonomic classification of organisms: kingdom, phylum, class, order, family, genus, species.

The natural world also contains patterns like cracks, stripes, spirals, waves, and symmetries. These are visible and predictable regularities that can be observed. For example, animals may have bilateral symmetry, where if divided in half, each side is a mirror image of itself. Similarly, spirals can be observed in snail shells, the growth patterns of some animals' antlers, and even the way in which some vegetables, like cabbage, grow.

Scientists use the characteristics of organisms to sort them into a variety of **classifications** using a system called taxonomy. The highest level of taxonomic classification is the **kingdom**, and each kingdom is then broken down into smaller categories. The smallest level of classification is a **species**, which includes individuals with similar genetics that are capable of breeding. The entire taxonomic classification system is as follows:

- kingdom
- phylum
- class
- order
- family
- genus
- species

All organisms are sorted into one of five kingdoms: Monera, Protista, Fungi, Plantae, and Animalia. The **Monera** kingdom includes bacteria, which are unicellular organisms that have no nucleus. **Protists** are also unicellular organisms, but they have a nucleus. Both Monera and Protists reproduce **asexually** by cellular division.

Fungi are a group of unicellular and multicellular organisms that have cell walls and reproduction strategies that differ from those in the other kingdoms. This kingdom includes common organisms like mushrooms and molds. Fungi can reproduce both asexually by cellular division and **sexually** through spores. Many species of fungi are decomposers and attain energy by breaking down organic matter in the environment.

Plants are a kingdom of organisms that use the energy from sunlight to make food (the sugar glucose) through the process of photosynthesis.

Plants are multicellular eukaryotic organisms that belong to the Plantae kingdom and produce energy primarily by photosynthesis. **Photosynthesis** is a process in which a chemical called **chlorophyll** uses energy from sunlight to convert water and carbon dioxide in the air into sugars. The chlorophyll is contained in special organelles called chloroplasts and is responsible for the green color of most plants' leaves.

One way in which plants are grouped is by how they transport water and nutrients throughout the plant. Some plants are vascular, which means that they have special tissues that transport water and nutrients, while others are nonvascular and distribute water and nutrients by passing them from cell to cell through osmosis or diffusion.

Vascular plants have three basic parts: leaves, a stem, and roots. **Leaves** are the organ where sunlight is captured and used by the chlorophyll to produce food for the plant through photosynthesis. They come in many different shapes and sizes but are often broad and flat in order to capture as much sunlight as possible. Most leaves are green because of the chlorophyll they contain. The **stem** is the part of the plant that provides structure and supports the weight of the plant. The stem has special tissues that transport nutrients throughout the plant and is where plants store food. The special tissue that plants use to transport water and minerals is called **xylem**. **Phloem** is another special tissue that transports sugar and other nutrients throughout the plant. The **roots** anchor the plant and absorb water and nutrients from the soil.

The **Animalia** kingdom contains multicellular organisms that can move around and must consume other organisms for energy. The kingdom includes several notable classifications that divide organisms based on important features. These include whether the organism has a backbone or spine: **vertebrates** do; **invertebrates** do not. Animals are also classified based on whether they are **ectotherms**, meaning their source of body heat comes from the environment, or **endotherms**, meaning their body heat is derived from metabolic processes within the body. Ectothermic animals are sometimes known as cold-blooded, and endothermic animals as warm-blooded. Animal classification also looks at animal reproduction: some animals lay eggs; others give birth to live young.

Helpful Hint

The acronym ***LAWN*** represents the requirements for plants: light, air, water, nutrients.

Amphibians are ectothermic vertebrates that have gills when they hatch from eggs but develop lungs as adults. Examples of amphibians include frogs, toads, newts, and salamanders. **Reptiles**, such as snakes, lizards, crocodiles, turtles, and tortoises, are cold-blooded vertebrates that have scales and lay eggs on land. **Birds** are endothermic vertebrate animals that have wings, feathers, scaly legs, beaks, no teeth, and bear their young in a hard-shelled egg. **Mammals** are endothermic vertebrate animals that have hair, give live birth (with a few exceptions), and produce milk for the nourishment of their young.

All organisms have a **life cycle**, or stages of life. Every organism is born, matures, reproduces, and dies. However, the stages in this life cycle vary from organism to organism. Plants, for example, often go through a cycle of seed, germination, maturing, pollination, and fruiting.

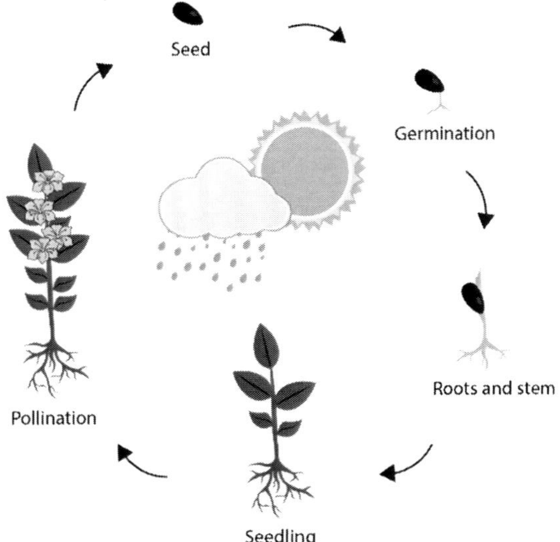

Figure 7.1. The Plant Life Cycle

In contrast, when a frog lays eggs in water, the eggs hatch to become tadpoles with gills. The tadpoles eventually grow legs and develop lungs, and the tail is absorbed into the body. At this point, a tadpole has become an adult frog. The frog life cycle is an example of **metamorphosis**, or a change in the body of the organism during its life cycle.

Practice Question

3) How could a second-grade teacher BEST use a graphic organizer to help students understand plants and animals?

A. by showing how they are similar and different using a Venn diagram
B. by showing how they have both form and structure using a two-column chart
C. by showing how they come in different types using a Frayer model
D. by showing how they can be divided into categories using a web

Plant Reproduction

Vascular plants are grouped as flowering or nonflowering based on how they reproduce. Flowering plants use flowers as their reproductive organs. Flowers are made from special brightly colored leaves called **petals** that together form the **corolla**. The petals are supported by other special leaves called **sepals** that together form the **calyx**. Inside the flower are both male and female reproductive organs. The male reproductive organ is called the **stamen** and has two parts, the **anther** and the **filament**. The male reproductive cells, called **pollen**, are produced in the stamen and stored in the anther. The anther is located at the end of a stalk called the filament.

The female reproductive organ is called the **pistil**, and is usually located in the center of the flower. The pistil has two parts, the **carpel** and the **stigma**. The carpel is the ovary of the flower, where **ova** (eggs)—

the female reproductive cells—are produced. The stigma is where the pollen (the male reproductive cell) is received and is sometimes extended on a stalk called the **style**. Flowering plants are brightly colored to attract insects that move pollen from the anther to the stigma to fertilize the eggs.

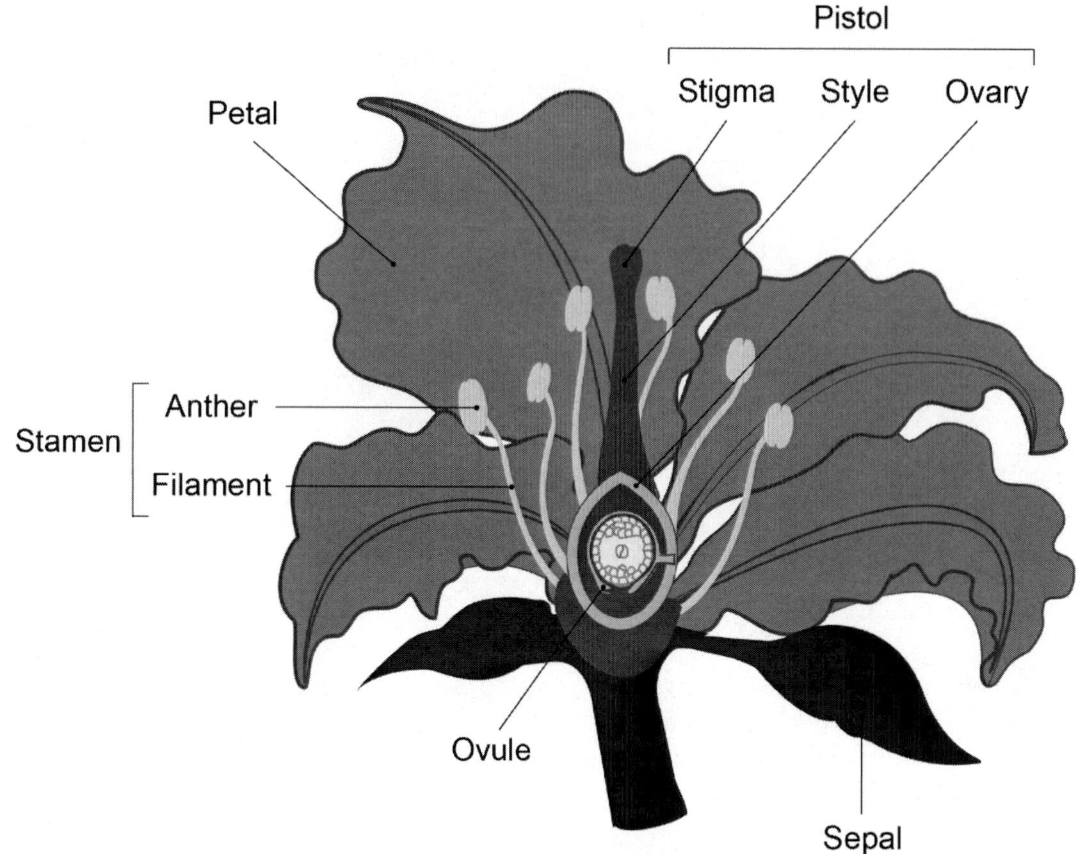

Figure 7.2. Flower with Male and Female Reproductive Structures

After **fertilization** occurs, the flower forms a fruit that contains the seeds that grow from the fertilized eggs. **Seeds** are the plant embryo and come in a variety of shapes, sizes, and colors. The **fruit** provides nutrients and protects the seeds as they grow. It also attracts birds and animals that help distribute the seeds away from the plant. Seeds can also be distributed by air and water. The seeds are protected by a waxy layer called the seed coat.

Once the seed is distributed, it needs air, water, and soil to grow. **Germination** is when seeds begin to grow. The seed begins to form small roots and uses nutrients stored in a special organ called the **endosperm** for energy until it can form leaves and generate energy through photosynthesis. Flowering plants are also divided based on the number of embryos, or **cotyledons**, in their seeds. Plants with only one embryo in each seed, like corn or wheat, are called **monocots**. Those with two embryos in each seed, like beans, are called **dicots**. When the seed develops leaves, it is called a sprout or seedling. It continues to grow until it becomes a mature plant and can reproduce again by growing flowers.

Nonflowering plants are divided into two groups: those that use seeds to reproduce and those that use spores to reproduce. Non-flowering plants that use seeds to reproduce are called **gymnosperms,** which literally means *naked seeds*. These plants produce seeds that do not have a covering like the fruits produced by flowering plants. **Conifers** are a major group of gymnosperm plants that use woody cones to protect their seeds. Most conifers are trees like pine, cedar, or redwood. Conifers produce male and female cones. The male cones produce pollen that is distributed by the wind, and if the pollen falls on a female cone, the female cone produces seeds that are protected by the cone. The seeds produced by conifers have winged structures on them that allow them to be carried by the wind. Once they reach the ground, the seeds germinate and grow.

Practice Question

4) A first-grade teacher wants to illustrate for students the way in which plant seeds are protected. What could the teacher use to illustrate this?

A. a bean sprout
B. an apple
C. a bean bag
D. an oak leaf

Animal Reproduction

Animals may reproduce sexually or asexually. Asexual reproduction has the primary disadvantage of producing an organism genetically identical to the parent. Asexual reproduction may involve fission or **binary fission**, where an organisms seems to divide itself in two and regenerate lost parts. Flatworms and sea anemones are two examples of organisms that reproduce via fission. **Budding** is a form of asexual reproduction just like it sounds: the organism forms a bud that then breaks off from the "parent." Some invertebrates (e.g., coral) reproduce via budding. **Parthenogenesis** is another type of asexual reproduction wherein an unfertilized egg grows into an adult organism. Some insects, fish, reptiles, and amphibians reproduce in this manner.

Sexual reproduction differs from asexual reproduction in that offspring that are genetically different from their parent or parents are produced. **Hermaphroditism** is a form of sexual reproduction in which the organism has female and male sex organs in one individual. Snails and clams are examples. Most organisms reproduce with two individuals: a male that provides sperm and a female that provides the egg. This type of reproduction is often divided into organisms that use external fertilization or internal fertilization. In most **external fertilization**, females release eggs and males release sperm into water in what is known as spawning. Most fish and many other aquatic animals practice external fertilization.

In **internal fertilization**, sperm is placed directly into the female via mating. Mating may result in the female laying a fertilized egg that develops outside the body; this is known as **oviparity** and is the practice of all birds and some other animals. Unlike oviparity, in **ovoviparity**, the fertilized egg stays in the body of the female for protection until it hatches or right before it hatches. Some fish and snakes use this type of reproduction. Like humans, many mammals reproduce via **viviparity**, where offspring do not hatch from eggs but rather remain in the mother until a live birth.

When organisms reproduce, **genetic** information is passed to the next generation through deoxyribonucleic acid, or DNA. Within DNA are blocks of nucleotides called **genes**, each of which contains the code needed to produce a specific protein. Genes are responsible for **traits**, or characteristics, in organisms such as eye color, height, and flower color. During sexual **reproduction**, the child receives two copies of each gene, one each from the mother and the father. Some of these genes will be **dominant**, meaning they are expressed, and some will be **recessive**, meaning they are not expressed. Each child will have a mix of its parents' traits.

A special chart that shows all of the possible genetic combinations from parents with given genotypes is called a **Punnett square**. A Punnett square is a grid with four squares, where the possible genes from one parent are written along the top and the possible genes from the other parent are written down the side. Each square is filled in with the corresponding letters from the top and side of the grid, with capital letters representing dominant genetic traits listed first, followed by lowercase letters representing recessive traits.

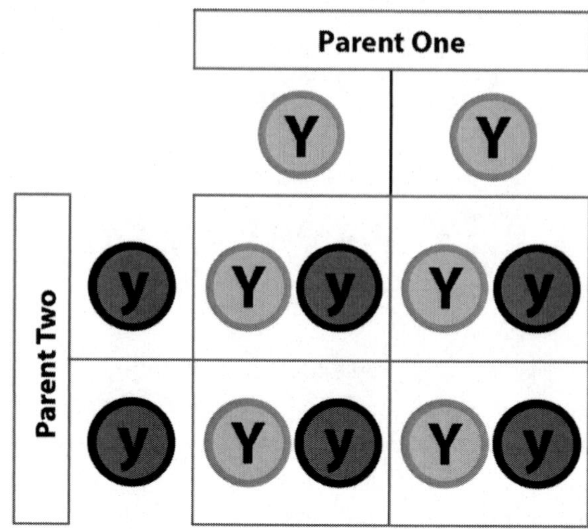

Figure 7.3. Punnett Square

When an individual's genetic code is damaged, that organism may have a **genetic disorder**. For example, cystic fibrosis, which causes difficulty with basic bodily functions such as breathing and eating, results from damage to the gene which codes for a protein called CFTR. Down syndrome, which causes developmental delays, occurs when a person has three copies of chromosome twenty-one (meaning they received two copies from one parent as a result of an error in meiosis).

> **Helpful Hint**
>
> Many of the rules of genetics were discovered by Gregor Mendel, a nineteenth-century abbot who used pea plants to show how traits are passed down through generations.

Genes are not static. Over time, **mutations**—changes in the genetic code—occur that can affect an organism's ability to survive. Four common types of genetic mutations are substitution, insertion, deletion, and frameshift. Substitution mutations occur when one nucleotide is exchanged with another (such as switching the bases adenine and cytosine). Insertion mutations happen when extra nucleotide pairs are inserted into the DNA sequence. Removal of nucleotide pairs from the DNA sequence results in deletion mutations. Finally, frameshift mutations occur when the insertion or deletion of nucleotides causes the gene to be misread. Harmful mutations will appear less often in a population or be removed entirely because organisms with those mutations will be less likely to reproduce and thus will not pass on that trait.

> **Consider This**
>
> Why might a harmful mutation continue to exist in a population?

Beneficial mutations, called **adaptations**, may help an organism thrive in a particular environment. This means that the organism is more likely to reproduce, and thus that trait or adaptation will appear more often. Over time, this process, called **natural selection**, results in the **evolution** of new species. The theory of evolution was developed by naturalist Charles Darwin when he observed how finches on the

Galapagos Islands had a variety of beak shapes and sizes that corresponded to different food sources, allowing the birds to coexist.

Inherited traits—those that pass from parents to children—such as hair or eye color, are different from learned characteristics. **Learned characteristics** are things that organisms acquire during their lives. For example, if, after straying too close to a lion, a gazelle is chided by its mother, it will learn to keep its distance. Learned characteristics are distinct from **instincts,** which are inherited. For example, fish are born knowing how to swim instinctually, and human babies are born knowing how to cry.

Similar to learned characteristics are **environmental factors** that impact how traits are expressed differently. Drugs, chemicals, temperature, and light are all environmental factors that can impact gene expression. For example, a person may be genetically predisposed to large muscle mass, but this trait may only be expressed after the use of steroids. The light a caterpillar is exposed to can impact the color of a butterfly's wings. Some rabbits also develop black noses, tails, feet, and ears in response to cold temperatures.

Humans may also interfere with the reproduction of plants or animals by **selective breeding**. In selective breeding, organisms with desirable characteristics (such as watermelons with few seeds or dogs with high intelligence) are bred intentionally to produce offspring with the same characteristics.

Practice Question

5) A third-grade teacher wants to use an informal assessment to determine whether students understand the difference between recessive and dominant genes. Which technique is likely to be the MOST effective?

A. asking students to identify the color eyes both of their parents have

B. giving a quick quiz where students write one sentence using the words *dominant* and *recessive*

C. having students research and present about common inherited traits that are heterozygous recessive

D. using an exit ticket where students fill in blanks in sentences using the word *dominan*t or *recessive*

Ecology and the Environment

Living Things and the Environment

Ecology is the study of organisms' interactions with each other and the environment. As with the study of organisms, ecology includes a classification hierarchy Groups of organisms of the same species living in the same geographic area are called **populations**. These organisms compete with each other for resources and mates and display characteristic patterns in growth related to their interactions with the environment. For example, many populations exhibit a **carrying capacity,** which is the highest number of individuals the resources in a given environment can support. Populations that outgrow their carrying capacity are likely to experience increased death rates until the population reaches a stable level again.

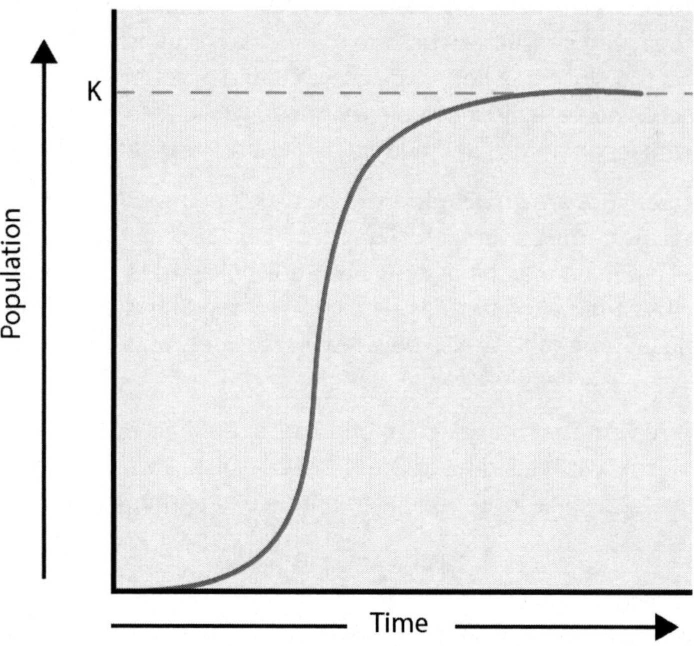

Figure 7.4. Carrying Capacity

Populations of different species living together in the same geographic region are called **communities**. Within a community many different interactions among species occur. **Predators** consume **prey** for food, and some species are in **competition** for the same limited pool of resources. Two species may also have a **parasitic** relationship in which one organism benefits to the detriment of the other, such as ticks feeding off a dog. Organisms may also be involved in **symbiosis,** or a close relationship between two very different organisms. They may also engage in **mutualism**, which benefits both organisms, or **commensalism**, where only one organism benefits but leaves the other unharmed.

Helpful Hint

The five levels of ecology, from smallest to largest (organisms, populations, communities, ecosystems, biosphere), can be remembered using the phrase *"**O**ld **p**eople **c**atch **e**asy **b**reaks."*

The lowest trophic level in the web is occupied by **producers,** which include plants and algae that produce energy directly from the sun. The next level are **primary consumers** (herbivores), which consume plant matter. The next trophic level includes **secondary consumers** (carnivores), which consume herbivores. A food web may also contain another level of **tertiary consumers** (carnivores that consume other carnivores). In a real community, these webs can be extremely complex, with species existing on multiple trophic levels. Communities also include **decomposers**, which are organisms that break down dead matter.

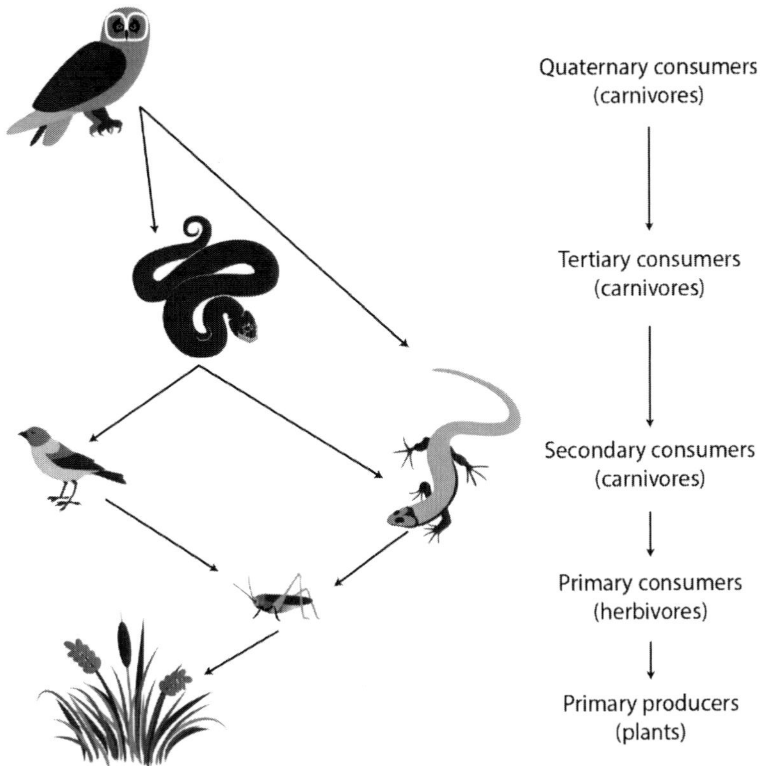

Figure 7.5. Food Web

The collection of biotic (living) and abiotic (nonliving) features in a geographic area is called an **ecosystem**. In a forest, for example, the ecosystem consists of all the organisms—animals, plants, fungi, bacteria, and so on—in addition to the soil, groundwater, rocks, and other abiotic features. Ecosystems are constantly developing and changing through a process called **ecological succession**. There are two types of ecological succession: primary and secondary. **Primary succession** describes the development and changes that occur during colonization of a new habitat, such as newly exposed rock. **Secondary succession** describes changes to previously colonized habitats that have been disrupted by events such as forest fires.

Check Your Understanding

What would happen if all of the decomposers disappeared from an ecosystem?

Ecosystems contain the resources that life within them rely on, such as water, soil, and temperatures conducive to survival of the organisms that live there. One crucial part of any ecosystem and of all life on Earth is carbon. Plants take carbon from their environment; this carbon is found and moved between plants, the soil, the ocean, and the atmosphere in what is known as the **carbon cycle**. Carbon is often referred to as the foundation for all life because of its central role in photosynthesis and its presence in DNA.

Biomes are collections of plant and animal communities that exist within specific climates. They are similar to ecosystems, but they do not include abiotic components and can exist within and across continents. For example, the Amazon rainforest is a specific ecosystem, while tropical rainforests in general are considered a biome that includes a set of similar communities across the world. Together, all the living and nonliving parts of the earth are known as the **biosphere**.

Terrestrial biomes are usually defined by distinctive patterns in temperature and rainfall, and aquatic biomes are defined by the type of water and organisms found there. Examples of biomes include the following:

- **desert:** a biome with extreme temperatures, very low rainfall, and specialized vegetation and small mammals
- **tropical rainforest:** a hot and wet biome with an extremely high diversity of species
- **temperate grassland:** a biome with moderate precipitation, distinct seasons, and grasses and shrubs that dominate
- **temperate broadleaf forest:** a biome with moderate precipitation and temperatures; dominated by deciduous trees
- **tundra:** a biome with extremely low temperatures, short growing seasons, and little or no tree growth
- **coral reef:** a marine (saltwater) system with high levels of diversity

wetland: an area of land saturated with water; includes five types—ocean, estuary, river, lake, and marsh

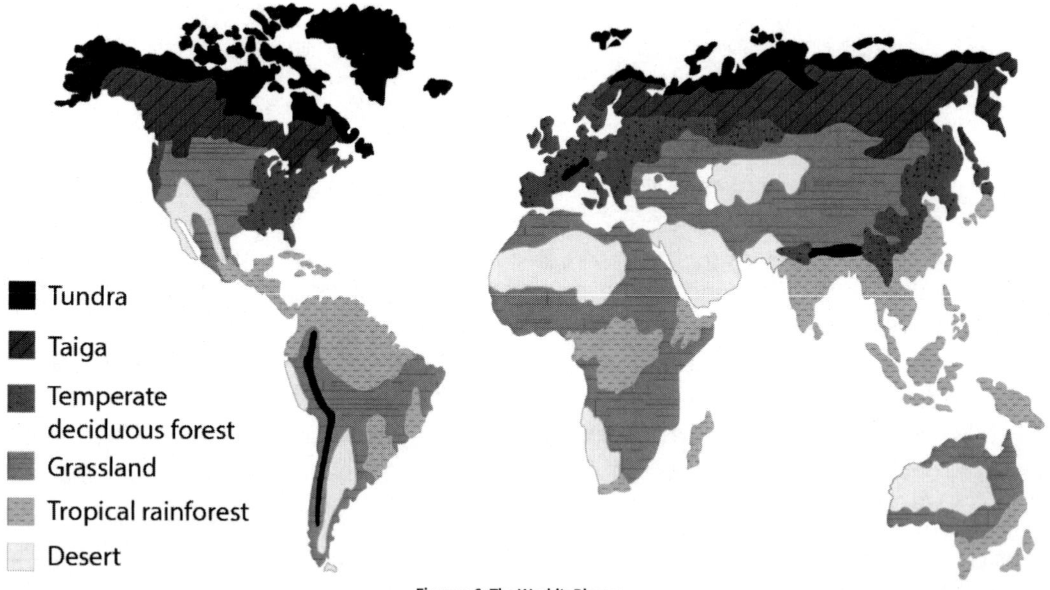

Figure 7.6. The World's Biomes

Ecosystems are not static environments but rather sites of constant change. The organisms within an ecosystem must therefore constantly shift and change as temperature, water, and soil change over time. For example, some organisms migrate with seasonal temperature shifts or when water in one area becomes scarce.

Practice Question

6) A first-grade teacher wants to introduce the class to the idea of producers and consumers. Which of the following activities would provide the MOST appropriate introduction to the life science concept of producers and consumers for this age group?

A. watching cattle graze in a field
B. comparing the Venus fly trap and the oak tree
C. identifying where their school lunch came from
D. sorting pictures of plants and animals into a T-chart

Humans and the Environment

Humans have impacted the environment in myriad ways. While the start of agriculture is generally credited with allowing human populations to stay in one place and build cities with advanced cultures, it has wreaked havoc on the environment. As lands were cleared for farming, ecosystems changed. With advances in farming like use of pesticides and fertilizers, chemical run-off caused changes in marine ecosystems as well.

In response, **integrated pest management** (IPM) has become more popular. IPM is an approach to managing pests based on knowledge of pests themselves, including their life cycles and environmental interactions. This approach can be more cost effective and more environmentally friendly as use of noxious pesticides is kept to a minimum. IPM is based on four steps:

1. Identifying pest thresholds that necessitate action: This limits the use of pesticides when they are not truly needed.

2. Monitoring and assessing pests: Some insects and weeds are actually not harmful to agricultural output and need no intervention; others may require action.

3. Preventing pests from becoming a problem: Strategies like crop rotation may limit pest presence.

4. Controlling via the least risky but still effective methods: This may involve non-chemical methods as a first line of action, but chemical pesticides may be used if other methods have proved ineffective.

Agriculture is one way in which humans are impacting the environment, but it is not the only way. Urbanization, sprawl, road and dam construction, and human population growth are all threats to wildlife. Even small changes can have an impact: once the delicate balance of an ecosystem is disrupted, the system may not function properly. For example, if all the secondary consumers disappear, the population of primary consumers would increase, causing the primary consumers to overeat the producers and eventually starve. Species called **keystone species** are especially important in a particular community, and removing them decreases the overall diversity of the ecosystem.

Human activity is a major cause of species loss because humans often encroach upon existing ecosystems. Other times, humans overhunt or overuse a species. Sometimes species become threatened when a disease breaks out. When a species has less than 2,500 adults or when it declines by 20 percent within five years or two generations, it is considered an **endangered species**. When there are no more of a specific species, it is said to be **extinct**.

Species extinction is occurring at an alarming rate beyond what is expected through natural processes. This strongly suggests that humans are to blame. The Endangered Species Act of 1973 was passed to protect vulnerable plants and animals in the United States; however, the problem is a global issue and continues as many developing nations struggle to balance economic growth and environmental protections.

> **Did You Know?**
>
> The northern flying squirrel is one of the animals on the Pennsylvania Endangered Species List. Its decline is largely due to the loss of forest habitats in the Pocono region.

A major contemporary concern for virtually every ecosystem on Earth is **climate change**. Most scholars define climate change as long-term shifts or changes in weather patterns. Climate change can have impacts on local ecosystems, such as a group of apes living in a small area, or on far broader groups of organisms. For example, climate change in an island area, such as Indonesia, could impact every organism in that area.

Climate change has both natural and human causes. Natural causes of climate change include changes in Earth's orbit and axis of rotation, changes in the sun's energy, volcanic activity, and natural changes in Earth's surface and carbon dioxide concentrations. However, natural causes do not explain all climate change. Human activities, like the burning of fossil fuels and agricultural and industrial processes, have increased greenhouse gases in what is known as the **greenhouse effect**. Increased levels of carbon dioxide, methane, nitrous oxide, and chlorofluorocarbons contribute to the greenhouse effect.

To impact climate change, experts advise two paths: mitigation and adaptation. **Mitigation** involves reducing or eliminating the release of greenhouse gases into the atmosphere. **Adaptation** is more about adapting to the changing climate. Mitigation strategies might include eliminating the use of fossil fuels and increasing the use of renewable resources, shifting to more sustainable agricultural practices, and improving energy efficiency in homes and businesses. Adaptation strategies might include shifting the growing season or growing location of certain crops due to changes in climate and reducing risks to populations from extreme weather events by building barriers and reinforcing buildings.

Practice Question

7) A third-grade teacher wants to illustrate that the same environment can be perfect for one organism but harmful to another. Which example might she use?

A. fish and coral living in an ocean environment
B. camels and cactuses living in a desert environment
C. humans and pigeons living in a city environment
D. humans and deer living in a city environment

Physical Science

Properties of Matter

Matter takes up space and has weight as well as physical and chemical properties. **Physical properties** of matter refer to observed or measured characteristics that do not change the matter's identity. These include boiling and melting points, density, conductivity, solubility, malleability, color, and hardness. **Chemical properties** refer to the ability of matter to chemically react or change. Chemical properties produce something new after the change or reaction. For example, a piece of paper that burns is turned to ash.

The basic unit of all **matter** is the **atom**. Atoms are composed of three subatomic particles: protons, electrons, and neutrons. **Protons** have a positive charge and are found in the nucleus, or center, of the atom. **Neutrons**, which have no charge, are also located in the nucleus. Negatively charged **electrons** orbit the nucleus. If an atom has the same number of protons and electrons, it will have no net charge. Charged atoms are called ions. Atoms that have more protons than electrons are positively charged and are called cations. Negatively charged atoms have more electrons than protons and are called anions.

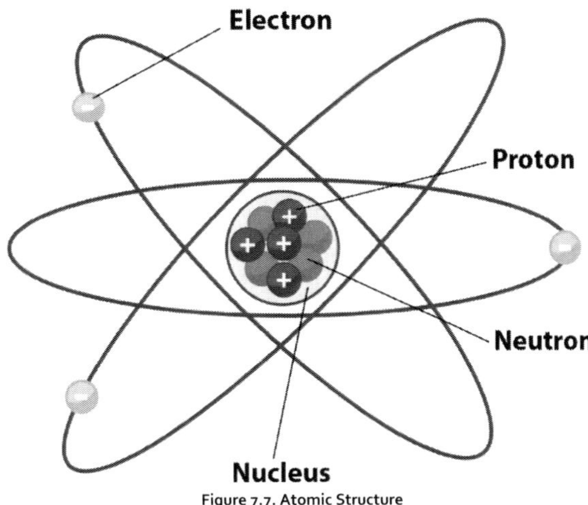

Figure 7.7. Atomic Structure

The mass of an atom is determined by adding the number of protons, neutrons, and electrons; however, electrons have very little mass, so the **atomic mass** is determined by adding just the mass of protons and neutrons.

Elements, such as hydrogen and oxygen, are substances in their simplest form that retain their unique characteristics. Each element has a distinct **atomic number** based on the number of protons in the nucleus. For example, hydrogen has one proton; oxygen has six. An element is defined by the number of protons it has, but variations of an element that have different numbers of neutrons are called **isotopes**. Some isotopes are unstable and emit radiation as they decay. These are called radioactive isotopes or radioisotopes. Others do not decay over time and are called stable isotopes. A table of chemical elements arranged by atomic number is called **the periodic table**.

> **Helpful Hint**
>
> The parts of an atom can be remembered using the acronym ***PEN***—protons, electrons, neutrons.

When two or more atoms join together they form a **molecule**. For example, O_3 (ozone) contains three oxygen atoms bound together, and H_2O (water) contains two hydrogen atoms and one oxygen atom. Water is a **compound** because it is made by combining two or more different elements. Atoms can be joined together by different types of bonds by sharing or exchanging **valence electrons**, which are electrons that can participate in chemical reactions with other elements. In a **covalent bond**, the atoms share one or more valence electrons. In an **ionic bond**, one or more electrons are transferred from one element to another to create two ions with opposite charges that are attracted to each other and bind together.

All matter exists in one of four **states**—solid, liquid, gas, or plasma:

- **Solid** matter has densely packed molecules and does not change volume or shape.

- **Liquids** have more loosely packed molecules and can change shape but not volume.
- **Gas** molecules are widely dispersed and can change both shape and volume.

Plasma is similar to gas but contains freely moving charged particles (although its overall charge is neutral).

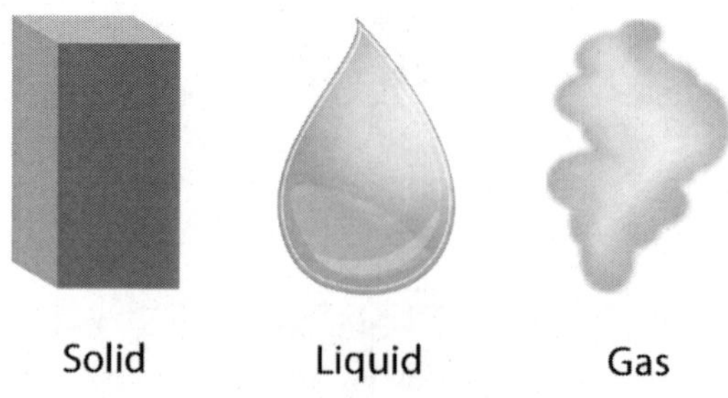

Figure 7.9. States of Matter

Changes in temperature and pressure can cause matter to change states. Generally, adding energy (in the form of heat) changes a substance to a higher-energy state (e.g., solid to liquid). Transitions from a high- to lower-energy state (e.g., liquid to solid) release energy. Each of these changes has a specific name:

- solid to liquid: melting (energy added)
- liquid to solid: freezing (energy removed)
- liquid to gas: evaporation (energy added)
- gas to liquid: condensation (energy removed)
- solid to gas: sublimation (energy added)
- gas to solid: deposition (energy removed)

When matter changes states, energy is added or removed as noted above.

Matter changing state is an example of a **physical change**, which is a change that does not alter the chemical composition of a substance. The state of matter changes, but the underlying chemical nature of the substance itself does not change. Other examples of physical changes include cutting, heating, or changing the shape of a substance.

When substances are combined without a chemical reaction to bond them, the resulting substance is called a **mixture**. In a mixture, the components can be unevenly distributed, such as in trail mix or soil. Alternatively, the components can be uniformly distributed, as in salt water. When the distribution is uniform, the mixture is called a **solution**. The substance being dissolved is the **solute**, and the substance in which it is being dissolved is the **solvent**. Physical changes can be used to separate mixtures. For example, heating salt water until the water evaporates will separate a salt water solution, leaving the salt behind.

In contrast to a physical change, a **chemical change** occurs when bonds between atoms are made or broken, resulting in a new substance or substances. Chemical changes are also called **chemical reactions**. Chemical reactions are either **exothermic,** meaning energy (heat) is released, or **endothermic,** meaning energy (heat) is required for the reaction to take place. Photosynthesis is an

> **Helpful Hint**
>
> In both physical and chemical changes, matter is always conserved, meaning it can never be created or destroyed.

endothermic reaction that converts electromagnetic energy from the sun into chemical energy. Cellular respiration is an exothermic reaction where oxygen and glucose are changed into carbon dioxide and water. Chemical reactions are represented by written mathematical equations. The **reactants,** the substances that are changing in the chemical reaction, are represented on the left side of the equation. The **products,** the new substances formed during the chemical reaction, are represented on the right side of the equation. The law of conservation of mass says that the amount of each element cannot change during a chemical reaction, so the same amount of each element must be represented on each side of the equation (i.e., the reactants and products must have the same amount of each element). This is called a **balanced equation**. For example, the production of water from two molecules of hydrogen gas and one molecule of oxygen gas can be written as: $2H_2 + O_2 = 2H_2O$.

The substances on the left side of the equations are called the reactants. The plus sign (+) sign means "reacts with," and the arrow ( ) means "produces." The substances on the right side of the equations are called the products. The number in front of the substances tells how many molecules of the substance are used, although the number is only written if it is more than one.

Common reactions include the following:

- **reduction/oxidation (redox):** a chemical change in which a substance loses electrons, as when iron rusts when exposed to oxygen, forming iron oxide
- **combustion:** a chemical reaction that produces heat, carbon dioxide, and water, usually by burning a fuel
- **synthesis:** a chemical reaction in which two substances combine to form a single substance
- **decomposition:** a chemical reaction in which a single substance is broken down into two or more substances (e.g., the digestion of food)
- **neutralization:** a chemical reaction that occurs when an acid and a base react to produce a salt and water

Matter is classified by its **properties**, or characteristics. These properties include mass, weight, density, solubility, conductivity, and pH. **Mass** refers to the amount of matter in an object. Although the terms are often used interchangeably, mass is distinct from **weight**, which is the force of the gravitational pull on an object. Unlike weight, mass stays the same no matter where an object is located. When two objects of the same mass are on Earth and on the moon, the object on the moon will weigh less because the force of gravity on the moon is less than it is on Earth.

Density is the mass of the object divided by its volume, or the amount of space the object occupies. A denser object contains the same amount of mass in a smaller space than a less dense object. This is why a dense object, such as a bowling ball, feels heavier than a less dense object, like a soccer ball. The density of an object determines whether it will sink or float in a fluid. For example, the bowling ball will sink because it is denser than water, while the soccer ball will float.

Solubility refers to the amount of a solute that will dissolve in a solvent. **Conductivity** describes how well a material conducts heat or electricity. Silver, copper, aluminum, and iron are good conductors, while rubber, glass, and wood are poor conductors. Poor conductors are also called **insulators**.

Finally, the **pH scale** is used to describe the acidity of a substance. **Acids** are compounds that contribute a hydrogen ion (H+) when in a solution, and **bases** are compounds that contribute a hydroxide ion (OH−) in a solution. The pH scale goes from 1 to 14, with 7 considered neutral. Acids (such as lemon juice) have a pH lower than 7; bases (such as soap) have a pH greater than 7. Water is neutral with a pH of 7.

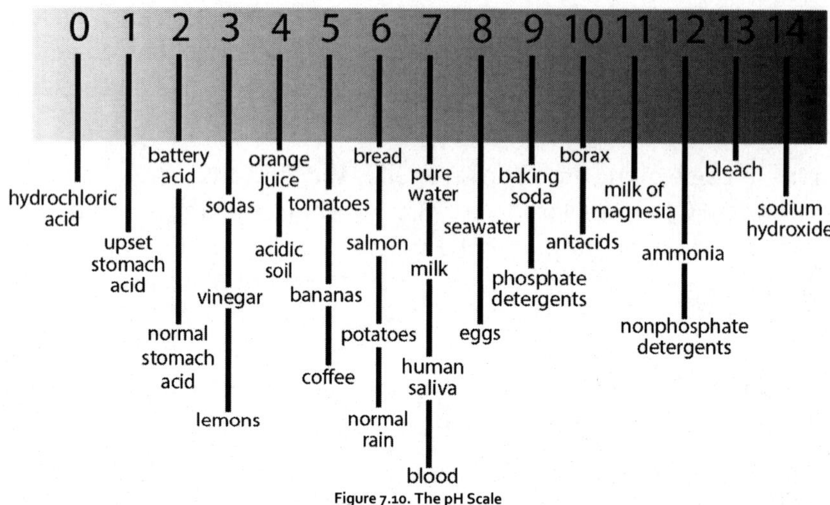

Figure 7.10. The pH Scale

Practice Question

8) A first-grade student notices that there is dew on the grass in the morning but not in the afternoon after the sun has come out. The student is noticing which two phenomena?

A. deposition and sublimation
B. melting and evaporation
C. condensation and evaporation
D. freezing and evaporation

Force and Motion

The motion of objects can be measured using a number of different variables, including speed, displacement, velocity, and acceleration. These variables are either **vector** (magnitude and direction) or **scalar** (magnitude only) measurements.

Speed is a scalar measure that describes how quickly something moves using the following equation:

- speed = distance/time

Displacement is a vector measure of the shortest distance between the initial and final locations of a moving point as calculated using the following equation where v is the velocity, v_0 is the initial velocity, and t is the elapsed time.

- displacement $= \frac{1}{2}(v + v_0)t$

Velocity is a vector quantity that describes the rate at which an object changes position according to the following equation:

- velocity = displacement/time

An object that travels a certain distance and then returns to its starting point has a velocity of zero because its final position did not change. Its speed, however, can be found by dividing the total distance it traveled by the time it took to make the trip.

Acceleration is also a vector quantity and describes how quickly an object changes velocity. It is found using the following equation:

- acceleration = change in velocity/time

A push or pull that causes an object to move or change direction is called a **force**. Forces can arise from a number of different sources. **Gravity** is the attraction of one mass to another mass. For example, the earth's gravitational field pulls objects toward it, and the sun's gravitational field keeps planets in motion around it. Electrically charged objects create a field that causes other charged objects in that field to move. Other forces include **tension**, which is found in ropes pulling or holding up an object; **friction**, which is created by two objects moving against each other; and the **normal force**, which occurs when an object is resting on another object.

An object that is at rest or moving with a constant speed has a net force of zero, meaning all of the forces acting on it cancel each other out. Such an object is said to be at **equilibrium**. Isaac Newton proposed three **laws of motion** that govern forces:

- **Newton's first law:** An object at rest stays at rest and an object in motion stays in motion unless acted on by a force.
- **Newton's second law:** Force is equal to the mass of an object multiplied by its acceleration ($F = ma$).
- **Newton's third law:** For every action there is an equal and opposite reaction.

Helpful Hint

The normal force balances out gravity in resting objects. When a book rests on a table, gravity pulls down on it and the normal force pushes up, canceling each other out and holding the book still.

The laws of motion have made it possible to build **simple machines**, which take advantage of those laws to make work easier to perform. Simple machines include the inclined plane, wheel and axle, pulley, screw, wedge, and lever.

Figure 7.11. Simple Machines

Practice Question

9) A second-grade teacher wants to combine the study of simple machines with a social studies topic. Which activity would be MOST appropriate?

A. matching community helpers to the machines they are most likely to use
B. building a replica of the pyramids with a pulley system
C. rolling a ball down an incline plane in the neighborhood park
D. identifying the new activities human civilizations could do with each machine

Energy

Energy is the capacity of an object to do work, or, in other words, to cause some sort of movement or change. There are two kinds of energy: kinetic and potential. Objects in motion have **kinetic energy**, and objects that have the potential to be in motion due to their position have **potential energy**. Potential energy is defined in relation to a specific point. For example, a book held ten feet off the ground has more potential energy than a book held five feet off the ground because it has the potential to fall farther (i.e., to do more work).

Kinetic energy can be turned into potential energy and vice versa. In the example above, dropping one of the books turns its potential energy into kinetic energy. Conversely, picking up a book and placing it on a table turns kinetic energy into potential energy. In another example, a pendulum—an object with mass hanging from a fixed point—is able to swing indefinitely after an initial input of mechanical energy to start the motion by repeatedly converting potential energy to kinetic energy and back again.

> **Helpful Hint**
>
> Like matter, energy is always conserved. It can be changed from one form to another but never created or destroyed.

There are several types of potential energy. The energy stored in a book placed on a table is **gravitational potential energy** and is derived from the pull of the earth's gravity on the book. **Electric potential energy** is derived from the interaction between positive and negative charges. Because opposite charges attract each other, and like charges repel, energy can be stored when opposite charges are moved apart or when like charges are pushed together. Similarly, compressing a spring stores **elastic potential energy,** which is then converted to kinetic energy when the compressed spring is released. Energy is also stored in chemical bonds as **chemical potential energy**.

Temperature is the name given to the kinetic energy of all the atoms or molecules in a substance. While it might look like a substance is perfectly still, its atoms are actually constantly spinning and vibrating. The more energy the atoms have, the higher the substance's temperature. **Heat** is the movement of energy from one substance to another. Energy will spontaneously move from high energy (high temperature) substances to low energy (low temperature) substances.

The measurement of temperature is known as **thermometry**. Various scales are used to measure temperature. **Fahrenheit**, where water freezes at 32 degrees, is one such scale as is **Celsius**, where water freezes at zero degrees. **Kelvin** is another common scale, often used in scientific study. Zero degrees Celsius equals 273.15 K or kelvin.

This heat energy can be transferred by radiation, conduction, or convection. **Radiation** does not need a medium; the sun radiates energy to Earth through the vacuum of space. **Conduction** occurs when two substances are in contact with each other. When a pan is placed on a hot stove, the heat energy is conducted from the stove to the pan and then to the food in the pan. **Convection** transfers energy through circular movement of air or liquids. For example, a convection oven transfers heat through the circular movement caused by hot air rising and cold air sinking.

Energy in today's world comes from many sources. Energy sources are classified as **renewable**, or self-replenishing over time, and **nonrenewable**, or finite resources that will be used up completely at one point in time. Renewable energy sources include wind, solar, hydropower (water energy), geothermal energy, and biomass energy. Nonrenewable energy sources include oil, coal, natural gas, and nuclear energy.

Renewable energy sources are generally regarded as better for the earth and its people; however, renewable energy sources may present some disadvantages. Solar energy, for example, is an abundant and renewable source of energy that does not pollute water or air. It is, however, more expensive in its initial installation and requires a large space. Wind energy also requires a high up-front cost and may impact local wildlife, especially birds and bats. Like solar power, wind energy has low ongoing operating costs and may have great potential (like solar energy) for powering homes and businesses in the future.

Practice Question

10) A teacher could BEST illustrate which type of potential energy using a compressed spring?

A. chemical potential energy
B. electric potential energy
C. gravitational potential energy
D. elastic potential energy

Earth Science

Earth Structure

The outermost layer of Earth is called the **crust**—a very thin and broken surface layer. Beneath the crust is the **mantle,** a dense layer of rock. The mantle has an upper layer that is cooler and more rigid, and a deep mantle that is hotter and more liquid. Under the mantle is the **core**, which also includes two parts: a liquid outer core and an inner core composed of solid iron. Scientists believe the inner core spins at a rate slightly different from the rest of the planet, which creates Earth's magnetic field.

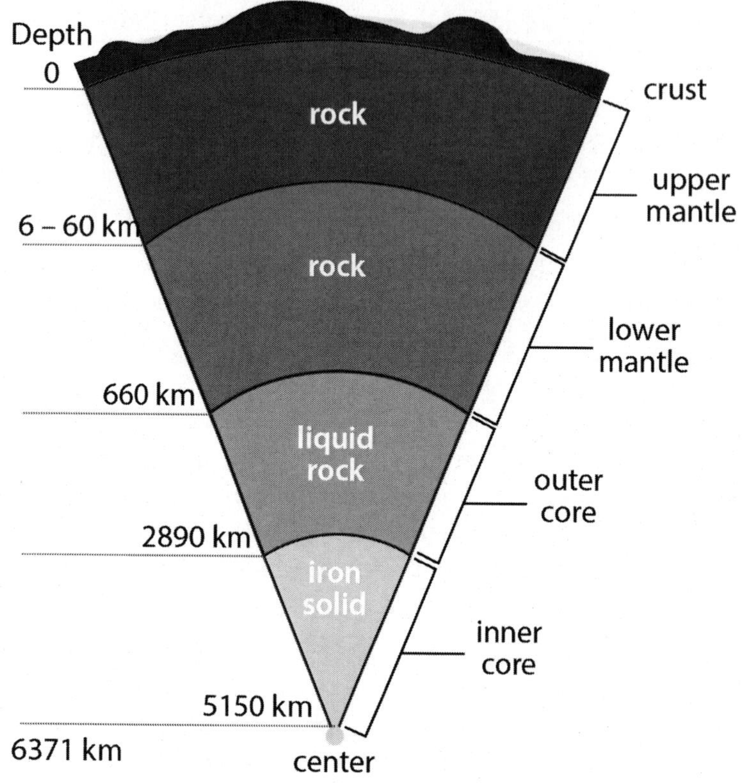

Figure 7.12. Layers of Earth

The crust and upper layer of the mantle make up the **lithosphere**, the planet's surface layer. Under the lithosphere is a hot, semisolid part of the mantle called the **asthenosphere**. The lithosphere includes **tectonic plates,** which are the broken pieces of Earth's solid outer crust. The tectonic plates float on top of the more liquid asthenosphere that flows very slowly beneath them.

Earth's surface is divided into seven large land masses called **continents,** which are often separated by oceans. Scientists believe that over 200 million years ago the continents were joined together in one giant landmass called Pangaea. Due to **continental drift** (the slow movement of the tectonic plates), the continents gradually shifted to their current positions—and are still moving.

Earth's surface includes many bodies of water that together form the **hydrosphere**; the study of water on Earth is called **hydrology**. The hydrosphere is distinct but interconnected with other Earth systems. The largest bodies in the hydrosphere are saltwater **oceans**. There are five oceans: the Arctic, Atlantic,

Indian, Pacific, and Southern. Together, the oceans account for 71 percent of Earth's surface and 97 percent of Earth's water.

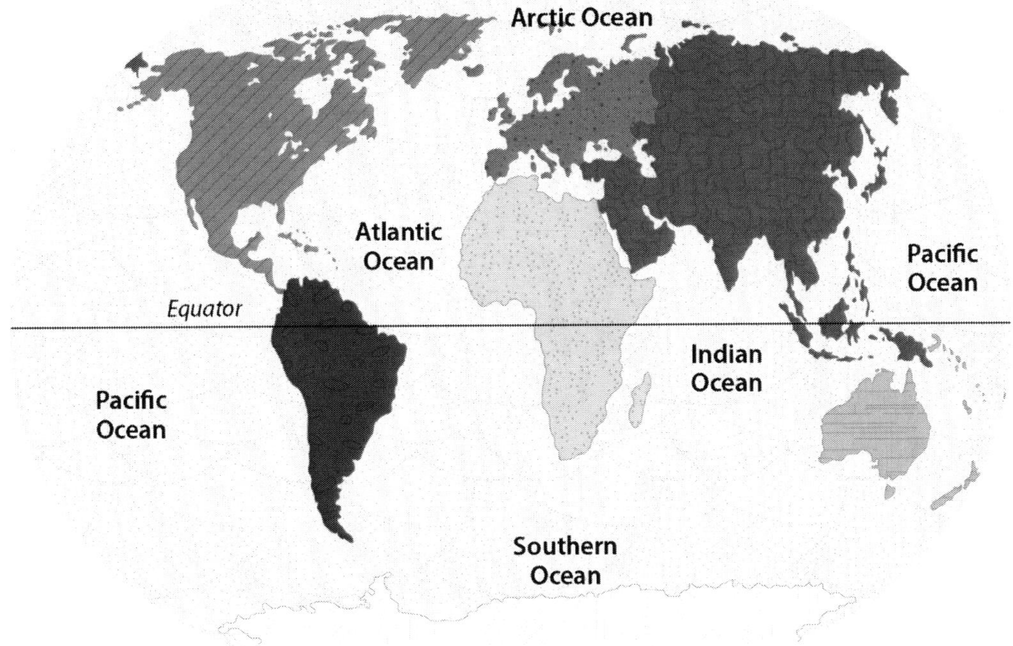

Figure 7.13. Earth's Oceans

Oceans are subject to **tides**, cyclic rising and falling water levels at shorelines, which are the result of the gravitational pull of the moon and sun. **Currents** are movements of the ocean water caused by differences in salt content or temperature and winds. **Waves** carry energy through the water and are caused by wind blowing across the surface of the ocean. Tides shape coastal topography as they cause erosion, which may create new landforms like platforms or notches.

Other bodies of water include **lakes**, usually fresh water, and **seas**, mainly salt water. Rain that falls on the land flows into **rivers** and **streams**, which are moving bodies of water that flow into lakes, seas, and oceans. The areas where rivers and streams meet salt water are called **estuaries**. Estuaries often contain brackish water, or the mix between salt and fresh water; estuaries often boast ecosystems full of unique organisms specially adapted to this salinity.

When all the rain that falls on a given area of land flows into a single body of water, that land area is called a **watershed** or **drainage basin**. The earth also contains **groundwater**, or water that is stored underground in rock formations called **aquifers**. Groundwater is key to the exchange of water between the land and subsurface. Water from the surface moves into the subsurface and fills aquifers. The water stored in these aquifers eventually makes its way back to the surface.

Much of Earth's water is stored as ice. The North and South Poles are usually covered in large sheets of ice called **polar ice**. **Glaciers** are large masses of ice and snow that move. Over long periods of time, they scour Earth's surface, creating features such as lakes and valleys. Large chunks of ice that break off from glaciers are called **icebergs**.

Although a **rock** is also a naturally occurring solid, it can be either organic or inorganic and is composed of one or more minerals. Rocks are classified based on how they were formed. The three types of rocks are igneous,

> **Did You Know?**
>
> Most of Pennsylvania's water comes from the Ohio, Susquehanna, and Delaware River Basins.

sedimentary, and metamorphic. **Igneous rocks** are the result of tectonic processes that bring **magma,** or melted rock, to the earth's surface; they can form either above or below the surface. **Sedimentary rocks** are formed when rock fragments are compacted as a result of weathering and erosion. Lastly, **metamorphic rocks** form when extreme temperatures and pressure change the structure of preexisting rocks.

Practice Question

11) Which water-related topic would be appropriate to introduce to a kindergarten class?
   A. turning off the tap while brushing teeth in order to save water
   B. determining the salinity in a sample of water from a drainage basin
   C. understanding costs and benefits of using hydroelectric power for industry
   D. calculating the force of the ocean at high tide

Earth Cycles

The rock cycle describes how rocks form and break down. Typically, the cooling and solidification of magma as it rises to the surface creates igneous rocks. These rocks are then subject to **weathering,** the mechanical and/or chemical processes by which rocks break down. During **erosion,** the resulting sediment is deposited in a new location. This **deposition** creates new sedimentary rocks. As new layers are added, rocks and minerals are forced closer to the earth's core where they are subject to heat and pressure, resulting in metamorphic rock. Eventually, they will reach their melting point and return to magma, starting the cycle over again. This process takes place over hundreds of thousands or even millions of years.

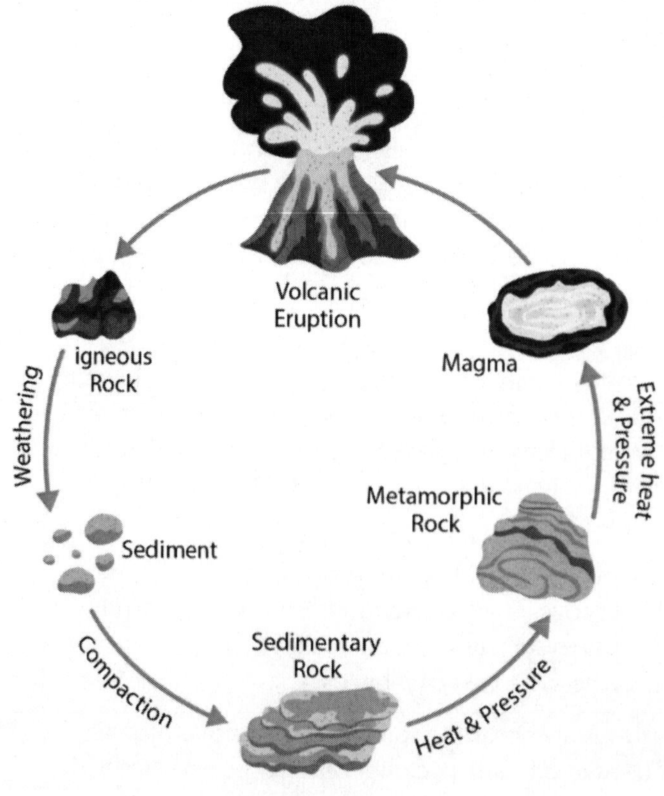

Figure 7.14. The Rock Cycle

Ecosystems contain resources that the lives within them rely on, such as water, soil, and temperatures conducive to the survival of the organisms that live there. One crucial part of any ecosystem and of all life on Earth is carbon. Plants take carbon from their environment; this carbon is found and moved between plants, the soil, the ocean, and the atmosphere in what is known as the **carbon cycle**. Carbon is often referred to as the foundation for all life because of its central role in photosynthesis and its presence in DNA.

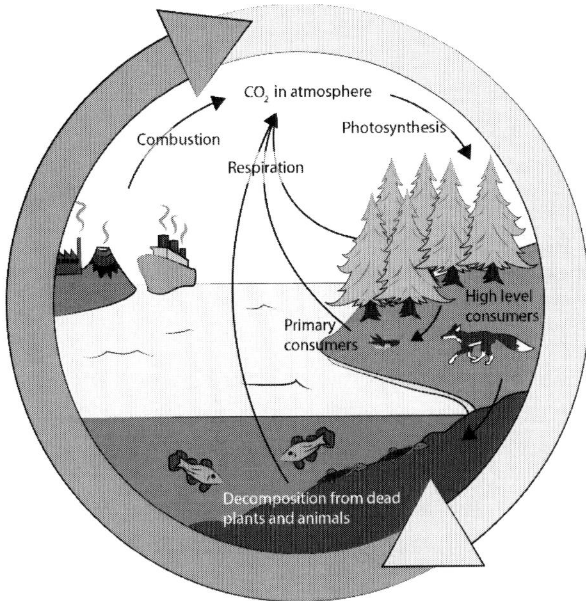

Figure 7.15. The Carbon Cycle

The **water cycle** is the circulation of water throughout the earth's surface, atmosphere, and hydrosphere. Water on the earth's surface **evaporates,** or changes from a liquid to a gas, and becomes water vapor. Water vapor in the air then comes together to form **clouds**. When it cools, this water vapor condenses into a liquid and falls from the sky as **precipitation**, which includes rain, sleet, snow, and hail. Precipitation replenishes groundwater and the water found in features such as lakes and rivers, starting the cycle over again.

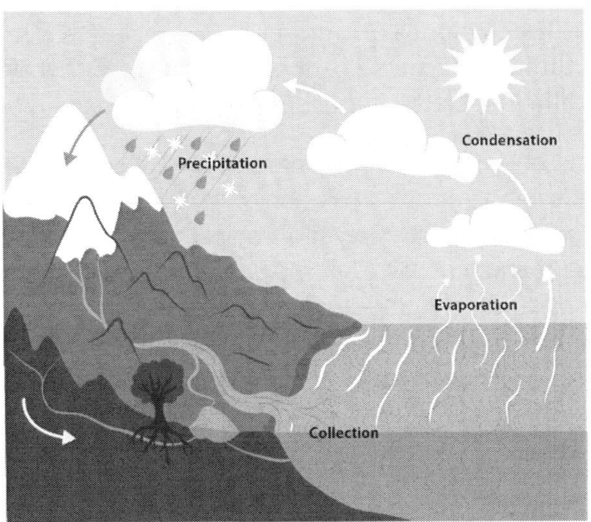

Figure 7.16. The Water Cycle

Most of these cycles of Earth's systems are natural, and human activity can alter these systems. Dams and irrigation systems built by humans can alter the water cycle. Land clearing for agriculture or other human activities can accelerate erosion and impact the rock cycle. Burning fossil fuels releases carbon dioxide into the atmosphere and impacts the carbon cycle. It is important for humans to consider the broader impacts of their actions on Earth's systems and processes.

Practice Question

12) A fourth-grade teacher watches as student groups work to create a poster showing the water cycle. The teacher wants to extend student thinking to include human impact on the environment. Which question should the teacher ask?

A. What is meant by the word *precipitation*?
B. Why is water in the air called *humidity*?
C. How might a new subdivision change the way in which water moves?
D. Why is it important for drinking water to be purified?

Weather and Climate

The study of weather is known as **meteorology**. A warm front occurs when warm air moves over and replaces a cold air mass, causing the air at the front to feel warmer and more humid. A cold front occurs when cold air moves under and replaces a warm air mass, causing a drop in temperature.

Sometimes, weather turns violent. Tropical cyclones, or **hurricanes**, originate over warm ocean water. Hurricanes have destructive winds of 74 miles per hour or more and create large storm surges, when sea water rises above the normal tide level, that can cause extensive damage along coastlines. Hurricanes, typhoons, and cyclones are all the same type of storm; they just have different names based on where the storm is located. Hurricanes originate in the Atlantic or Eastern Pacific Ocean, typhoons in the Western Pacific Ocean, and cyclones in the Indian Ocean. **Tornadoes** occur when unstable warm and cold air masses collide and a rotation is created by fast-moving winds.

Did You Know?

Flooding is the most common natural disaster in Pennsylvania.

Severe weather has many unfortunate impacts, but technological tools can help predict such events so that people can prepare. **Doppler radar**, which detects wind strength and direction as well as precipitation, is one such tool. Satellite imagery also helps meteorologists study and predict weather. **Weather balloons** or radiosondes, collect data from the upper stratosphere. **Automated surface-observing systems (ASOS)** also monitor and track weather on Earth's surface. Computers help analyze all of this data and make

The long-term weather conditions in a geographic location are called **climate**. A **climate zone** is a large area that experiences similar average temperature and precipitation. The three major climate zones, based on temperature, are the polar, temperate, and tropical zones. Each climate zone is divided into subclimates that have unique characteristics. The tropical climate zone (warm temperatures) can be divided into tropical wet, tropical wet and dry, semiarid, and arid. The temperate climate zones (moderate temperatures) include Mediterranean, humid subtropical, marine West Coast, humid continental, and subarctic. The polar climate zones (cold temperatures) include tundra, highlands, nonpermanent ice, and ice cap. Polar climates are cold and experience prolonged, dark winters due to the tilt of Earth's axis.

Practice Question

13) To help a student understand the difference between weather and climate, what could a teacher do?

A. ask how the landscapes of Pennsylvania and New Mexico are different
B. ask what the weather is usually like in Pennsylvania and what it is on a single day
C. ask what the record temperatures were in Pennsylvania and New Mexico over the past five years
D. ask what type of natural disasters are most likely to occur in Pennsylvania

Space Science

Astronomy is the study of space. Earth is just one of a group of **planets** that orbit the **sun**, which is the star at the center of Earth's **solar system**. The planets in the solar system are Mercury, Venus, Earth, Mars, Jupiter, Saturn, Uranus, and Neptune. Every planet, except Mercury and Venus, has **moons**, or naturally occurring satellites that orbit a planet. The solar system also includes **asteroids** and **comets**, small rocky or icy objects that orbit the sun. Many of these are clustered in the asteroid belt, which is located between the orbits of Mars and Jupiter.

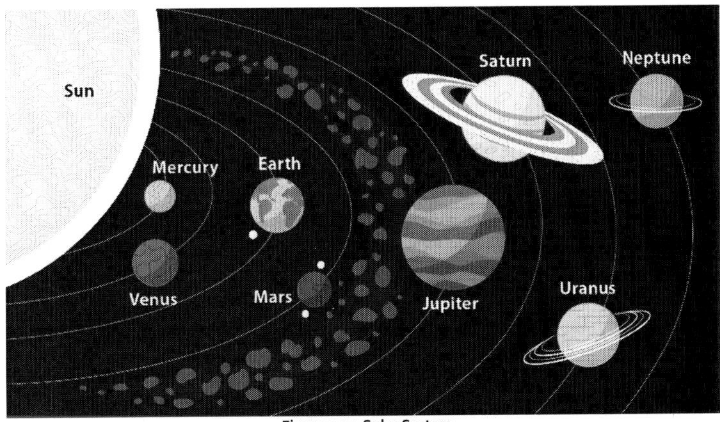

Figure 7.17. Solar System

The solar system is a small part of a bigger star system called a galaxy. (The galaxy that is home to Earth is called the Milky Way.) **Galaxies** consist of gas, dust, and hundreds of billions of **stars**, which are hot balls of plasma and gases, all held together by gravity. The universe has many types of stars, including supergiants, giants, white dwarfs, and neutron stars.

The closer and larger the star is to Earth, the brighter it will appear. Generally stars are only apparent in the night sky when a person's portion of the earth is pointed away from the sun. This phenomenon also makes the Moon visible at night and the sun visible during the day. Additionally, because Earth orbits the sun through the course of a year, we see different parts of the night sky during different seasons. This is why different constellations are visible at different times.

> **Helpful Hint**
>
> The phrase "**M**y **V**ery **E**ducated **M**other **J**ust **S**erved **U**s **N**oodles" can help students remember the order of the planets: **M**ercury, **V**enus, **E**arth, **M**ars, **J**upiter, **S**aturn, **U**ranus, **N**eptune.

Stars form in nebulas, which are large clouds of dust and gas. When very large stars collapse, they create **black holes**, which have a gravitational force so strong that even light cannot escape.

Earth, the moon, and the sun interact in a number of ways that impact the planet. The moon reflects sunlight in what are called **lunar phases**. A **new moon** occurs when sunlight is hitting the far side of the moon that cannot be seen from Earth; sunlight reflecting off the near side we can see is called a **full moon**. During the other lunar phases (waxing crescent, first quarter, waxing gibbous, waning gibbous, third quarter, and waning crescent), people on Earth see only a portion of the moon.

When the positions of the earth, moon, and sun align, **eclipses** occur. A **lunar eclipse** occurs when planet Earth lines up between the moon and the sun: the moon moves into the shadow of Earth and appears dark in color. A **solar eclipse** occurs when the moon lines up between Earth and the sun: the moon covers the sun, blocking sunlight.

The cycle of day and night and the seasonal cycle are determined by Earth's motion around the sun. It takes approximately 365 days, or one year, for Earth to revolve around the sun. While Earth is revolving around the sun, it is also rotating on its axis, which takes approximately 24 hours, or one day. As the planet rotates, different areas alternately face toward the sun and away from the sun, creating night and day.

Earth's axis is not directly perpendicular to its orbit, meaning the planet is tilted. The seasons are caused by this tilt. When the Northern Hemisphere is tilted toward the sun, it receives more sunlight and experiences summer. At the same time that the Northern Hemisphere experiences summer, the Southern Hemisphere, which receives less direct sunlight, experiences winter. As the earth revolves, the Northern Hemisphere tilts away from the sun and moves into winter, while the Southern Hemisphere tilts toward the sun and moves into summer.

Practice Question

14) At the start of a fourth-grade unit on the solar system, a student asks why it is winter in some places and summer in other places. Which concept should the teacher cover in order to answer the student's question?

A. eclipses
B. lunar phases
C. axial tilt
D. time zones

Health and Motor Development

Health

Lessons on health help students learn about wellness and unhealthy behaviors. Students gain the ability to explain the importance of physical activity, what contributes to disease in the body, and how nutrition, stress, and substance use affect their growth and well-being.

Helpful Hint

Planting a garden is a great hands-on activity for teaching early elementary students about food and nutrition.

In the earliest grades, students might first be introduced to health concepts by studying the **five senses:** sight, smell, hearing, touch, and taste.

Teaching students about the physical systems in the body is another great introduction to the theories of health and gives them the fundamental knowledge to better understand **nutrition** and fitness. In the early elementary grades, the focus should be on the elements of a

balanced diet. Looking at the healthy eating plate and identifying nutrients helps students learn how their choices affect their bodies.

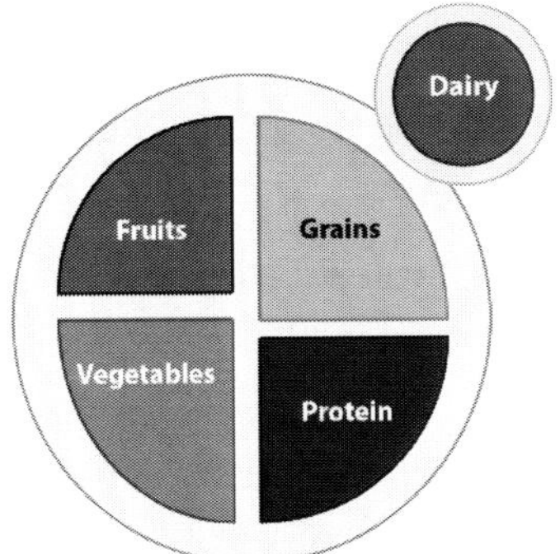

Figure 7.18. MyPlate Food Guide

Students should learn about the basic nutrients:

- water
- carbohydrates
- protein
- fat
- vitamins
- minerals

Did You Know?

Some research suggests that the type of food we routinely eat is what we crave. This means people who are healthy eaters may actually crave healthy foods.

They should be able to identify foods and drinks that contain various nutrients and which foods and drinks to avoid for their lack of nutrient content.

Nutrition is tied to growth and body composition, but it is not the only factor. **Body type,** which is inherited and largely unchangeable, will also impact the shape of the human body. Similarly, human **growth spurts**, or sudden increases in height and weight, are also a natural part of growing up.

Disease prevention and control is another part of human health. Students should learn about practical ways to prevent diseases, such as practicing **personal hygiene**, identifying symptoms of diseases and how they affect the body, and how to prevent diseases.

There are four main disease types:

- infectious
- hereditary
- physiological
- deficiency

Infectious diseases, which are transmitted to a person from the environment, can be limited through vaccines, handwashing, avoiding close contact with sick people, and basic practices such as not coughing or sneezing on others; however, they cannot always be entirely avoided. Hereditary diseases come from a genetic predisposition and cannot be prevented—only treated. Deficiency diseases arise when an individual does not have enough of something (e.g., a vitamin or mineral), and other physiological diseases are those that are not from the other categories (e.g., cancer, stroke, heart disease).

The cause of many diseases is known, though the cause of others is unknown. Nevertheless, students should understand that a healthy lifestyle, including proper nutrition and exercise, reduces the risk for many diseases. Because some degree of illness is unavoidable, students will need to know the warning signs. These include: fever, nausea, rash, diarrhea, lethargy, and pain, among other symptoms.

Most diseases can be treated by health care professionals. Seeing a doctor annually can help prevent future disease.

Students may also learn about injury prevention and safety. Topics would include basic safety rules, reacting to emergencies, and understanding strategies for self-protection.

As part of this, students also need to understand that their **mental health** contributes to social and emotional well-being. Students should learn different strategies and skills to improve their relationships with others and themselves. Topics can include

- friends and family,
- effective communication,
- appropriate emotional responses, and
- assuming responsibility for their own decisions.

Activities on goal-setting (both short and long-term), problem-solving, and decision-making are all highly appropriate for health classrooms. As students make decisions and solve problems, tolerance, respect, empathy, and self-control should be central.

Older students will learn about stress, its effects on the body, and identifying resources and constructive ways of dealing with it. Instruction in bullying prevention will also be part of the health curriculum. Most schools have policies on bullying, which should be part of this discussion. Cyberbullying or online harassment of others online should also be discussed with particular emphasis on its negative effects and how one should respond if this occurs.

Overall health is also impacted by mental processes. Of particular importance is the development of a positive **self-image**, or the way in which a person perceives him or herself. A healthy mind and body can contribute to a positive self-image, but students must be prompted to recognize that no body is perfect.

Practice Question

15) A third-grade teacher wants to help students recognize the early signs of illness. Which activity is MOST appropriate?

A. Students write in a journal about the last time they felt nauseous.
B. Students feel each other's foreheads to see if they have a fever.
C. Students create an infographic about common symptoms of colds and flu.
D. Students complete a questionnaire about how they are feeling.

Movement

Learning movement fundamentals requires understanding movement concepts and possessing fundamental motor skills. Motor skills involve both fine motor skills, or the use of the small muscles in the hands, and gross motor skills involve larger muscle groups. Teaching **movement concepts** helps children increase their understanding of body awareness and management.

The objective of **body awareness** is for students to explore the body's capabilities. In early childhood, students learn to identify and understand the locations of different body parts. They also practice the many shapes and positions they can form with their bodies. Teachers should be aware that development in children follows a **proximodistal** pattern, wherein development begins in the torso and moves outward. It also typically occurs in a **cephalocaudal** pattern, or from the top of the body downward.

Spatial awareness is understanding where the body can move. Teachers should provide ample opportunities for students to explore the spatial qualities of movement. Examples include self-space, general space, pathways, range, and the direction of movement. Students should not only recognize these examples, but also respect the space of others, travel through space in a purposeful manner, and adjust their range of movement depending on the task.

The goal in teaching the **qualities of movement** is for students to understand how balance affects movement and the qualities of static and dynamic balance. Teachers should also help students generate and modify force to accomplish assigned tasks as well as differentiate among speeds so they can move more quickly or slowly. As students progress through the elementary grades, teachers should encourage them to accomplish movements within a certain amount of time and space.

Helpful Hint

Developing body management skills means integrating agility, coordination, balance, and flexibility to create effective movement.

Non-locomotor skills are movements that do not require moving through space. These include bending, stretching, twisting, turning, pushing, and pulling. Object **manipulation skills**, such as volleying, dribbling, punting, or striking a ball are also part of non-locomotor skills development. As students develop their movement skills, teachers should give children ample opportunities to explore them, as well as combine them with locomotor skills so these can be applied to all physical education activities.

Locomotor skills are the numerous ways in which the body can move through space. They include walking, skipping, running, jumping, sliding, galloping, and leaping. Students should be given ample time to practice skills repeatedly after observing a proper demonstration. Students' **rhythmic skills**, or movements to a defined beat while skipping, for example, will also develop with time if given sufficient practice.

When instructing students on walking skills, teachers should demonstrate that each foot alternates and that there is always one foot touching the floor. Instruct students to point toes straight head, keep their eyes forward with their heads up, and with their weight transferred from the heel to the ball of the foot. Students can also practice walking at different speeds, on their toes, or with bent legs.

Students should also be instructed in **basic movement skills** beyond walking, such as how to step with the opposite foot when throwing a ball or completing the kick when using the foot to move a ball. Teachers should be aware that **mature movement patterns**, or the ability to perform a movement skill smoothly and continuously, will take time. Students must master body **control**, or the ability to stabilize and balance the body in a variety of movements.

Sliding involves students moving sideways with a leading foot. Students should focus on keeping the weight on the balls of their feet, eyes focused on the direction of travel, with hips and shoulders pointing to the front. This **locomotor pattern** is commonly used in sports such as softball, basketball, and racquet games. In the younger grades, the focus should be on introducing the basic movements so that students can develop proficiency in different sports as they get older.

Practice Question

16) A teacher wants to create an obstacle course that helps young students develop both fine and gross motor skills. Which stations accomplish both of these goals?

A. small hurdles and a climb-through tunnel
B. skipping and moving clothespins on a line
C. sprinting and jogging for a sustained period
D. doing five sit-ups and then galloping to the finish

Fitness

Health-related fitness includes the development of flexibility, cardiorespiratory endurance, muscular strength, and endurance. **Flexibility** refers to the body's range of motion of joints and can be developed through activities like stretching, yoga, and gymnastics. **Cardiorespiratory endurance** refers to the ongoing ability of the cardiorespiratory organs to get oxygen to the muscles during activity. This type of endurance is an important part of overall health; it is best developed through running, swimming, cycling, and other aerobic exercises. Exercises that promote cardiorespiratory endurance are referred to as **conditioning**.

Muscular strength involves the amount of weight a muscle can move or the amount of force it can produce. Weight training and bodyweight exercises such as push-ups and planks help build muscular strength. General **endurance** refers to the body's ability to sustain a certain physical activity over time, either strength or cardio. Endurance typically improves as physical fitness increases with time.

When designing lessons to promote fitness, teachers should keep in mind the **FITT** (frequency, intensity, time, type) **principle**. This acronym describes guidelines for a fitness plan, and it can be applied to the whole class or to individual students if necessary.

> **Helpful Hint**
>
> Each class and grade level's fitness goals will be different; modifications may be needed to match a lesson plan with the students' current fitness levels.

Frequency refers to how often students should exercise. For example, lifestyle exercises may be scheduled more often rather than endurance ones. The **intensity** of the activity describes how hard students need to work during each class. **Time** refers to how long students should participate in the activity. Students should participate in at least thirty to sixty minutes of age-appropriate physical activity daily, ten minutes of which should be moderate to vigorous activity. The **type** of activity describes the kinds of activities students practice or play. Teachers should create different lessons incorporating a wide variety of lifestyle and recreational activities, active aerobics, flexibility, sports activities, and strength and muscular endurance exercises.

Technology can easily be integrated into physical education as appropriate. Wearable fitness technology, from basic pedometers to advanced heartrate trackers, are one tool. Other technologies include virtual reality fitness programs and fitness gaming.

Practice Question

17) Which movement activity would BEST allow for an integrated unit on Newton's laws of motion?
   A. softball
   B. cross-country running
   C. hurdles
   D. high-intensity interval training

Social Elements of Movement and Fitness

The goal of any physical education program should be to engage all students so that they can improve their physical fitness, learn to enjoy movement and recreation, and develop appropriate social skills. To help students obtain these goals, teachers should be aware of important social aspects related to physical education which may vary based on the individual student.

Research suggests that opportunities to engage in physical activity can improve student confidence and even reduce certain delinquent behaviors. Athletic participation has been proven to foster a positive **school climate**, sense of belonging, and school pride. For maximum benefits, physical education should always be **developmentally appropriate**, or tailored to the developmental level of participants.

In planning developmentally appropriate activities, teachers should consider the physical and social-emotional development of students with a focus on inclusion. Activities that require a high degree of existing physical fitness or specific training are likely to be least appropriate for younger students and may lead to frustration. Similarly, games or activities that students have already mastered may quickly become stale.

Activities will likely include both those that involve **competition**, such as group sports like kickball, soccer, or basketball, and those that do not, such as stretching and dance. While there is some debate about the role of competition in physical education programs, many experts believe that the most important factor is how competitive sports and activities are facilitated. Students must be taught **sportsmanship**, or the belief that sport is, above all, a social interaction that should be enjoyed for its own sake.

There are drawbacks to competition in sports, such as stress and a possible loss of confidence. Students should be encouraged to focus on their own efforts and their own improvement over time versus the outcome of a game reflected in a score. Furthermore, **cooperation** should be emphasized over competition whenever possible. Opportunities for students to work together with each other toward a goal and improve communication and teamwork skills should be nurtured as part of group activities.

As part of participation in physical education activities, teachers should also be aware of differences between cultures. Of particular relevance is the difference between **individualist versus collectivist cultures**. Individualist cultures, like the United States, often value individual achievement and competition. In contrast, collectivist cultures, common in many Asian, African, and Latin American nations, value group success. Teachers should consider both value systems when designing activities so that students have opportunities to learn in familiar and new ways.

Students will also have various fitness levels and activity preferences as well as varied physical abilities. To accommodate all students, some classes employ a station or center approach where students can select from various activities. Other classes use adapted or modified activities. Additionally, teachers should be aware that standards of dress for physical education, such as shorts and t-shirts, may not be aligned with cultural norms that prioritize modesty. Flexibility to accommodate the modesty needs of all students may be required.

Practice Question

18) A first-grade teacher wants to encourage cooperation while building students' movement skills. Which activity would be the MOST appropriate?

A. a kickball game
B. a dodgeball game
C. a relay race
D. a sack race

Answer Key

1) C: Putting a plant in a closet out of the sun and describing how it changes over time will allow students to observe slight changes in a plant through careful observation.

2) C: Having students list two tasks that could be done with each type of simple machine will assesses whether or not students understand the purpose of simple machines in making tasks easier.

3) A: Showing the similarities and differences between plants and animals by using a Venn diagram could help students understand how they both have needs like all living things (e.g., food, water); how they both reproduce and have a life cycle; how they differ in the ways in which they get food; and how they differ in their overall structure or form.

4) B: Seeds are protected in fruits. An apple would illustrate this concept for students since they will be able to see the small seeds inside the larger apple.

5) D: Using an exit ticket where students fill in blanks in sentences using the word *dominant* or *recessive* is an informal assessment. Such sentences can help teachers gauge what students do and do not understand. One example sentence could be, "_________traits are traits for which a person has a gene that is not expressed."

6) D: Sorting pictures of plants and animals into a T- chart would be developmentally appropriate for this age group and help students grasp the concept of plants being producers and animals being consumers.

7) D: Deer would not be able to find the vegetation they need to eat in order to survive and might be hit by cars in an urban environment. On the other hand, humans do just fine in an urban environment. The other options describe organisms that are well-suited to their environments.

8) C: Dew is water vapor in the air that condenses as liquid on the ground; it then evaporates back into gas as the day heats up.

9) D: Identifying the new activities human civilizations could do with each machine connects human interactions with their environment and technology use with the study of simple machines. Students could note how the wheel and axle changed farming and travel and how the screw, pulley, and wedge changed how buildings could be built.

10) A: Gasoline stored in a car's gas tank is an example of chemical potential energy.

11) A: Turning off the tap while brushing teeth in order to save water is the most developmentally appropriate water-related topic for this age range and something that kindergarten students could easily do to make a difference.

12) C: Asking how a new subdivision might change the way in which water moves will extend the students' thinking by getting them to consider how human activities—such as development—can impact the water cycle by creating new paths for water drainage.

13) B: Climate is the overall weather pattern, but weather is a specific event or condition at a certain time.

14) C: When one part of Earth is titled towards the sun, it gets more sunlight and will be summer. Conversely, where there is less sunlight because of the tilt, it will be colder/winter.

15) C: Having students create an infographic about common symptoms of colds and flu is an activity that aligns directly with the goal of helping students recognize the early signs of illness since it helps students learn and internalize the warning signs they should look for.

16) B: Skipping develops large muscle groups (gross motor skills), and moving clothespins develops smaller muscle groups (fine motor skills) in the hands.

17) A: Students could observe the way in which force on the ball (e.g., throwing it, hitting it) leads to the motion of the ball.

18) D: In a sack race, students have to work together, which would encourage cooperation while building students' movement skills.

Practice Test #1

Module 1

1) A kindergartener teacher is using developmentally appropriate ways to instruct his students on the complex concept of physics by letting them observe the speeds at which different objects slide down a ramp. The teacher is implementing the ideas of which theorist?

A. Lev Vygotsky
B. Jerome Bruner
C. Abraham Maslow
D. Howard Gardner

2) Diana, a third-grade student, has a temperature of 102°F and has been vomiting. When the teacher calls home, Diana's mother tells her they just moved to the area, cannot afford health insurance, and do not have a family doctor. The teacher might provide Diana's family with information regarding which of the following?

A. fever-reducing medication
B. how to apply for CHIP or Medicaid
C. local pediatricians
D. the flu shot

3) A teacher is conducting an observation of Jack, one of his first-grade students, to see how many times he engages in aggressive behavior over the course of the morning. Every thirty minutes, he observes Jack for one minute and records each aggressive behavior. The teacher is conducting which type of informal assessment?

A. time-sampling
B. anecdotal notes
C. checklist
D. educator rankings

4) When choosing manipulatives for a kindergarten class, a teacher should choose those that

A. focus on only one skill at a time.
B. can only be used by one child at a time.
C. support learning through observation.
D. support learning through problem-solving.

5) If children are allowed to participate in the development of classroom rules, they will

A. disregard the rules since they were not developed by the teacher.
B. only choose rules that are easy to follow.
C. choose so many rules that they will have a difficult time remembering.
D. be more motivated to follow the rules.

6) Which type of assessment is not driven by data but still measures performance and is used to drive instruction?

A. informal assessment
B. formal assessment
C. norm-referenced assessment
D. criterion-referenced assessment

7) In order for assessments to BEST support learning and development, they should

A. be administered whenever the teacher feels they are necessary.
B. only be administered at the end of each unit.
C. correspond to the dates children are expected to master certain concepts.
D. only be administered at the beginning, middle, and end of the year.

8) Which of the following describes the idea that all experiences are learned through interactions with the environment by way of classical or operant conditioning, and that the mind is a *tabula rasa* at birth?

A. behaviorism
B. cognitive development theory
C. constructivism
D. social development theory

9) A second-grade teacher wants to assess student retainment of skills at the end of a small-group intervention aimed at vocabulary acquisition. Which method of assessment should the teacher use?

A. administer a norm-referenced assessment
B. ask students to write two sentences using two new words they learned
C. ask students to write a list of all the new words that were introduced in the session
D. administer a standardized achievement test

10) Which of the following children is MOST clearly in need of further assessment for an apparent delay in physical development?

A. a third grader who struggles to hold a pencil
B. a first grader who runs more slowly than her older sister
C. a fifth grader who cannot do a pull up
D. a kindergartner who can only catch with both hands

11) Which of the following may be an indication of atypical language development?

A. frequent hunger
B. insubordinate behavior
C. limited working memory
D. an interest in visual images

12) A third-grade teacher wants to develop an assessment tool to evaluate student's oral presentations. Which tool would be MOST appropriate?

A. anecdotal notes
B. portfolio
C. analytical checklist
D. rubric

13) A fourth-grade teacher wants to offer multiple means of engagement in the classroom. Which assignment BEST embodies this principle?

A. writing a formal essay with MLA citations about a literary work that you have read
B. recording a video that includes sound and visual effects describing your educational background
C. creating a digital schedule of when you will study for tests
D. writing a letter to the editor or recording a public service message about an issue you see as a problem

14) Which of the following is the MOST common way to assess students for appropriate social-emotional development?

A. rating scale
B. observation
C. anecdotal notes
D. parent conferences

15) The parent of a kindergarten student informs the teacher that the student's brother is having surgery in the coming weeks. How should the teacher respond?

A. with an awareness that such an event in the student's microsystem may have an impact on the student
B. with concern that the student's macrosystem may be unable to offer the student support during this time
C. with indifference because exosystem relationships do not impact the student directly
D. with appreciation because the parent is inviting the teacher into a new and lasting chronosystem

16) A teacher using Bandura's social learning theory would need to ensure that students have which of the following?

A. motivation to learn what is being taught
B. others who are more capable and can demonstrate new ideas
C. opportunities for intrapersonal reflection
D. multiple exposures to information

17) A prekindergarten teacher notes that a student who has been in multiple foster homes since birth exhibits extreme anxiety and insecurity. What can the teacher conclude about this student per Erikson's stages of psychosocial development?

A. that the student was not given adequate opportunities to exert independence
B. that the student has become mistrusting because of unpredictable relationships
C. that the student has lacked encouragement to engage with peers
D. that the student has had to rebel against authority figures as part of self-advocacy

18) The school cafeteria runs out of standard 8 oz. cups, so it gives some students the standard 6 oz. of milk in a 12 oz. cup. A kindergarten student becomes very upset by this claiming that others "got more milk" than she did. What does this student not yet understand?

A. object permanence
B. volume versus mass
C. conservation
D. weight versus mass

19) When does MOST of a child's brain development occur?
   A. in the first eighteen months
   B. in the first five years
   C. in the first seven years
   D. in the first twelve years

20) According to Bowen's family systems theory, what happens when parents believe something is wrong with their child?
   A. The child may distance herself from the parent.
   B. The parent may pressure the spouse to change.
   C. The parent may try to control the child.
   D. The child may begin to actually exhibit the problem.

21) A young child had only seen brown horses in videos. After being taken to a farm and seeing a gray horse, the child has a new understanding that horses come in several colors other than brown. Which word describes this event?
   A. assimilation
   B. transference
   C. scaffolding
   D. synapsing

22) What is the predictable sequence of physical development in children?
   A. development from the inner body to the outer body
   B. development from the bottom of the body to the top
   C. development of the fingers and toes before the arms and legs
   D. development of fine motor skills before gross motor skills

23) A teacher is considering multiple passages for use on a curriculum-based assessment to evaluate inferencing skills. Which passage would be MOST appropriate?
   A. one that includes a glossary or footnoted vocabulary words
   B. one that contains text features, like headings and italics
   C. one that presents few graphics or illustrations
   D. one that requires limited background knowledge to understand

24) A prekindergarten teacher is having a conference with a student's mother, who has expressed concern that the child frequently misspells words that she uses to label pictures she draws. Which of the following is the advice the teacher should give the student's mother?
   A. have the student focus on a few target spelling words each week until she begins to label her pictures correctly
   B. not to worry since the student is in the invented spelling phase, which is a natural part of literacy development
   C. not to worry since the student is receiving lots of targeted phonics practice in school but that the child should still go back and correct these pictures
   D. have the student focus on learning new vocabulary each day as this will help with her overall spelling development

25) In a conference with the parents of a second-grade student, a teacher wants to provide suggestions for practice at home to improve fluency. Which strategy should the teacher suggest?

A. timed silent reading
B. cloze exercises
C. reading aloud to a younger sibling
D. listening to an older sibling read aloud

26) Per FERPA, to whom can a student's assessment results be released?

A. any immediate family member
B. any school official
C. a school to which the student is transferring
D. a school that plans to use it for comparison purposes

27) What does the research base suggest about the overrepresentation of Black and Latino students in special education programs?

A. The overrepresentation is largely due to cultural factors that prioritize collectivism versus individualism.
B. The overrepresentation is largely due to systemic bias in identification procedures.
C. The overrepresentation is largely exaggerated, and most students are placed appropriately.
D. The overrepresentation is largely because of inefficient classroom management in urban school settings.

28) An IEP annual review meeting has been scheduled for a third-grade student who is currently in a general education classroom full time. How would the student's general education teacher MOST likely participate in this meeting?

A. by recommending additional ancillary supports, such as one-on-one instruction
B. by presenting information on what to expect on the upcoming PSSA test
C. by explaining how the student is performing in the classroom
D. by analyzing the IEP for possible omissions

29) A fourth-grade teacher is planning a hands-on activity where students take a walk on the school grounds to identify a service project they can undertake. One of the students in the class has an orthopedic impairment and uses a wheelchair. Which of the following accommodations would BEST help this student participate in this activity?

A. videorecording the walk and showing the video to the student at a later time
B. having two students designated to carry the student and the wheelchair through inaccessible spaces
C. stopping frequently during the walk to allow the student to rest
D. preplanning the route to ensure that the student can access it freely in the wheelchair

30) A kindergarten student with autism spectrum disorder (ASD) is in a general education classroom most of the time but also receives specialized behavioral interventions from a behavioral specialist. How could the general education teacher BEST partner with the specialist?

A. by recording videos of model behaviors to show to the student
B. by experimenting with new consequences for undesirable behaviors
C. by reinforcing the techniques being used by the specialist
D. by encouraging the specialist to observe other students in the classroom

31) A third-grade teacher wants to help students become self-directed learners who set and meet learning goals. To this end, the teacher begins posting students' grades on a poster in the classroom so that they can see their progress. What is the primary reason for which this practice is NOT appropriate?

A. It encourages students to focus on grades over other indicators of growth.
B. It infringes on the rights of students to have their grades to be kept confidential.
C. It may lead to academic competition among students.
D. It provides students with limited information on how they can improve.

32) Before planning a unit on different foods and dress from around the world, a first-grade teacher sends a letter to parents asking for their input and assistance in planning an end-of-unit multicultural celebration. This practice is likely to be MOST effective in helping the teacher achieve which of the following goals?

A. reinforcing to families an awareness of a shared global culture
B. connecting families with each other to share resources
C. providing resources beyond what the school itself can provide
D. showing families a desire to form beneficial partnerships

33) In a routine conference with the parents of a kindergarten student, a teacher discovers that many of the academic expectations the parents have for their child—a very bright five-year old—are unreasonable. What is the BEST course of action for the teacher to take?

A. to discuss the importance of developmental appropriateness in learning goals
B. to emphasize the progress the student has already made
C. to encourage the family to focus more on moral development than academics
D. to highlight the dangers of untrained professionals teaching a child

34) Professional development for teachers is likely to NOT be effective when it

A. is sustained over a long period of time.
B. involves staff from multiple departments.
C. lacks clear alignment with classroom practices.
D. involves few opportunities for action research.

35) A group of teachers with diverse philosophies and teaching styles has come together at an elementary school to evaluate a new suite of instructional materials for possible adoption. What is MOST important for the group to consider?

A. whether the materials can calibrate teaching among the different classrooms
B. whether the materials are aligned with the universal design for learning
C. whether the materials contain both digital and paper components
D. whether the materials will be updated with regularity by the publisher

36) A second-grade general education teacher is assigned a paraprofessional to assist in the implementation of IEP goals for two students in the class. What can the teacher do to BEST support the paraprofessional?

A. limit the duties of the paraprofessional to interaction solely with these two students
B. provide the paraprofessional with a daily list of administrative duties to complete
C. encourage the paraprofessional to provide whole-group instruction
D. give the paraprofessional information on the core curriculum and classroom resources

37) What is the MOST important reason for teachers to develop cross-cultural competence?
- A. to establish a positive climate for learning
- B. to understand parent concerns
- C. to develop global citizens
- D. to comply with federal guidelines

Module 2

1) Which assessment technique would MOST effectively measure a student's expressive vocabulary?
- A. having the student point to the picture that matches a spoken word
- B. asking the student to describe her family or some topic about which she is familiar
- C. having the student read aloud a paragraph that contains many new words
- D. asking the student to write down as many words as possible in a two-minute period

2) A teacher working with emergent readers asks, "What word am I trying to say, /p/ /i/ /n/?" and instructs students to say the word. Which strategy is the teacher using to build phoneme awareness?
- A. phoneme blending
- B. phoneme deletion
- C. phoneme segmentation
- D. phoneme substitution

3) A first-grade student is sounding out the word *flat*. He sounds out the word *f-l-a-t*. Which of the following is true about this student?
- A. He lacks basic knowledge of the alphabetic principle.
- B. He needs more practice with affixes.
- C. He sounded out each letter individually versus the onset and rime.
- D. He has a strong knowledge of consonant blends.

4) What is the purpose of sight word instruction in an elementary classroom?
- A. to help students learn letter-sound correspondences to improve accuracy
- B. to help students manipulate sounds in words to improve auditory skills
- C. to help students recognize words automatically to improve fluency
- D. to help students use word parts to improve reading comprehension

5) A teacher is working on a unit on forming the past tenses of verbs with his second-grade class. Which of the following would be the MOST appropriate writing assignment to ensure sufficient practice with this skill?
- A. writing a paragraph that compares and contrasts cars and trucks
- B. writing a paragraph about what students did over the winter break
- C. writing a description of students' living rooms
- D. writing a persuasive paragraph about students' favorite colors

6) In a unit on morphology, a fourth-grade teacher wants to give students a list of the most common roots. Most of the English roots on the list will have originally come from which languages?
- A. German or French
- B. Spanish or French
- C. Latin or Greek
- D. French or Greek

7) A third-grade teacher wants to model the process of metacognition during reading as a precursor to fix-up strategies. Which question would she MOST likely use?

A. What genre is this?
B. How are the characters developed?
C. Do I understand this paragraph?
D. Where can I learn more about this topic?

8) A teacher wants to give first-grade students a summative sight word assessment. Which of the following is the BEST way to conduct this assessment?

A. direct the students to write the sight words from memory within a given time limit
B. ask the students to read from a sight word list while the teacher circles the words they know
C. have students sound out each sight word as the teacher presents it to them on a note card
D. encourage students to clap out the beats as they repeat each word after the teacher

9) A second-grade teacher wants to improve students' decoding skills. Which of the following would be the MOST effective instructional strategy?

A. introducing character analysis
B. teaching word families
C. encouraging finger tracking
D. demonstrating think-alouds

10) A fourth-grade student often drops the *-s* in verbs while speaking ("She go to the store.") This is consistent with the way her parents speak. How is this BEST described?

A. dialect
B. bridging
C. code-switching
D. preproduction

11) Which assessment tool is MOST effective for tracking progress in oral reading fluency?

A. portfolios
B. reader's theater
C. running records
D. phonics screeners

12) A third-grade teacher wants students to practice evaluative comprehension after reading an argumentative essay on school uniforms. Which activity BEST meets this goal?

A. Students write a summary of the author's main claim and list the support the author provided.
B. Students identify and label all of the facts and opinions in the essay.
C. Students get in pairs and discuss the strengths and weaknesses of the author's argument.
D. Students get in groups and write a list of questions they have after reading the essay.

13) A second-grade teacher is reading and responding to student writing. The teacher reads the following sentence written by a student:

Lucy thought the first movie was better then the second one.

What feedback should the teacher give the student?

A. The verbs should be in the present tense.
B. *Then* indicates time, not comparison.
C. *One* is a dangling modifier.
D. The subject is misplaced.

14) Which types of words should students be able to spell correctly by the end of third grade?

A. most four syllable words
B. most contractions
C. most cognates
D. most multi-meaning words

15) A fourth-grade teacher uses the Frayer model in both reading and content-area instruction. How is this tool helpful to students?

A. It aids in vocabulary acquisition.
B. It teaches fix-up strategies.
C. It aids in the annotation of key details.
D. It teaches the synthesis of information throughout the text.

16) At mid-year, a third-grade teacher receives a new student with expanding English language proficiency. During the ten minutes of sustained silent reading time that the class participates in every afternoon, what is the MOST important factor for this teacher to consider?

A. whether the reading material given to the student has idioms
B. whether the reading material given to the student is appropriately leveled
C. whether the student will understand how to read silently
D. whether the student will feel uncomfortable with the silence in the classroom

17) A third-grade teacher wants to model inferencing strategies while reading an informational text. Which strategy is MOST appropriate?

A. drawing a plot pyramid
B. filling in a KWL chart
C. conducting a think-aloud
D. showing fix-up strategies

18) After giving a benchmark assessment, a fourth-grade teacher determines that students need more practice with writing a cohesive paragraph. Which activity is MOST likely to meet this goal?

A. instruction in task and audience
B. practicing both self and peer revision strategies
C. using the COPS mnemonic
D. identifying relevant support for the topic sentence

19) At which age are children with typical development able to name familiar objects?
   A. six months
   B. twelve months
   C. two years
   D. three years

20) A kindergarten teacher notes that a student struggles to remember the sounds that letters make. What kind of exercises would BEST benefit this student?
   A. those aimed at graphophonemic skills
   B. those aimed at print awareness
   C. those aimed at orthographic processing
   D. those aimed at phonological processing

21) At the beginning of the year, a prekindergarten teacher wants to assess students' understanding of concepts of print. Which assessment is MOST likely to glean this data?
   A. having students select a book of interest off a shelf
   B. having students identify a letter and word in a text
   C. having students write their names using invented spelling
   D. having students point to a letter as its sound is said orally

22) A second-grade teacher has a student with dyslexia in the general education classroom. The student often struggles with losing her place while reading a connected text. Which strategy is MOST likely to help this student?
   A. the use of audio texts
   B. teaching fix-up strategies
   C. text annotation
   D. finger tracking

23) One similarity between first and second language development is that they BOTH
   A. require explicit instruction.
   B. include interlanguage effects.
   C. involve a silent period.
   D. center around morphology.

24) During the first week of school, a third-grade teacher observes students' oral language skills. What is the MOST important reason for this?
   A. to identify the level of familiarity with academic language
   B. to determine whether students have a particular dialect
   C. to plan opportunities for social-emotional development
   D. to note familiarity with appropriate intonation

25) A student in a first-grade class is struggling to sound out basic CVC words because of phonological deficits. What will this student MOST likely also find difficult?
   A. print awareness
   B. encoding
   C. previewing
   D. listening skills

26) A second-grade teacher is using running records to track oral reading fluency. In addition to tracking skipped words, repeated words, and other errors, the teacher assigns a holistic score of 1, 2, or 3 as an assessment of student expressiveness while reading. This primarily focuses on which aspect of reading fluency?

A. automaticity
B. rate
C. prosody
D. decoding

27) A third-grade teacher wants to help students improve their writing by using a voice appropriate for an academic context. Which revision strategies could BEST help students as they work to refine their work?

A. looking for simple sentences that could be combined to form compound sentences
B. identifying the writing task and deleting any sentences not supporting that task
C. reorganizing the piece using a general-to-specific framework
D. adding appropriate topic sentences near the beginning of each paragraph

28) In an integrated ELA and social studies unit, fourth-grade students will research and compose a report on an important figure in Pennsylvania history. Which step should students take before they write the report?

A. create a bibliography of primary and secondary sources
B. decide on which graphic elements to include
C. search for reliable sources
D. identify an appropriate citation style

29) A fourth-grade teacher wants to help students better understand the role of commas as a punctuation convention in writing. Which activity would promote this understanding?

A. reading poems with commas at the end of each line
B. reading written work aloud and pausing at each comma
C. composing a formal letter that includes at least one comma
D. interviewing a professional writer about the use of commas

30) To help students expand their vocabulary based on root words they already know, they can be instructed in

A. common derivational morphemes
B. etymologies
C. creating and using word walls
D. syllabication

31) A teacher is searching online and in her curriculum resources for a map to introduce her second-grade class to the idea of a legend. Which map would be the BEST resource for her to use?

A. a political map of the United States showing each state in the same color
B. a topographical map showing different elevations
C. a map that uses corncob icons to denote the major corn-producing states in the United States
D. a map that includes latitude and longitude

32) A teacher wants to integrate math standards into a third-grade social studies lesson on charts. Which question will BEST accomplish this goal?

A. What is the difference between the populations of the two cities with the highest and lowest populations?
B. Why are the columns and rows on each part of the chart labeled in different colors?
C. After calculating the mean population of all the cities on the chart, is this country at risk of overpopulation?
D. What information (columns or rows) could be added to the chart to give additional information about each city?

33) A second-grade teacher asks her class the following question: "What kind of houses would people living in forests most likely build?" What is she trying to help students understand?

A. the relationship between conservation and resource depletion
B. economic interdependence
C. how people use natural resources
D. the ways in which the global economy and the environment impact each other

34) A second-grade teacher wants to show how a feeling of security might be different in another culture. Which example would BEST illustrate this?

A. a typical American home that is safe and warm
B. different clothing styles worn by members of a South American cultural group
C. a mud hut located in a small rural village
D. a person who does not get along with her parents

35) A third-grade class reads an article about a community of people in a rain forest environment who are experiencing dramatic changes in their way of life because loggers are cutting down the trees in their home. What concept is the class learning?

A. that economic development is never as important as maintaining biodiversity
B. that part of global citizenship is taking action
C. that humans are dependent on their environments
D. that there can always be compromise when different cultures interact

36) Teachers could BEST use a history unit on the founding of Pennsylvania to promote student understanding of which of the following principles?

A. republicanism
B. freedom of religion
C. free enterprise
D. abolition

37) A fourth-grade teacher wants to plan an activity to address the following social studies standard: *Explain the role of buyers and sellers in determining prices of products.*

Which activity is MOST likely to meet this goal?

A. having students interview an entrepreneur about business operations
B. having students work the register at the school store
C. having students create a multimedia presentation on supply and demand
D. having students perform a skit where a buyer makes a car purchase

38) A sorting exercise would likely provide the most appropriate and effective means of assessing student mastery of which of the following first-grade social studies standards?

A. describing which tools are necessary to complete a task
B. identifying individuals who work for wages in the community
C. identifying classroom wants and needs
D. explaining why cultures celebrate

39) A kindergarten teacher wants to promote the development of a sense of belonging in the classroom. Which of the following activities BEST meets this goal?

A. having an event where parents visit during the school day
B. inviting an administrator to give a talk about the importance of school pride
C. reading a story to the class about different ways to celebrate birthdays
D. giving students roles in the classroom, such as updating the date or weather chart

40) Which of the following would be an appropriate activity for first graders during a simple lesson on rhythm?

A. The teacher makes loud and soft sounds on a drum.
B. The teacher plays a pattern on the drum, and students try to repeat it.
C. Students listen to different percussion instruments.
D. The teacher plays music at different speeds and students clap to indicate the tempo.

41) A first-grade art teacher wants to encourage her students to use texture in their art. Which medium/project would be BEST for this purpose?

A. a pastel drawing
B. an acrylic painting
C. a feather collage
D. a pinch pot vase

42) On a field trip to an art museum, a third-grade teacher stops the class in front of a canvas painted half black and half white. What principles of art might he discuss as they pertain to this painting?

A. contrast and proportion
B. movement and balance
C. pattern and emphasis
D. emphasis and movement

43) A first-grade teacher wants to integrate an art and math lesson with the objective of having students determine which shape comes next in a sequence. Which principle of art could she apply?

A. unity
B. emphasis
C. pattern
D. contrast

44) A student with limited verbal skills could participate in a theatrical production by

A. developing a unique character tag
B. providing sound effects on cue with percussion instruments
C. performing a soliloquy to an empty room
D. delivering a monologue that has been memorized ahead of time

45) During a dance rehearsal, students are continually bumping into each other. What do they need more practice with?
A. keeping sufficient negative space
B. identifying personal space
C. kinesthetic awareness
D. synchronization

Module 3

1) A second-grade class is learning about the properties of two-dimensional shapes. Which of the following activities would BEST reinforce the concept of perimeter?
A. using modeling clay to make solid figures
B. working on a jigsaw puzzle
C. using toilet paper tubes to create a windsock
D. throwing a basketball through a hoop

2) A second-grade teacher is teaching her students how to count money. Which of the following skills should students have before starting the lesson?
A. decomposing numbers
B. subitizing
C. division
D. skip counting

3) Decomposing helps reinforce which of the following mathematical concepts?
A. place value
B. cardinality
C. addition
D. skip counting

4) A teacher is introducing equivalent fractions. Which of the following could he use to show an application of this skill?
A. reducing a very large fraction
B. finding the reciprocal of a fraction
C. drawing a visual fraction model
D. working with unit fractions

5) Which of the following equations could a teacher use as an example of the commutative property?
A. $5 + 3 = 4 + 4$
B. $5 + 3 = 3 + 5$
C. $5 \times 3 = 15 \times 1$
D. $5 + 3 = 3 \times 5$

6) A second-grade teacher wants to have her students collect data and create a bar graph. Which of the following would be the BEST question for her to give her students?
A. How does the temperature outside change during the day?
B. What percentage of students like different types of ice cream?
C. What is the relationship between a plant's age and height?
D. Which classroom has the largest number of students?

7) A teacher wants students to think critically about mean, median, mode, and range, so he presents them with the following problem:
Kelly took three quizzes. She scored 80 on quiz 1, 90 on quiz 2, and 82 on quiz 3. Her final midterm grade was 84.

If students understand the definitions of each term correctly, they should be able to determine that Kelly's midterm score is based on which of the following?

A. mode
B. median
C. range
D. mean

8) After exploring the properties of cubes, a teacher asks students to suggest a method for finding the surface area. Which of the following answers demonstrates an understanding of both the properties of cubes and the concept of surface area?

A. Multiply the length by the height of one of its faces.
B. Find the area of one face and multiply by 6 since a cube has six square faces.
C. Measure the amount of space occupied inside it.
D. Find the area of the faces that are visible when the cube is resting on a table.

9) A student was asked to find the factors of 36. She writes "36, 72, 108, ..." Which of the following is the MOST likely reason for the student's error?

A. She does not know her multiplication facts.
B. She does not know the difference between prime factors and composite factors.
C. She has confused the terms *factors* and *multiples*.
D. She does not recognize the relationship between multiplication and division.

10) A student gave the following answer to an addition problem:

$$\begin{array}{r} 27 \\ \underline{+\,57} \\ 714 \end{array}$$

Which of the following values will the student likely give as the answer to the problem *392 + 273*?

A. 84
B. 104
C. 1,539
D. 5,165

11) A first-grade teacher asked the students in her class to place 8 counters on each of their desks. She then asked them to add counters to their pile so that there were 12 counters. Some students placed 4 more counters on their desks; however, other students counted out 12 more counters to add to their piles. Which of the following MOST likely explains the error of the second group of students?

A. They do not know their addition facts for sums greater than 10.
B. They do not fully understand one-to-one correspondence between numbers and objects.
C. They do not yet have a concept of the number 12.
D. They do not yet understand that one quantity can be composed of two smaller quantities.

12) A teacher is introducing students to rounding decimal places. A student's work is shown below:
Round 3689.247 to the nearest tenth. 3689.2

Which of the following problems would provide the teacher with additional information about this student's understanding of rounding?

A. Round 6.914 to the nearest tenth.
B. Round 73.241 to the nearest hundredth.
C. Round 24.3785 to the nearest thousandth.
D. Round 2.719 to the nearest tenth.

13) Which of the following operations is needed to solve the problem shown below?
Dave has 312 feet of trim. If he cuts the trim into 10 equal pieces, how long will each piece be?

A. division
B. multiplication
C. addition
D. subtraction

14) For the problem shown below, a student writes the answer as 15:20. Which question below should the teacher ask the student to help him correct his own work?
15 out of 20 students passed the test. What is the ratio of passing grades to failing grades in lowest terms?

A. What is considered a passing grade?
B. How many students failed the test?
C. Will the ratio reduce?
D. In what other forms can the ratio be written?

15) Which of the following tools would be MOST useful for promoting preschool students' skills in identifying shapes?

A. a sand table where students can draw with fingers
B. developmentally appropriate puzzles
C. manipulatives
D. clay

16) A teacher gives the students the following images and puts them in pairs with the task of describing the relationship they see:

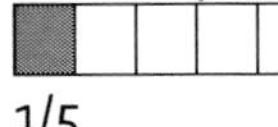

1/5

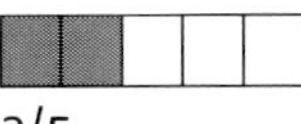

2/5

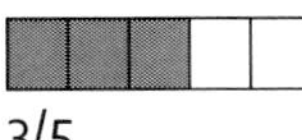

3/5

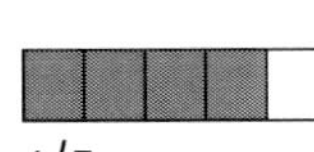

4/5

Which of the following is the relationship students are MOST likely meant to glean?

A. When the numerator stays the same and the denominator increases, the fraction increases.
B. When the numerator increases and the denominator stays the same, the fraction increases.
C. When the numerator and the denominator increase, the fraction decreases.
D. When the numerator stays the same and the denominator decreases, the fraction decreases.

17) Which of the following life-cycle topics is the MOST developmentally appropriate for prekindergarten students?

A. the life cycle of a pumpkin
B. the life cycle of the stars
C. the evolution of reproduction and heredity
D. the metamorphosis of a butterfly

18) A kindergarten teacher sets up a science center with an activity that asks students to sort objects into magnetic and nonmagnetic piles. Which of the following is the teacher trying to develop in students through the science center?

A. hypothesizing
B. exploration
C. confirming
D. classification

19) Which of the following learning activities would be MOST authentic in teaching second graders the life cycle of a plant?

A. The students use an interactive computer program to see the life cycle of a plant.
B. The students plant a seed and record what happens as the plant grows.
C. The students draw a diagram and label the parts of the plant.
D. The students listen to a story and learn about the life cycle of a plant.

20) A second-grade teacher sets up a science center with an activity that has 4 candy canes and 4 glasses, each filled with a different liquid. The liquids are warm water, cold water, oil, and vinegar. The students are instructed to hypothesize which liquid they think will dissolve a candy cane the quickest and then test their predictions. The teacher is trying to encourage student predictions on which of the following?

A. physical properties
B. physical change
C. density
D. reactions

21) A first-grade teacher wants to use a summative assessment tool to track student scientific growth over time. Which tool BEST meets this goal?

A. a benchmark test
B. a portfolio
C. an exit ticket
D. a discussion

22) After a lesson on photosynthesis, a third-grade teacher notes that several students are confusing the role of carbon dioxide. Which reteaching strategy is MOST appropriate?

A. having students research photosynthesis on their own and present what they learned
B. going back to fill in knowledge gaps about organic chemical compounds
C. using visual models that reinforce an understanding of the compounds created
D. encouraging students to observe plants in the process of photosynthesis

23) A fourth-grade class helps manage the school's garden. After hearing about integrated pest management (IPM), the teacher decides to help students employ this approach. Which step would students MOST likely complete?

A. setting target output for the garden
B. identifying pest thresholds for action
C. introducing predator pests into the garden
D. removing problem plants that deplete soil

24) A second-grade teacher is holding a class discussion on renewable and nonrenewable energy. A student does not understand why oil is considered a nonrenewable energy source because more can be taken from the ground when the gas station runs out. Which of the following facts about fossil fuels should the teacher cover in order to aid the student's understanding?

A. the role of fossil fuels in environmental degradation and the greenhouse effect
B. the explanation of how fossil fuels come from organisms that lived long ago
C. the prediction of scientists about when fossil fuel resources will be depleted
D. the properties of fossil fuels that make them suitable for combustion

25) As part of a hands-on lab activity, a second-grade teacher sets up a station with salt, sugar, oil, sports drink powder, and food coloring. She asks students to add a tablespoon of each of these substances to a clear glass with 6 ounces of water in it. Which topic is the teacher MOST likely introducing?

A. physical and chemical properties
B. states of matter
C. density
D. solubility

26) A third-grade teacher wants to introduce the topic of erosion. Which social studies topic could be integrated?

A. the Silk Road
B. the Dust Bowl
C. the Revolutionary War
D. the Civil War

27) A fourth-grade teacher wants to help students understand the role of humans in the water cycle. Which illustration BEST meets this goal?

A. a dam that changes the path of a river
B. increases and decreases in annual rainfall
C. the need for refrigeration to keep food cold
D. an aquifer that is used for swimming

28) Which of the following assessment methods would be MOST appropriate for a prekindergarten teacher wanting to evaluate student understanding of weather?

A. asking students to predict the temperature outside based on how hot or cool it feels
B. having students use a weather map to determine high and low pressure areas
C. asking students to orally explain the difference between weather and climate
D. having students point to a picture that shows how the weather is on that day

29) While on the playground, a second-grade class notices that even though a building and a fence seem to be blocking its way, a large tree has simply grown its branches around the obstructions. Using the students' observations would be an appropriate way to introduce which of the following life science concepts?

A. keystone species
B. primary succession
C. adaptation
D. heredity

30) A third-grade teacher is planning to introduce the following standard:
Explore how energy can be found in moving objects, light, sound, and heat.

How could this standard be BEST integrated with another science concept?

A. a discussion of why speed limits are necessary
B. an exploration of solar panels
C. a description of why food is cooked
D. an explanation of why music sounds different live

31) A third-grade student believes that the moon changes shape. What information should the teacher introduce to help the student understand why the moon appears to change shape?

A. information about eclipses and the moon's appearance
B. an explanation of Earth's axial tilt and the moon
C. an explanation of how sunlight hits the moon
D. information about how weather impacts the moon

32) Science lessons in a classroom guided by constructivist learning theory are MOST likely to involve which of the following?

A. direct instruction followed by guided practice
B. peer tutoring
C. exploration stations
D. independent practice and flexible grouping

33) A kindergarten teacher hoping to integrate physical education into everyday instruction tosses a beanbag to students each morning during circle time. Which skill is she helping her students develop?

A. spatial awareness
B. fundamental motor skills
C. body awareness
D. self-care skills

34) Which of the following is a good practice for first-grade teachers to employ during outside play or recess time?

A. ensuring that all play is structured
B. providing constant scaffolding to students
C. encouraging students to stretch their bodies to their physical limits
D. signaling the beginning and end of play time with both visual and verbal cues

35) For optimum health, how much physical activity should children participate in each day?

A. 30 – 60 minutes
B. 60 – 90 minutes
C. 90 – 120 minutes
D. more than 120 minutes

36) Which of the following is true of the process of students developing new locomotor patterns?

A. They frequently lose skills they once had.
B. They can develop these skills on their own without instruction.
C. They will need repetition to master these skills.
D. They will struggle to apply these skills in unstructured play.

37) Which of the following activities would be appropriate for a first-grade class to participate in to work on understanding mental health?

A. filling out a questionnaire to determine their conflict resolution style
B. learning about different types of psychiatric disorders and how they are treated
C. a discussion of how to maintain healthy relationships with friends and family members
D. organizing a guest speaker to talk to the class about life in an inpatient psychiatric facility

38) Which of the following goals is MOST important to develop in students participating in movement education programs?

A. proficiencies in multiple sports and games
B. enough cardiorespiratory endurance to run half a mile without stopping
C. a lifelong commitment to participation in physical activity
D. an ability to lead a team in a physical activity

39) A five-year-old child's *inability* to perform which of the following tasks could indicate a need for further assessment of the child's motor development?

A. hitting a tennis ball with a racket
B. picking up a tennis ball
C. doing a cartwheel
D. running a quarter of a mile without stopping

40) A fourth-grade class makes a weekly exercise schedule as part of a health assignment. The primary benefit of this type of activity is that it

A. promotes a positive self-image
B. drives responsible decision-making
C. encourages responsibility and accountability
D. builds a connection between home and school

41) The focus of lessons on healthy eating for early elementary students should be primarily be based upon which of the following?

A. daily caloric intake
B. vitamin deficiencies
C. eating disorders
D. a balanced diet

42) A first-grade teacher notices that as students are moving from center to center in the classroom, they frequently bump into furniture and chairs. What type of movement lessons would help these students BEST?

A. spatial awareness activities
B. manipulation skills
C. locomotor skills
D. movement pattern activities

43) A second-grade teacher has a student who uses a wheelchair in her class. The movement activities MOST appropriate for this student are those that

A. involve non-locomotor skills.
B. require mature movement patterns.
C. focus only on fine motor skills.
D. can be completed in isolation.

44) A kindergarten teacher wanting to teach students appropriate emotional regulation would first need to ensure that students are able to do which of the following?

A. react unemotionally to mistakes
B. identify their emotions
C. sort emotions into categories
D. learn to solve problems without emotions

Practice Test #1 Answer Key

Module 1

1) B: Bruner's modes of representation are not age based and present the idea that any subject can be taught at any age, as long as it is modified for the appropriate form and stage of the learner.

2) B: Since Diana's family cannot afford health insurance, sharing information about the community's free or income-based health clinics would be most appropriate in this situation.

3) A: Mr. Winter is conducting a time-sampling assessment. With this type of evaluation, a teacher observes and records the number of times in which a student engages in a skill or behavior at different time intervals.

4) D: Class materials should support learning through problem-solving.

5) D: If children are allowed to participate in the development of classroom rules, they will be more motivated to follow them.

6) A: Informal assessments are not data-driven but still measure performance and are used to plan instruction. The other answer options are data-driven assessment types.

7) C: In order to gain accurate information and plan for instruction, assessments should be administered according to the dates during which children are learning certain concepts.

8) A: Behaviorism presents the idea that all of our experiences are learned through interactions with our environment by way of classical or operant conditioning and that, at birth, our mind is a blank slate—a *tabula rasa*.

9) B: Asking students to write two sentences using two new words they learned is a short, informal assessment that gives the teacher the needed data about what has been retained from the session.

10) A: The ability to hold a pencil is a fine motor skill that should be developed well before third grade.

11) C: Though this may not seem directly related to language, struggles with working memory can—but not always—be indicative of atypical language development.

12) D: A rubric would help to not only score the presentations in a consistent manner but also to help students prepare their presentations if they are given the rubric beforehand and know the criteria on which they will be evaluated.

13) D: Writing a letter to the editor or recording a public service message about an issue you see as a problem is an authentic context and allows student choice, so this is multiple means of engagement per the universal design for learning (UDL).

14) B: Most problems with social-emotional development are apparent during everyday interactions and classroom observations as students interact with each other.

15) A: Per the ecological systems theory, the family is a key part of the child's microsystem; therefore, what happens in the family can have a huge impact on the individual.

16) A: Motivation is a key part of Bandura's theory because people will not perform a learned behavior unless they have the motivation to do so.

17) B: The student has likely experienced inconsistent and unreliable care during the earliest months of life (trust versus mistrust), which has resulted in the child being mistrusting.

18) C: The child does not yet understand the concept of conservation—the idea that weight, volume, and numbers stay the same even if there are changes in appearance.

19) B: Ninety percent of a child's brain develops in the first five years of life, making early education essential.

20) D: According to Bowen, the "family projection process" is when a parent's belief that there is a problem with the child becomes a self-fulfilling prophecy.

21) A: Per Piaget, assimilation means taking in new knowledge and combining it with existing knowledge. The child knew of horses but did not know that they come in multiple colors. The child assimilated this new information into existing schema.

22) A: Typical physical development is from the inner body to the outer body and from the top of the body to the bottom.

23) D: A text that requires limited background knowledge to understand is the least biased text to use for an assessment to evaluate inferencing skills. This is because it will not put students who do not have this specific type of background knowledge at a disadvantage.

24) B: The mother likely just needs the teacher's reassurance that this is a natural part of the child's development.

25) C: Reading aloud to a younger sibling is most likely to improve fluency and be achievable in a home environment.

26) C: Any of the other releases would be unlawful under the Family Educational Rights and Privacy Act (FERPA).

27) B: Research suggests that Black and Latino students are overrepresented in special education programs because of problems in assessment, such as standardized test instruments that do not account for cultural or language differences and subjective evaluators who may be unconsciously biased.

28) C: Since the general education teacher best speaks to the student's academic performance in the classroom, the teacher would most likely participate in an individualized education program (IEP) annual review meeting by explaining how the student is performing in the general education classroom.

29) D: The student must be given the same access to the activity, so preplanning the route to ensure that the student can access it freely in the wheelchair is the best course of action.

30) C: Reinforcing the techniques being used by the specialist will aid in continuity and help the student receive consistent interventions.

31) B: Per the Family Educational Rights and Privacy Act (FERPA), student academic records, including grades, may not be shared with the class.

32) D: Families can share information about their own cultural backgrounds; asking for their input and assistance is important in helping to show them that their partnership is desired and valued.

33) A: Developmentally inappropriate activities may reduce confidence and actually hinder development, so the parents should be aware of this.

34) C: Effective professional development (PD) is clearly aligned with a teacher's ongoing needs in authentic teaching contexts.

35) B: The universal design for learning (UDL) is essential for meeting the needs of all learners, so any instructional materials should allow for multiple means of engagement, representation, action and expression.

36) D: The paraprofessional can best be supported by understanding the core curriculum and the resources available to help students meet goals.

37) A: All students, regardless of cultural background, should feel welcome and safe in the classroom. This gives them the readiness to learn.

Module 2

1) B: Expressive vocabulary refers to the words that students are able to use in speech or writing, so asking the student to describe her family or some topic about which she is familiar would be most appropriate.

2) A: The strategy of phoneme blending requires students to combine phonemes to make a word.

3) C: He did not sound out the word into onset *fl* and rime *at*.

4) C: Sight word instruction is designed to help students recognize high-frequency words automatically, without decoding, so that they can read with fluency.

5) B: Writing a paragraph about what students did over the winter break would most logically be written in the past tense and would provide practice with forming the past tense.

6) C: The roots of most English words are Greek or Latin.

7) C: Part of metacognition is assessing one's own understanding; this would be the first step before applying fix-up strategies.

8) B: Asking the students to read from a sight word list while the teacher circles the words they know will help the teacher identify which words the students know and which words they need to practice more.

9) B: Word family instruction is a decoding strategy that reinforces student understanding of word patterns.

10) A: In some dialects, such as African American Vernacular English, (AAVE), subjects and verbs do not always agree and singular subjects may take plural verbs.

11) C: Running records allow teachers to track oral reading progress over time.

12) C: Evaluative comprehension involves an analysis of the quality of the text and the reader's response to it.

13) B: The word *than,* which is a conjunction used to make comparisons, should be used instead of *then*, which is an adverb that means *at that time*.

14) B: By the end of third grade, students should be able to spell most contractions.

15) A: The Frayer model is a four-part diagram that helps students break down vocabulary words in terms of their definitions and characteristics as well as examples and non-examples.

16) B: Silent reading for English language learners (ELLs) is generally only effective when it is appropriately matched with the student's current English language development.

17) C: A think-aloud will model for students the thought process behind inferencing, such as finding relevant text evidence that supports an inference.

18) D: Paragraphs that lack cohesion do not have ideas that stick together, so identifying relevant (and irrelevant) support for topic sentences would aid students.

19) B: Typically developing children can name familiar objects at around a year old.

20) D: Phonological process includes phonological awareness, phonological memory, and phonological retrieval, so these exercises would be most relevant.

21) B: A key part of concepts of print is student understanding of letters, words, and sentences.

22) D: Finger tracking would likely help the student to better keep track of the specific part of the text being read.

23) C: In both first and second language development, the learner listens for a while, has more receptive vocabulary than expressive vocabulary, and tends to go through a silent period.

24) A: Students may have various backgrounds with academic language, or the language skills necessary for academic success. Identifying this is important so that instruction can be tailored accordingly.

25) B: Encoding or translating sounds into letters will also be a problem with a student who is struggling to decode because the two processes are related.

26) C: Prosody refers to the expressiveness of oral reading.

27) A: Part of voice is syntax. Academic writing usually contains a variety of sentence structures.

28) C: Prior to writing a research report, students should search for reliable sources on the topic.

29) B: Reading written work aloud and pausing at each comma would help students connect commas to one of their uses, which is to show a pause.

30) A: Derivational morphemes are affixes that are added to root words. Knowing these would help students build on vocabulary knowledge they already have by learning new forms of a word.

31) C: A map that uses corncob icons to denote the major corn-producing states in the US will include a legend that explains that the corncobs are symbols representing areas of corn production.

32) A: Asking about the difference between the populations of the two cities is an appropriate integration of math computation and social studies skills for a third-grade class.

33) C: The students should understand that people use what is available in their environment. In this scenario, the people would use wood from trees to build houses.

34) C: A mud hut might seem simple and unfamiliar to students who live in houses built of wood or brick, but it represents how different types of housing still create a similar feeling of security for the people who live in them.

35) C: The people in the rain forest environment are dependent on its resources for survival, so cutting down trees changes their lives dramatically.

36) B: Pennsylvania was founded in part to be a haven for European Quakers to practice their religion free of judgment.

37) C: Supply and demand is central to determining the price of a good or service, so having students create a multimedia presentation on supply and demand will meet this goal.

38) C: Students could sort wants into one category and needs into another category to show mastery of this standard.

39) D: Giving students roles in the classroom, such as updating the date or weather chart, will make students feel a part of the daily functioning of the classroom and promotes a sense of belonging and responsibility.

40) B: Teaching patterns is an appropriate introduction to the concept of rhythm.

41) C: Feathers in a collage would create very unique textures, and students could explore this through touch.

42) A: This painting shows the contrast of black and white and has equal proportions of one half of each.

43) C: The teacher could integrate the art concept of patterns of shapes into an activity in which students draw or choose the shape that comes next in the sequence.

44) B: Providing sound effects on cue with percussion instruments does not require oral language skills.

45) A: Negative space is the space between dancers, so these students need practice with keeping enough negative space.

Module 3

1) B: The shape of the jigsaw puzzle pieces can be used to teach students about perimeter. The other options focus on three-dimensional shapes.

2) D: Knowledge of skip counting will help children count the different denominations of money by their values (e.g., nickels are skip counted in fives).

3) A: Decomposing a number refers to breaking it down into its individual place values.

4) A: A large fraction can be simplified by finding an equivalent fraction.

5) B: The commutative property states that the order of the numbers in an addition or multiplication equation does not matter.

6) D: Comparing the number of items in different categories is done on a bar graph.

7) D: The mean or average is the sum of all values divided by the number of values (80 + 90 + 82)/3 = 84.

8) B: Finding the area of one face and multiplying by 6 (since a cube has six square faces) gives the surface area of the entire cube.

9) C: The student has listed the *multiples* of 36—not its factors.

10) D: The student is not regrouping when necessary. A similar error would produce the work shown below:

$$\begin{array}{r} 392 \\ \underline{+\,273} \\ 5{,}165 \end{array}$$

11) D: The students counted out 12 more counters, not realizing that 12 could be composed of two smaller quantities (4 and 8).

12) C: A problem that requires rounding up will reveal whether the student is really reasoning about which direction to round or merely truncating the decimal number after the specified place.

13) A: The 3 1/2 feet of trim need to be divided into 10 pieces: $3\ 1/2 \div 10 = 7/20$ feet.

14) B: The student made a ratio out of the numbers given in the problem; however, the problem asks for a ratio involving a quantity not mentioned in the problem—the number of failing grades. Asking the student what that number is will likely lead him to see his mistake.

15) C: Manipulatives in different shapes are likely to help students' shape identification skills.

16) B: The images show the numerator increasing while the denominator stays the same; meanwhile, the fraction is increasing.

17) A: The life cycle of a pumpkin is basic and developmentally appropriate for toddlers; the other topics are too advanced.

18) D: Students are classifying objects by sorting.

19) B: Planting a seed and recording what happens as the plant grows is an authentic, hands-on lesson that allows the students to understand the life cycle of a plant.

20) D: The experiment is showing students how a liquid can dissolve an object. Some liquids create a reaction that will make the candy cane dissolve more quickly than others.

21) B: Portfolios involve work samples from various points in time, which can reveal growth and progress over time.

22) C: Using visual models that reinforce an understanding of the compounds created is the best reteaching strategy as such visual models can help students see carbon dioxide going into the plant and oxygen coming out.

23) B: Identifying pest thresholds for action is the first step in integrated pest management (IPM) so that action can then be taken as needed.

24) C: Most predictions are that fossil fuels will be completely depleted in this century.

25) D: The teacher is asking students to observe whether these things dissolve in the water to create a solution.

26) B: The Dust Bowl involved long-term non-sustainable farming practices that led to widespread erosion and decimation of farmland in the American Midwest.

27) A: This option describes how human activity (a dam) changes the path of water.

28) D: Weather charts, where students move clouds, rain, sun, snow, and so forth into a box to show the day's weather, are quite common in preschool classrooms.

29) C: The tree has adapted to its environment by growing around the building and fence.

30) B: This easily integrates the idea of energy from the sun and objectives related to renewable energy sources.

31) C: What we see is just sunlight hitting and reflecting off different parts of the moon.

32) C: Constructivism posits that students learn by exploring their world and making meaning. Thus, a science classroom rooted in this idea would likely involve lots of hands-on exploration.

33) B: The ability to catch something that is thrown is a part of fundamental motor skills.

34) D: Signaling with visual *and* verbal cues ensures safety and that all students can be rapidly brought back to attention by the teacher.

35) A: The recommended amount of daily physical activity for children is 30 – 60 minutes. At least 10 of those minutes should be devoted to moderate to vigorous activity.

36) C: Students will need repeated practice to master new locomotor patterns.

37) C: Discussing healthy relationships would be a developmentally appropriate activity for a first-grade class.

38) C: In light of information on long-term health outcomes, encouraging students to have a lifelong commitment to participation in physical activity is a very important goal for any physical education program.

39) B: A five-year old should be able to pick up and grasp most objects that are the size of a tennis ball.

40) C: This type of assignment helps students take personal accountability for health and fitness.

41) D: Learning about a balanced diet is the most developmentally appropriate lesson for this age group.

42) A: Spatial awareness is an awareness of how the body moves in space in relation to other objects in that space. Activities where students have to move carefully around over, under, or near objects can build spatial awareness.

43) A: Non-locomotor skills do not involve the body moving with the legs, so these would be most appropriate.

44) B: Awareness of one's emotions is the first step to emotional regulation because if emotions cannot effectively be identified, they cannot be regulated.

Practice Test #2

Module 1

1) A teacher guided by social development theory and the zone of proximal development would MOST likely use which approach?
   A. homogenous grouping
   B. heterogenous grouping
   C. flipped classroom
   D. direct instruction

2) A kindergarten teacher observes students on the playground the first day of school. Which situation is an indication that a child may have atypical physical development?
   A. The student is afraid to swing as high as the others.
   B. The student puts down his feet to stop himself while going down the slide.
   C. The student trips over untied shoelaces.
   D. The student is unable to climb up three steps to the top of the slide.

3) A third-grade teacher is assisting the school in researching and selecting an instrument to be used for universal screening for students with potential reading difficulties that require further intervention. What should the teacher look for in potential assessment tools?
   A. whether they can be easily modified to meet the needs of all students
   B. whether they contain information in multiple modalities
   C. whether they are sensitive enough to identify knowledge gaps
   D. whether they report results in percentile rank

4) According to family systems theory, which factor is MOST relevant to individual functioning?
   A. sibling position
   B. time spent in recreation
   C. parental self-image
   D. rewards for good behavior

5) A school has developed partnerships with many community service agencies. One of these agencies focuses on maternal health and ensuring pregnant women have access to nutritious foods and health information. What is the MOST important justification for this?
   A. Few pregnant women have the necessary information to make good choices.
   B. Maternal nutrition can impact the development of the fetus.
   C. Women may not realize they are pregnant early enough to change health habits.
   D. Health education can make the labor and delivery process less daunting.

6) A second-grade teacher wants to create a warm, welcoming, and inclusive classroom environment. Which action is MOST likely to promote this?

A. researching students' ethnic backgrounds and placing a flag from their native countries on their desks
B. decorating the classroom in neutral colors and limiting the use of posters and bulletin boards
C. ensuring the correct pronunciation of each student's name
D. avoiding the posting of classroom rules or expectations

7) A first-grade teacher notes that one of her students who has just arrived from Haiti and who is an ELL is very quiet and avoids most conversations. What is the BEST course of action for this teacher to take?

A. to make a referral for special education services because of a suspected language delay
B. to do more to encourage the student to speak with classmates by assigning group activities
C. to give the student opportunities to develop expressive language but recognize that a silent period is expected
D. to use a variety of different assessment instruments to determine whether the student has a phonological processing deficit

8) Which of the following describes atypical development for a first-grade student?

A. frequent changes in the friend group
B. a recurring fear and crying when dropped off at school by a parent
C. challenging rules, such as the established bedtime
D. a desire to do many things independently

9) A third grader is struggling with identification of sight words and letter-sound correspondence. What can be said about this student?

A. His cognitive development is typical of his age and grade.
B. He is ready to begin the transition from learning to read to reading to learn.
C. He could benefit from further practice with phonemic awareness.
D. He should be targeted for intervention since his development is atypical.

10) A kindergarten teacher notices that after one of the students in the class begins wearing the macaroni necklace she made in art class on her head, several other students also put their necklaces on their heads. Which learning theory might she be observing in action?

A. social learning theory
B. the sensorimotor stage
C. operant conditioning
D. the cognitive theory of development

11) Which of the following is one of the criticisms of behaviorism?

A. It lacks any empirical evidence.
B. It fails to account for both positive and negative behaviors.
C. It does not explain change over time.
D. It does not make any distinction between humans and animals.

12) A preschool teacher puts labels on many common classroom items, such as the whiteboard, the trash can, and the window. Why is this strategy helpful to students?

A. Labels help students learn decoding strategies.
B. Labels help students understand text-meaning associations.
C. Labels reinforce location and directionality skills.
D. Labels encourage students to develop oral language skills

13) A third-grade teacher has asked his students to write a short narrative about something interesting that happened to them during the week. What accommodation could he make for an ELL to enable her to BEST participate in this activity?

A. He could ask the student to write only two sentences instead of the full narrative.
B. He could have the student dictate the narrative into an audio recorder.
C. He could give the student a graphic organizer to organize her thoughts first before she writes.
D. He could allow the student to use an English picture dictionary or an electronic translating device.

14) During an oral assessment, a first-grade teacher presents a student with a language impairment with words on flash cards and asks him to stomp out the syllables in each word with his feet. In which part of the UDL is the teacher engaging?

A. culturally competent teaching
B. multiple means of representation
C. multiple means of expression
D. multiple means of engagement

15) A second-grade teacher notices that many of her ELL students are more likely to practice oral reading when someone sits next to them and helps them with challenging vocabulary. Which instructional strategy might benefit these students?

A. assistive technology
B. assignment modifications
C. peer tutoring
D. progress monitoring

16) A fourth-grade teacher is creating a social studies assessment at the end of a unit on economics. Which question would be at the remember or recall level of Bloom's taxonomy?

A. How is a planned economy different from a market economy?
B. Would you want to start a business? Why or why not?
C. What is the definition of the word *producer*?
D. Who do you think should pay the highest taxes?

17) According to Abraham Maslow, if a child's needs of love and belonging are not fulfilled, he or she may

A. continue to progress through the hierarchy as normal.
B. move back and forth between levels.
C. stop progressing up the hierarchy.
D. skip the needs of love and belonging to continue moving up the hierarchy.

18) A new second-grade teacher teaches a unit on homographs and is shocked at the poor summative assessment results. Which strategy is MOST likely to avoid this situation in the future?

A. giving frequent formative assessments and modifying instruction as needed
B. administering a diagnostic assessment prior to each unit of study
C. modifying the summative assessment to better meet the needs of each student
D. ensuring the assessment offers response possibilities in multiple modalities

19) A fourth-grade teacher has a student with an emotional disturbance who is sometimes disruptive when he becomes frustrated. Which strategy would MOST likely help this student?

A. enforcing consistent consequences with this student
B. removing the student from the classroom during these outbursts
C. providing the student with a cool-down zone in the classroom
D. limiting the opportunities this student has to do challenging work

20) A fourth-grade teacher wants to encourage students' social-emotional development and problem-solving skills. Which instructional strategy is MOST likely to meet this aim?

A. project-based learning
B. think-pair-share
C. guided instruction
D. reciprocal teaching

22) A prekindergarten classroom employing a constructivist learning approach is MOST likely to contain which of the following?

A. desks organized into rows
B. learning centers or stations
C. workbooks and worksheets
D. leveled readers

21) If a teacher wanted to know how the class's knowledge of third-grade math skills compares to other third graders throughout the nation, which of the following assessments would she use?

A. a standards-based assessment
B. a screening assessment
C. a norm-referenced assessment
D. an authentic assessment

23) Per the Pennsylvania Code of Professional Practice and Conduct for Educators, professional relationships must be maintained with students

A. in the classroom
B. on school grounds
C. both in and out of the classroom
D. both in the classroom and at school-sponsored events

24) Per the Pennsylvania Code of Professional Practice and Conduct for Educators, educators must

A. keep health and personnel records of colleagues confidential.
B. inform administrators of collegial political activities conducted off campus.
C. make a commitment to mentor colleagues when asked.
D. limit contact with colleagues outside of school.

25) A teacher has made an initial request for an evaluation for a kindergartener in his class whom he suspects may have a disability. After the initial request for evaluation, the evaluation must be completed within what time period?

A. as soon as a team becomes available
B. one week
C. sixty days
D. within the same school year

26) A teacher overhears some of her first-grade students saying they always have to read the same books during independent reading because the classroom library has so few books. Funding for the school year has been tight. The BEST way for the teacher to impact change in this situation is to do which of the following?

A. buy books herself for the classroom library
B. require students to bring books from home
C. limit independent reading time to one day per week.
D. ask other classrooms to participate in a book rotation program

27) A teacher wants to collaborate with the families of his prekindergarten students to ensure they are prepared for kindergarten the next school year. Which of the following is an effective way to do this?

A. send home the list of the kindergarten state standards for parents to review
B. organize a parent meeting to discuss kindergarten expectations and provide parents with strategies and materials
C. send home books or handouts with kindergarten-level sight words to have children read to their families
D. inform parents in a newsletter that kindergarten is quickly approaching so they should start preparing their children

28) Which of the following commitments is a part of ESSA?

A. providing every student with adequate school supplies
B. ensuring that all students are taught to high academic standards
C. requiring all students to have a 90 percent attendance rate
D. ensuring all teachers have the required amount of professional development hours

29) Which of the following is included in the National Association for the Education of Young Children (NAEYC) Code of Ethical Conduct?

A. requirements for student-to-teacher ratios
B. responsibilities to community and society
C. dress code recommendations
D. best practices for special education services

31) Per law, Pennsylvania teachers are

A. mandated reporters of child abuse or neglect
B. required to offer asynchronous learning opportunities
C. mandated reporters of suspected educator ineffectiveness
D. required to limit direct instruction to less than one third of class time

32) A student with ADHD is in a fourth-grade general education classroom. Which educational practice should the teacher AVOID with this student?

A. a highly structured classroom environment with predictable routines
B. allowing frequent breaks during independent work time
C. permitting flexible seating arrangements
D. giving highly-detailed oral directions with multiple steps

33) A first-grade teacher is asked to plan a professional development event for teachers at an elementary school. Which step should the teacher take first?

A. asking teachers what their needs are
B. reviewing schoolwide assessment data
C. researching online tools and resources
D. identifying her own teaching weaknesses

34) Who would the general education teacher MOST likely need to partner with to understand and implement the provided supports for a student with a speech or language impairment?

A. the school psychologist or counselor
B. the instructional specialist
C. the speech-language pathologist
D. the school social worker

35) A third-grade teacher is seeking out the help of a school counselor for a student with behavioral problems in her class. What data should the teacher gather and bring to the meeting?

A. dates and times of parent conferences
B. standardized test information
C. a portfolio of work samples
D. anecdotal or observational notes

36) In developing cross-cultural competence, a first-grade teacher conducts research on collectivist and individualist cultures. Per this research, she decides to change some classroom practices to better align with students from collectivist cultures. Which practice is she MOST likely to eliminate?

A. competitive games
B. peer tutoring
C. self-assessment
D. independent reading

Module 2

1) Which of the following strategies would be MOST beneficial for second-grade students who are at the beginning stage of writing a story?

A. revising the story's first paragraph
B. organizing ideas in a story element chart
C. drafting the exposition of the story
D. sharing the story with a classmate

2) A fourth-grade teacher teaches students what is meant by the word *paraphrase* and gives practice with this skill during a unit on research methods. What is the MOST likely reason for students to learn this skill?

A. to expedite drafting
B. to include relevant support
C. to avoid plagiarism
D. to condense writing

3) A teacher has her first-grade students complete a daily journal page. They draw pictures and write descriptions of their pictures, spelling the words as well as they can. How does this activity contribute to the students' phonics proficiency?

A. Students connect letters to sounds.
B. Students practice authentic decoding.
C. Students build fine motor skills.
D. Students identify orthographic patterns.

4) Which of the following describes systematic phonics instruction?

A. a series of lessons on sound-letter concepts that begins with the letter *a* and words that begin with *a*, then progresses sequentially through the alphabet to the letter *z* and words that begin with *z*
B. a series of logically sequenced lessons on sound-letter concepts that begins with the simplest sound-letter correspondences and progresses to the more complex, from single letters to words
C. a series of logically sequenced lessons that develop student understanding of how sounds, syllables, words, and word parts can be orally manipulated to break apart words, make new words, and create rhymes
D. a series of lessons on roots and affixes derived from Greek or Latin, beginning with the most common prefixes and suffixes and progressing in a logical sequence to more complex word structures

5) Each weekend, a different student in a second-grade class takes home the classroom's stuffed animal mascot. On the following Monday, the student is required to give a short speech about the mascot's weekend adventures. How can the teacher BEST support student preparedness to meet the assignment's specific criteria?

A. by administering a summative assessment of speaking ability
B. by including a speech rubric with the mascot when it is sent home
C. by issuing exit tickets with questions about oral presentations
D. by reserving the mascot for students with effective speaking skills

6) A third-grade teacher encourages her students to check out and read books on any topics of interest to them and helps students identify books that are appropriate for their current reading level. The most important benefit of this approach is that students can

A. read independently without the need for teacher scaffolding.
B. learn new vocabulary via implicit means.
C. use authentic materials as mentor texts.
D. begin developing the habit of reading for pleasure.

7) A young child is able to identify the front and back cover of a book, point to the book's title, and identify words on a page. What skill is the student ready for *next*?

A. print awareness
B. phonemic awareness
C. literal comprehension
D. oral fluency

8) In an oral assessment, a first-grade student reads the following sentence:
I am g-l-a-d to h-e-l-p you b-r-i-n-g c-oo-k-/e/-s.

The teacher can determine that this student

A. has not yet mastered consonant blends.
B. cannot distinguish between long and short vowels sounds.
C. recognizes orthographic patterns.
D. needs further sight word instruction.

9) During the first week of first grade, a teacher gives a diagnostic assessment asking students to read a list of five simple CVC words. One student is unable to sound out any of the words. What action should the student's teacher take?

A. determine if she knows the name of each letter
B. assess her knowledge of individual letter sounds
C. give the assessment again with picture cues
D. ask her to write any words that she can read

10) A third-grade teacher wants to build a trusting classroom environment where students from all backgrounds are respected and valued. When introducing the concept of academic language to students, what should this teacher emphasize?

A. the importance of academic language for success in middle and high schools
B. the need for students to stop using slang or a certain dialect while at school
C. the fact that different types of language are used in different contexts
D. the judgments people make based on the formality of language used

11) A lesson in a second-grade classroom on prereading strategies is MOST likely to involve which topic?

A. morphology
B. predicting
C. evaluative comprehension
D. phonological processing

12) A fourth-grade teacher assigns students to write a personal narrative about an important event in their lives. After reading the narratives, she determines that many students are using sentence fragments and run-on sentences. Which grammatical topic would be MOST appropriate to introduce to the class?

A. identifying subjects and verbs
B. diagramming complex sentences
C. recognizing dependent and independent clauses
D. common marks of punctuation (e.g., periods and exclamation points)

13) A first-grade teacher introduces new vocabulary each week by projecting the word, its definition, and a picture to the class; however, the teacher is concerned that students are not retaining this vocabulary knowledge. Which instructional strategy is MOST likely to help?

A. giving a written assessment immediately after the lesson
B. using the vocabulary words as the weekly spelling words
C. repeatedly using the words in context in her speech throughout the week
D. intentionally teaching students the root and etymology of each new word

14) The strategy of teaching phonics through spelling relies on which foundational principle?

A. the interconnection between decoding and encoding
B. the predictable stages of oral language development
C. the need for visual reinforcement in literacy learning
D. the need to teach the most useful sounds first

15) A third-grade teacher wants to help ELLs write a summary of a story. Which strategy is MOST likely to be effective?

A. helping students identify text evidence for key conclusions
B. providing sentence frames like "First,__________. Next,________. Last,________."
C. giving students a word list of transitional expressions (e.g., thus, furthermore, and also).
D. reviewing the difference between simple and complex sentences.

16) Which type of graphic organizer is MOST likely to help students analyze a literary text?

A. KWL Chart
B. semantic map
C. outline
D. plot diagram

17) A student in a first-grade class is struggling with oral fluency. The teacher believes part of the issue may involve the student's lack of confidence. Which strategy should the teacher try?

A. modeling appropriate rate and prosody
B. having the student participate in reader's theatre
C. giving the student a familiar text for oral assessments
D. encouraging the student to segment sentences

18) A third-grade teacher wants to help students develop an awareness of audience to adjust their writing accordingly. Which of the following activities would BEST meet this goal?

A. writing a letter to a friend about an issue and then modifying it to send to a public official
B. writing a response to an oral presentation given by classmates
C. identifying tone in a poem and attempting to match that tone in an essay
D. identifying when it is most appropriate to use first- and second-person points of view

19) A second-grade teacher is modeling fix-up strategies for students. As the teacher gets to a certain part of the text she says, "Oh, I don't know much about this. The words look pretty hard." What should the teacher say next?

A. "I probably need to slow down my reading speed here."
B. "I had better start over from the beginning."
C. "I think I should look for text evidence to make an inference."
D. "I need to find a different text that will be easier."

20) A third-grade teacher gives students a reading journal where students set goals, track the books they've read over the course of the year, and write a few sentences about each book after they've finished it. What is the PRIMARY purpose of this strategy?

A. to encourage students to read more books than their peers
B. to develop students' interest in books on diverse topics
C. to help students become self-directed learners
D. to assess how students are meeting state standards

21) A second-grade student asks a teacher: "Why do the words *say* and *weigh* have the same sound but a different spelling?" The teacher could use this question as a starting point for a mini-lesson on which of the following?

A. letter-sound correspondence
B. morphophonology
C. graphemes
D. homographs

22) How are the ELPs organized?

A. into content domains, language proficiency levels, and grade-level clusters
B. into content domains, language proficiency levels, and individual grade levels
C. into language proficiency levels and individual grade levels
D. into content domains and language proficiency levels

23) Which of the following is one of the five essential components of reading instruction per ESSA?

A. spelling
B. morphology
C. phonics
D. prosody

24) A kindergarten teacher is planning to read a storybook to the class during circle time. The book has many detailed pictures as well as sound effects when certain buttons on the page are pushed. How can the teacher prepare a student with ASD for this activity?

A. by asking the student to be the one to push the buttons
B. by having the student sit far away from the circle
C. by informing the student beforehand that the book will make noise
D. by giving the student his own copy of the book

25) A third-grade teacher wants to help a reader struggling with comprehension to select a book for independent reading time. Which type of book should the teacher direct the student toward?

A. a story with flashbacks and foreshadowing to drive interest
B. a nonfiction book with a word pronunciation guide
C. a book of rhyming poetry
D. a fiction book with a simple plot

26) A first-grade teacher continues to have students practice sight word recognition even after they have mastered the ability to sound out most words. What is MOST likely the teacher's goal?

A. to transition students from phonics to a whole-language approach to reading
B. to build student fluency by promoting a faster reading rate and automaticity
C. to encourage students to distinguish between decodable and non-decodable words
D. to help student awareness of the most common words used in everyday communications

27) A kindergarten teacher wants to help students go beyond literal comprehension as she reads a storybook to the class. Which guiding question BEST meets this goal?

A. Who is the main character?
B. What is the character's name?
C. What happened first in the story?
D. What do you think will happen next?

28) As part of a vocabulary exercise, a fourth-grade teacher allows students to draw a picture representing each word, write a sentence demonstrating the meaning of each word, or audio or video record a conversation of them using each word. This activity BEST shows this teacher's commitment to which of the following?

A. standards-based assessment
B. the universal design for learning
C. inquiry-based learning
D. criterion-referenced assessment

29) Which strategy should be used to help a third-grade class access a content-area text that contains many unfamiliar words?

A. having students annotate unknown words as they read
B. providing explicit instruction in new words beforehand
C. teaching students to preview the text for new words
D. helping students divide the words into syllables

30) A third-grade teacher begins a unit on affixes like *-ive*, *-ion*, and *-ly*. What other topic could be easily integrated into this unit?

A. academic language
B. sentence structure
C. parts of speech
D. active and passive voices

31) A second-grade teacher projects a picture of a sign on the freeway that says, "Pittsburgh 150 miles." What is the teacher illustrating?

A. absolute location
B. physical geography
C. human geography
D. relative location

32) A fourth-grade student completes a research project on significant events of the American Revolution. Which of the following is an appropriate method to determine the credibility of the resources he has used to conduct research?

A. checking the author and date of the source
B. reviewing website design and writing style
C. assuming all online resources are not credible
D. reviewing website design and domain name

34) A first-grade teacher is planning a lesson on civic participation. What should the teacher include as the FIRST step?

A. being willing to compromise
B. listening to other points of view
C. becoming informed on the issues
D. taking action by solving a problem

33) Which of the following illustrations could be used to show students the role of the physical environment in settlement patterns?

A. a map of the Appalachian Trail
B. a map of towns along rivers
C. an image of American Indians in tepees
D. an image of people in covered wagons

35) A fourth-grade teacher is planning instruction to meet the following standard:
Identify the services performed by local and state governments.

Which activity BEST meets this objective?

A. Students complete a chart showing who the governor, state attorney general, and state treasurer are.
B. Students watch a video recording of live city council proceedings.
C. Students work together to recommend changes to school rules.
D. Students go online to identify the fire and police stations located closest to the school.

36) Aligned with state standards, a fourth-grade teacher wants students to distinguish between fact and opinion in a primary source. Which document would be MOST effective?

A. the charter granted to William Penn
B. the Pennsylvania State Constitution
C. a speech given by John F. Kennedy about space exploration
D. a newspaper article from 1923 about heavy snows that year

37) A kindergarten teacher leads students in a song that is very loud in some places but very soft in others. Which concept is this teacher introducing?

A. pitch
B. melody
C. texture
D. dynamics

38) A third-grade teacher has pairs of students draw a topic out of a hat and present an unscripted duet scene. What is MOST likely the teacher's aim?

A. to encourage students to learn blocking
B. to help students practice improvisation
C. to allow students to integrate artforms
D. to promote student awareness of intention

39) A prekindergarten student is at the dramatic play center. The student puts on a stethoscope and a lab coat. Which of the following comments by the teacher would likely be MOST effective for extending the student's thinking during this dramatic play experience?

A. "What kind of sickness are you going to help with?"
B. "You're going to be a doctor!"
C. "Do you want me to help you find more costumes?"
D. "There are some scrubs in the costume box."

40) In a visual arts lesson, a fourth-grade teacher shows students images of age-appropriate paintings from the Renaissance. What background information should the teacher present to help students understand the artwork?

A. details about how painters of the time often also worked as marble sculptors
B. an explanation of how much of this artwork was produced in Italy
C. a description of how religion was central to life for many people of this time
D. details about the differences between abstract art and realism

42) Which instrument requires the LEAST amount of fine motor skills development?

A. keyboard
B. recorder
C. bongos
D. guitar

43) Which artistic medium would be MOST appropriate for a student with visual impairments to work with?

A. clay
B. string
C. watercolors
D. pencil

44) Which type of assessment would be MOST appropriate to evaluate progress in visual arts in a prekindergarten classroom?

A. rubric
B. exit ticket
C. running record
D. portfolio

45) In an integrated humanities and social studies lesson, a teacher wants to show students a video of a dance style from Latin America. Which type of video should the teacher look for?

A. waltz
B. jazz
C. swing
D. flamenco

Module 3

1) Which word problem is MOST appropriate when introducing percentages?

A. Saundra puts $2,000 in a savings account. The interest rate is 4.2%. How much interest does Saundra earn in a year?
B. Ryan gets 35 questions correct on a test and scores 70%. How many questions are on the test?
C. Amanda earns $200,000 and pays 19% income tax. How many dollars does Amanda pay in taxes?
D. There are 20 students in the class and 5 of the students have birthdays in June. What percentage of students were born in June?

2) A fourth-grade class wants to find the probability of pulling a red gumball out of a jar that contains 50 gumballs. What information do the students need to know to find the answer?

A. How many green gumballs are in the jar?
B. How many different colors of gumballs are in the jar?
C. How many red gumballs are in the jar?
D. How long have the gumballs been in the jar?

3) A student in a second-grade class answers the questions as shown below. If the student's error pattern continues, what is the answer to the third question?

1. $25 - 18 = 13$
2. $87 - 58 = 3$
3. $42 - 38 = ?$

A. 4
B. 14
C. 16
D. 80

4) Which activity is MOST appropriate for a student who is just being exposed to numeracy?

A. comparing integers on a number line
B. drawing pictures of combinations that equal 10
C. matching the numeral *10* to cards with 10 items on them
D. counting out three plastic bears

5) A third-grade teacher notices that sometimes students write unreasonable answers to multiplication problems. For example, for 12 × 22, one student put 264, 000. Which strategy is likely to be helpful to students?

A. confirming answers via estimation
B. backward problem-solving
C. using a place value chart to check answers
D. fluency with fast facts

6) A third-grade teacher wants to align instruction with the principles of UDL as well as students' learning preferences. Which instructional strategy pertaining to multiplication meets this goal?

A. having students connect multiplication and addition
B. having students use both visual arrays and standard algorithms to solve problems
C. having students first master multiplication facts up to 12× before attempting two by two digit multiplication
D. explicitly teaching students the phrases commonly used in word problems to signal multiplication

7) A fourth-grade math teacher wants to use a formative assessment tool during a math lesson on fractions to determine the students' level of understanding. Which technique is MOST appropriate?

A. encouraging students to ask questions during teacher modeling
B. encouraging students to hold up their work and answers to sample problems on small white boards
C. encouraging students to share their work and answers with the person sitting next to them
D. encouraging students to take notes in their notebooks and turn them in after the lesson

8) A prekindergarten teacher is setting up an exploratory math station that students can use during center rotations. Which item would be MOST appropriate to include?

A. base ten blocks
B. fraction strips
C. an abacus
D. a digital clock

9) The students in a second-grade class investigate if there is a relationship between the weather and the number of bus riders. What data do the students need to collect?

A. the mean number of bus riders during the first week of the month
B. the number of rainy days this month
C. the number of students who walk home from school when it is sunny
D. the mean number of bus riders on rainy days this month

10) A teacher gives each student a set of cards with numbers 1 – 10 on them. She asks the students to lay down two cards that add up to 10, and then she asks students to lay down three cards that add up to 10. What is this exercise designed to teach students?

A. fact families
B. properties of addition
C. decomposing numbers
D. standard algorithms

11) A second-grade teacher is planning activities to help students master the following standard: *Measure and estimate lengths in standard units using appropriate tools.*

The teacher would most likely need to introduce which concept FIRST?

A. borrowing
B. fractions
C. ratios
D. perimeter

12) A first-grade student is struggling to solve the following word problem:
Alina went to the store and bought 8 apples. She invited Todd over, and he ate 3 apples. How many apples does Alina have left?

Which guiding question could the teacher ask to help?

A. "What does 'have left' tell you?"
B. "What did Todd do?"
C. "What happened after Alina bought the apples?"
D. "What does 'bought 8 apples' tell you?"

13) A preschool student is completing an exercise with the teacher at the math table. The student looks at the printed card with four clocks on it and says, "One, two, three, four, five. Five clocks." How can the teacher help this student?

A. practice with dot pattern flashcards
B. writing the numbers 1 – 10 in sequence
C. pointing to each object while counting
D. decomposing the number 5

14) A prekindergarten teacher is assessing students' math knowledge. The teacher gives students both a short written assessment and an oral assessment. What is the BEST reason for doing this?

A. to integrate oral language goals
B. to build a positive student-teacher relationship
C. to have multiple sources of documentation for recommending interventions
D. to ensure that math skills alone—not fine motor skills—are being assessed

15) Which support would MOST likely assist a third-grade student with dyscalculia who is working on two-digit-by-one-digit multiplication?

A. use of a fact chart
B. use of manipulatives
C. recording answers orally
D. recording estimated answers

16) A kindergarten teacher sees a student drawing a heart and a star in the sand. The teacher comes up to the child with the goal of extending her mathematical thinking. Which strategy meets this goal in a developmentally appropriate way?

A. The teacher asks, "Are these two- or three-dimensional shapes?"
B. The teacher writes numbers in the sand and says, "How are numbers and shapes different?"
C. The teacher draws another heart and another star after the drawings and says, "What comes next?"
D. The teacher points to the heart and the star and says, "Let's draw lines of symmetry through these shapes."

17) A teacher opens a soda bottle and places a balloon over the top of the bottle. The class observes the bottle every ten minutes. Which concept is the experiment demonstrating?

A. force and motion
B. magnetic attraction
C. acids and bases
D. states of matter

18) A fourth-grade teacher wants to integrate information about renewable energy into a lesson on layers of the earth. Which type of renewable energy BEST meets this goal?

A. nuclear energy
B. geothermal energy
C. solar energy
D. hydropower

19) Which activity could be used to demonstrate Newton's third law of motion?

A. hitting the 8-ball with the cue ball in billiards
B. rolling two balls of different masses down a ramp
C. dropping a ping-pong ball
D. swinging a pendulum

20) A second-grade teacher is talking with students before an experiment. The teacher wants students to make a hypothesis. Which characteristic of a good hypothesis should the teacher emphasize?

A. A hypothesis must match the conclusion of an experiment.
B. A hypothesis must be from an unknown branch of science.
C. A hypothesis must be scientifically proven.
D. A hypothesis must be capable of being tested.

21) An elementary class completes the following heat conduction experiment:
Students take butter and place it on a metal spoon, a plastic spoon, and a pencil. They place the spoons and pencil in a glass and pour hot water in the glass. The students watch to see which object the butter melts on the fastest.

The teacher visits each team of students as they work and asks questions about heat conduction. Which student response shows an understanding of heat conduction?

A. Heat conduction is how heat travels from one object to another. The butter melted on the metal spoon the fastest. Metal is the best conductor.
B. Heat conduction is how heat travels from one object to another. The butter melted on the plastic spoon first. Plastic is the best conductor.
C. Heat conduction is how heat travels from one object to another. The butter melted on the pencil the fastest. Wood is the best conductor.
D. Heat conduction is how heat travels from one object to another. The butter melted on the metal spoon and the plastic spoon at the same time. Both of these are great conductors.

23) A third-grade teacher notes students looking at mushrooms growing in the grass at recess. The teacher wants to extend student's thinking about the role of mushrooms when they return for science after recess. Which question should the teacher ask?

A. Do mushrooms grow only in certain biomes?
B. What are the stages in mushroom reproduction?
C. How can mushrooms be handled safely?
D. What do mushrooms contribute to an ecosystem?

22) A teacher is designing an inquiry activity for her third-grade classroom that will require students to make a catapult. The students will use the catapult to shoot marshmallows to see whose marshmallows go the farthest.

The activity will BEST reinforce which of the following ideas?

A. types of energy
B. states of matter
C. force and motion
D. simple machines

24) A second-grade teacher is planning a unit on plant reproduction. How could the teacher integrate the idea of structure and function into this unit?

A. by asking students to look outside and note how many plants use flowering reproduction versus non-flowering reproduction
B. by asking students to think about why plants need to reproduce
C. by explaining to students that bees spread pollen for plant reproduction, so plants have bright flowers to attract bees
D. by explaining to students that the petals of flowering plants can be large or small but together they make up the corolla

25) A fourth-grade teacher wants to help students understand that just because an organism has a gene for a trait, it does not mean that trait will be expressed. Which illustration would be MOST effective?

A. encouraging students to trace their family lineage to see which hair and eye colors are most prominent
B. providing an example of learned characteristics and an example of environmental factors
C. drawing a Punnett square to illustrate the likelihood of a person with two heterogenous genes having blue eyes
D. showing the way frogs and butterflies cycle through their lives in stages where they have different body types but remain the same organism

26) At recess, second-grade students note that students wearing bulky, textured clothing go down the slide more slowly than students wearing smoother, more fitted clothing. This is a good time to introduce which content area word?

A. thermodynamic
B. friction
C. gravity
D. electromagnetic

27) A teacher wants to provide a material that will attract a magnet in a lab students are working on. Which material should the teacher choose?

A. iron
B. copper
C. silver
D. gold

28) A third-grade science teacher introduces chemical and physical changes of matter. What is the BEST way to assess students' understanding of these concepts?

A. having students describe the properties of objects in the classroom
B. having students think about experiments they could do with matter
C. asking students to sort the words *freezing*, *rusting*, and *burning* into categories
D. asking students to sort the words *color*, *solubility*, and *hardness* from most to least important

29) A fourth-grade teacher gives students the following scenario:
A stream that usually contains several hundred thousand gallons of water is impacted by a drought that significantly decreases its amount of water. What will most likely also occur?

Which response shows an accurate student understanding?

A. Less energy will be transferred between trophic levels.
B. The carrying capacity of the ecosystem will decrease.
C. Predators will increase in number.
D. Remaining organisms will change their niche.

30) A fourth-grade teacher wants to help students understand the process by which professional scientists conduct and publish research. Which activity would BEST meet this goal?

A. conducting a peer review of the lab report of another group of students
B. creating a timeline of important scientific discoveries of the past
C. interviewing another group of students about their lab experience
D. making a poster to describe lab safety rules

31) A kindergarten teacher sets up a science exploration center with magnifying glasses and small models of insects and other small objects, such as sand dollars and tiny shells. The BEST justification for this type of activity is that it allows students to do which of the following?

A. identify patterns in nature
B. form and test hypotheses
C. practice scientific observation
D. learn to work cooperatively

32) A first-grade class is learning about recycling. To encourage students to become responsible citizens who participate in recycling efforts, the teacher should

A. help students learn to identify whether common items are recyclable.
B. encourage students to begin weighing the trash and recycling containers at home.
C. take students on a field trip to a local recycling center.
D. show students a cartoon video that describes what recycling centers do.

33) A second-grade teacher wants to provide an illustration of a structural adaptation. Which of the following is the BEST example to use?

A. A lizard has camouflaged skin.
B. A skunk sprays a toxin to scare away prey.
C. A spider spins a web to trap food.
D. A bird migrates south in the winter.

34) In order to adhere to the universal design for learning (UDL), movement programs should

A. promote proficiencies in multiple sports and games.
B. involve activities in which all students can participate.
C. use performance-based assessments.
D. include both theoretical and practical subject matter.

35) A first-grade teacher is preparing students for a gymnastics unit that will involve the use of a balance beam. Which activity would help prepare students to use this piece of equipment?

A. object manipulation
B. locomotor skills development
C. hopping on one foot
D. doing push-ups

37) Which type of class structure is MOST likely to help students of all abilities participate in physical activity?

A. teacher-directed drills
B. student-choice stations
C. circuit training
D. free play time

38) Which of the following describes the phenomenon where a child's development begins in the torso and radiates outward?

A. cephalocaudal
B. proximodistal
C. biolocomotion
D. biomechanics

39) A preschool teacher is creating a proposal for new outdoor education equipment. Part of the proposal is a play tunnel. Which rationale should the teacher use for the play tunnel?

A. helping students develop static balance
B. helping students develop non-locomotor skills
C. helping students develop spatial awareness
D. helping students develop locomotor patterns

40) As part of an obstacle course, kindergarten students must grab a small rubber ball with a pair of plastic tweezers and move it to a container. How does this contribute to these children's physical development?

A. by encouraging the development of gross motor skills and locomotor patterns
B. by providing practice with fine motor skills and object manipulation
C. by developing muscular strength through repetition of one activity
D. by building joint flexibility by stretching and lengthening large muscle groups

41) What should children be taught about their weight and height?

A. It will change as they go through growth spurts.
B. Water intake can impact both metrics.
C. It will decrease as their cardiorespiratory endurance increases.
D. Protein intake will increase both metrics.

42) Which activity would BEST help students develop a positive self-image?

A. creating a schedule for daily hygiene rituals, such as brushing teeth
B. learning about the negative life outcomes associated with addiction
C. tracking progress over time in the development of strength and endurance
D. posting class-wide win-loss records on bulletin boards and websites

43) As prekindergarten students are lined up to wash hands before lunch, a student asks the teacher, "Why do we have to wash our hands before lunch?" The teacher could use this inquiry for a later lesson on which of the following?

A. the importance of daily routines
B. making responsible food choices
C. decision making
D. avoiding germs

44) A second-grade teacher is conducting a health lesson on disease prevention. Which activity is MOST appropriate for the students' current developmental level?

A. alcoholism and pregnancy
B. how to lower cholesterol
C. the use of sunscreen
D. maternal nutrition

Practice Test #2 Answer Key

Module 1

1) B: Heterogenous grouping places students in mixed-ability groups. Per Vygotsky's theories, this would allow "more capable others" to help students.

2) D: Kindergarten students who cannot climb up three steps may be experiencing atypical physical development and may need further assessment.

3) C: Screening assessments must be highly sensitive in order to accurately detect potential difficulties that may require early intervention.

4) A: Per family systems theory, whether one is the oldest, middle, or youngest child can impact the way in which that individual functions.

5) B: Adequate maternal nutrition is essential for the developing fetus and can have lasting impacts on the child.

6) C: Ensuring the correct pronunciation of each student's name is very important to show cross-cultural competence and make students feel valued and respected as individuals.

7) C: When first learning a new language, a silent period is natural and expected.

8) B: Most typically developing first graders will be able to separate easily from a parent at a familiar place, such as school.

9) D: By third grade, this student should definitely have mastered letter-sound-correspondence and recognition of most sight words.

10) A: Bandura's social learning theory suggests that children learn by observing and imitating the behavior of those around them.

11) D: True behaviorists are often criticized for lumping humans and animals together as having identical responses to stimuli.

12) B: Labels encourage a text-meaning association and increase high-frequency words (HFW) recognition skills.

13) D: The dictionary or translating device would help the student write the narrative in English.

14) C: The term *multiple means of expression* refers to the student being able to show what he knows in multiple ways.

15) C: In peer tutoring, a fluent peer can assist the English language learner (ELL) students with the challenging vocabulary.

16) C: Asking the students to define a word is the simplest question since it only asks students to recall or remember the definition of a term.

17) B: If a child's needs of love and belonging are not met, progress may be disrupted, causing the child to move back and forth between levels.

18) A: Formative assessments monitor ongoing learning. Had the teacher been giving formative assessments, she would have known that the students required more practice and were not ready for a summative assessment.

19) C: This keeps the student in the least restrictive environment and addresses the problem by having the student temporarily move away from the class when needed.

20) A: In project-based learning, student groups identify authentic problems and work to solve them, which encourages both social-emotional development and problem solving.

21) C: Norm-referenced assessments measure student performance against all other students of that same age and grade.

22) B: Learning centers or stations allow students to explore on their own and use intentionally organized learning materials.

23) C: Professional relationships must be maintained with students even if students are encountered outside of the classroom setting.

24) A: Rule 8 of 235.5b involves keeping health and personnel records of colleagues confidential; none of the other options are part of the Code.

25) C: The Individuals with Disabilities Education Act (IDEA) states that an initial request for evaluation must be completed within sixty days.

26) D: The teacher can call on colleagues to help take action on an issue in which students have expressed concern.

27) B: Organizing a parent meeting to discuss kindergarten expectations and provide parents with strategies and materials is an effective way for the teacher to advocate for his students' kindergarten success. By doing this, the teacher is raising families' awareness of what is expected and providing information and strategies to families so that they can help prepare their students as well.

28) B: Ensuring that all students are taught to high academic standards is stated in the law; the other options are not a part of the Every Student Succeeds Act (ESSA).

29) B: The Code includes ethical responsibilities to children, families, colleagues, and community and society.

30) C: General education teachers do not make the IEP, but they are required by law to implement it.

31) A: Failing to report suspected child abuse or neglect is illegal. The other statements are not legal requirements.

32) D: Highly-detailed oral directions with multiple steps will likely be hard for this student to follow.

33) A: Professional development is most effective when it is directly aligned with teacher needs, so asking teachers what their needs are is the best first step since it can guide all the subsequent planning.

34) C: The speech-language pathologist (SLP) and medical professionals typically guide the treatment of students with speech and language impairments.

35) D: Anecdotal or observational notes can help the counselor understand the student's specific behaviors.

36) A: Collectivist cultures typically value cooperation over competition, so the teacher will most likely consider eliminating competitive games.

Module 2

1) B: It is most beneficial for students to use graphic organizers to shape their ideas before writing.

2) C: Learning the importance of avoiding plagiarism is a critical component of writing instruction for school and career success.

3) A: Emergent writing activities, such as journaling, provide students with opportunities to connect the sounds they hear in words to the letters that represent those sounds.

4) B: Systematic phonics instruction is a series of logically sequenced lessons on sound-letter concepts, beginning with the simplest sound-letter correspondences and progressing to the more complex, from single letters to words.

5) B: A rubric provides students with specific criteria to consider and practice prior to their presentations.

6) D: These students are likely to become lifelong readers. The more a student reads, the more proficiently the student will read.

7) B: Early literacy development typically begins with print awareness, which this student has mastered, and then on to phonemic awareness, or the idea that language is made up of sounds.

8) A: These are all consonant blends: /gl/ /lp/ /br/ and /ng/; however, the student sounded out each letter individually, which indicates that he has not yet mastered consonant blends.

9) B: To determine how to best help this student, the teacher should assess whether or not she has mastered the letter sounds—knowledge that is needed to sound out consonant vowel consonant (CVC) words.

10) C: Emphasizing the fact that different types of language are used in different contexts can help respect all students' backgrounds and the slang or dialect they may use. It is not that academic language is "right" and other types of language "wrong"; it is that certain types of language are better for certain situations in order to communicate most effectively.

11) B: Before students read, they should predict what the text will be about based on the title, bolded words, heading, pictures, and so forth.

12) C: Fragments are generally dependent clauses and run-ons are fused independent clauses, so introducing how to recognize dependent and independent clauses would be appropriate.

13) C: Repeatedly using the words in her speech throughout the week will help the teacher's students generalize this knowledge and hear the words being used in context. It balances explicit vocabulary learning with implicit vocabulary learning since students will hear the words being used in an authentic context.

14) A: Decoding (reading) and encoding (spelling) are interconnected and related processes.

15) B: Providing sentence frames will help students by providing a framework so they are not simply writing ex nihilo (i.e., from out of nothing).

16) D: A plot diagram shows the story's main parts (exposition/rising action, conflict, falling action, resolution). This is best aimed at helping students analyze a literary text.

17) C: Giving the student a familiar text for oral assessments may help the student's confidence.

18) A: Writing a letter to a friend about an issue and then modifying it to send to a public official will help students see how writing must change when the audience changes.

19) A: Slowing down reading speed is a common and useful fix-up strategy. When texts are complicated or contain lots of new information, slowing down the reading speed can be highly effective.

20) C: When students set their own goals and track their progress it encourages self-directed learning.

21) C: Graphemes are ways of recording a sound, so the teacher could explain that sometimes the same sound has a different grapheme.

22) A: The English language proficiencies (ELPs) are divided into four over-arching content domains, four sub-domains, six proficiency levels, and five grade-level clusters.

23) C: The Every Student Succeeds Act (ESSA) specifies phonemic awareness, phonics, vocabulary development, reading fluency, and reading comprehension.

24) C: Informing the student beforehand that the book will make noise will prepare the student for what is to come and make it less likely that the sounds will upset or disturb him.

25) D: Genre is one factor that influences comprehension. A story with a simple and predictable plot will likely be most accessible to a student who is still developing comprehension.

26) B: Having a large bank of sight words that are immediately recognizable helps students build fluency by enabling them to read more quickly and more automatically.

27) D: Asking the students what will happen next in the story will allow them to make a prediction, which goes beyond simple recall or literal comprehension as in the other question options.

28) B: The teacher is giving students options of how they can complete the assignment, which is a key part of the universal design for learning (UDL).

29) B: Pre-teaching new vocabulary, particularly in a content-area text, is likely to drive student comprehension.

30) C: These affixes all change a base word into a different part of speech, so this could be easily integrated into a unit on affixes.

31) D: Relative location refers to the location of one place in relation to another place, in this case Pittsburgh.

32) A: Checking the author and date of research helps to determine if the information is credible and up-to-date.

33) B: A map of towns along rivers shows that people settle and live near desirable parts of the physical environment, like rivers, which help transportation and trade.

34) C: Before people take any civic action, they must inform themselves on the issues.

35) B: Having students watch a video recording of live city council proceedings is the only answer option that shows a local government in action.

36) C: This text is most likely to contain both facts about space exploration and opinions Kennedy has about space exploration.

37) D: Dynamics refers to how loud or soft music is.

38) B: Helping students practice improvisation allows students to spontaneously improvise a performance without any planning or scripting.

39) A: Asking the student about her costume will extend student thinking by encouraging the student to pretend she is a doctor who will help someone with an illness.

40) C: For students to make connections and fully understand these pieces, an awareness and appreciation of how important religion was at the time would be useful.

41) B: Kindergarten students can likely grasp and use crayons safely and without too much mess; they also will likely enjoy drawing a picture of themselves.

42) C: Moving individual fingers is not necessary to play the bongos, which is why percussion instruments are popular for young children.

43) A: Clay is tactile, so visually impaired students could likely still be successful using this medium.

44) D: A portfolio would show progress in students' artistic skills over time.

45) D: Flamenco is popular in various parts of Latin America.

Module 3

1) D: This is a simple question about percentages that helps students understand the process of finding percentages without complicated calculations and multiple steps.

2) C: It is important to know how many red gumballs there are since the class already knows how many gumballs there are in total.

3) C: This answer (16) follows the error pattern. Rather than regrouping, the student is confusing the minuend and the subtrahend in the ones column.

4) D: Counters and toys are concrete objects, which are most appropriate for students just learning introductory math skills.

5) A: This is far too large of an answer for this problem, so students could use estimation to determine that if 10 × 20 = 200, then the answer 264,000 is way too big.

6) B: Having students use both visual arrays and standard algorithms to solve problems allows them the choice of how to solve problems. For students who prefer visual learning, it also allows them to see and solve problems in their preferred format.

7) B: Encouraging students to hold up their work and answers to sample problems on small white boards is an ongoing, formative assessment during the lesson that will give the teacher valuable information on how many students are solving the problems correctly.

8) C: An abacus is most developmentally appropriate since it allows students to practice counting while moving the beads.

9) D: The students need to know the average number of bus riders on rainy days and compare that quantity to the average number of bus riders on days with fair weather.

10) C: Numbers can be decomposed or pulled apart in various fashions.

11) B: To estimate length, one would most likely say "about one and a half feet." Further rulers have portions of inches such as ¼, ½, and ¾ of an inch.

12) A: "Have left" is a key phrase that indicates to the student that this is a subtraction problem.

13) C: The student is counting "ahead" of the objects on the printed card, so pointing to each object while counting will help.

14) D: Students may still be developing fine motor skills in prekindergarten but may have more math knowledge than they are able to demonstrate in writing.

15) A: Dyscalculia often involves struggles with retrieving math facts, so a multiplication fact chart would likely help this student.

16) C: This promotes patterning, which is a developmentally appropriate skill for a kindergarten student to practice.

17) D: The teacher is showing different states of matter by illustrating the transition between the solid, liquid, and gas forms. The balloon will collect carbon dioxide gas that was once dissolved in the soda.

18) B: Geothermal energy is a renewable energy source that comes from the heat within the earth. A discussion about geothermal energy would be a good setting to introduce a geology unit on the layers of the earth.

19) A: Newton's third law of motion states that for every action there is an equal and opposite reaction. When the cue ball hits the 8-ball, the cue ball stops, and the 8-ball moves.

20) D: A hypothesis must be reasonable and testable by experiment.

21) A: Heat conduction does travel from one object to another. Metals have electrons that can carry a charge easily. The butter would melt first on the metal spoon.

22) C: Making a catapult to shoot marshmallows reinforces the ideas of force and motion because the students will see that the more force they use to fling the marshmallow, the further it will go.

23) D: This could help students confirm understanding of decomposers and how mushrooms help break down organic matter as part of the carbon cycle.

24) C: Discussing how bees spread pollen for plant reproduction explains how the structure of the plant (bright flowers) promotes the reproductive function by attracting bees.

25) C: A Punnett square will show that even if a person has a gene for blue eyes, the person may not actually have blue eyes based on which genes are dominant or recessive.

26) B: The bulkier clothing creates more friction, causing the object (the person sliding) to slow down.

27) A: Magnets readily attract iron.

28) C: This activity would allow students to show whether each term reflects a chemical or physical change.

29) B: The carrying capacity is the total number of individual organisms that an ecosystem can support. With less water, the stream will likely be able to hold fewer plants and animals.

30) A: Professional scientific research goes through peer review, so this would give students a taste of this process.

31) C: As students look at these objects, they are practicing making close and detailed observations. The other options are incorrect because these things may or may not happen at this station.

32) A: If students learn whether materials are recyclable, they are likely to be more effective recyclers themselves.

33) A: A structural adaptation is the way an animal looks, or the body parts or physical features it has in order to survive.

34) B: All students must be able to access the movement curriculum, even if they have disabilities that might limit some types of movement.

35) C: Hopping on one foot will help students develop balance, which they will need to walk on the balance beam.

36) C: Students at this age are likely not developmentally ready for the other options, but teaching students to know their parents' phone numbers is developmentally appropriate.

37) B: Student choice stations can be set up so that there are options for students of various fitness levels and physical abilities.

38) B: Proximodistal development explains why a young child can often sit up before being able to walk or hold a small object between her fingers.

39) C: Spatial awareness involves being aware of how the body can move through spaces. A play tunnel is a set space that must be moved through by crawling, helping children understand spatial awareness.

40) B: Tweezers are a great way to build fine motor skills in young children. They are also a somewhat nuanced object that opens and closes, which also helps to develop object manipulation skills.

41) A: Growth spurts are a natural part of childhood, and children should be prepared for them.

42) C: When students see progress toward goals, this positively impacts their self-image.

43) D: Hand-washing is a way to kill germs on the hands so that they will not be digested during lunch. This is a developmentally appropriate lesson for these students.

44) C: The use of sunscreen is a topic that would be appropriate for this grade level. The others options are not directly related to problems students in the second grade would be experiencing.

Online Resources

Trivium includes online resources with the purchase of this study guide to help you fully prepare for the exam.

Practice Test

The second practice test can be taken in the book or online for an interactive experience. Since many exams today are computer based, practicing your test-taking skills on the computer is a great way to prepare.

Flash Cards

Trivium's flash cards allow you to review important terms easily on your computer or smartphone.

From Stress to Success

Watch "From Stress to Success," a brief but insightful YouTube video that offers the tips, tricks, and secrets experts use to score higher on the exam.

Reviews

Leave a review, send us helpful feedback, or sign up for Cirrus promotions—including free books!

Access these materials at: www.cirrustestprep.com/pect-prek4-online-resources

Made in United States
North Haven, CT
27 May 2024